BOOKS BY ANNE EDWARDS

NOVELS

The Survivors
Miklos Alexandrovitch Is Missing
Shadow of a Lion
Haunted Summer
The Hesitant Heart
Child of Night

BIOGRAPHY

Judy Garlard: A Biography
Vivien Leigh: A Biography

AUTOBIOGRAPHY
The Inn and Us (with Stephen Citron)

CHILDREN'S BOOKS
A Child's Bible
The Great Houdini
P. T. Barnum

Vivien

A BIOGRAPHY

BY *Anne Edwards*

SIMON AND SCHUSTER · NEW YORK

Library of Congress Cataloging in Publication Data

Edwards, Anne, date.
Vivien Leigh.

Includes index.
1. Leigh, Vivien, 1913–1967.   2. Actors—Great Britain—Biography.
PN2598.L46E3   791'.092'4 [B]   76-58432
ISBN 0-671-22496-4

The author wishes to thank the following sources for permission to quote material in this book:

W. H. Allen & Co., Ltd., for material from *Alexander Korda* by Karol Kulick, copyright © 1975 by Karol Kulick.

Chappell Music Company for lyrics from "I Went to a Marvelous Party" by Noël Coward, copyright © 1939 by Chappell & Co., Inc., copyright renewed. International copyright secured. All rights reserved.

Hamish Hamilton, Ltd., for material from *Vivien Leigh—A Bouquet* by Alan Dent, copyright © 1969 by Alan Dent.

McGraw-Hill Book Company, for material from *Memoirs of the 40's* by Cecil Beaton, copyright © 1972 by Cecil Beaton.

New Directions Publishing Corporation, for material from *The Theatre of Tennessee Williams*, Vol. I, copyright © 1947 by Tennessee Williams.

Quadrangle/The New York Times Book Co., for material from "Dancing in the Dark" by Howard Dietz, copyright © 1974 by Howard Dietz.

The Viking Press, Inc., for material from *Memo from David O. Selznick* edited by Rudy Behlmer, copyright © 1972 by Selznick Properties, Ltd.

A. P. Watt & Son, for material from *The Oliviers* by Felix Barker, copyright © 1953 by Felix Barker.

*To Steve
who shared this writing experience with me
and never failed
in his loving encouragement*

Act One

This way the king will come;
    this is the way.

—Queen
    in Shakespeare's
    Richard II

Chapter One

The search for an actress to play Scarlett O'Hara had cost David O. Selznick $50,000 and lasted two and one half years. Yet, work would begin on *Gone With the Wind* this clear, cold December evening in 1938 with the role uncast, and the city of Atlanta would burn on the back lot of his studio with seven Technicolor cameras standing ready to roll. Doubles for Scarlett and Rhett waited on the sidelines for their cues to hop aboard the buckboard that would take them through the fiery streets of Atlanta, streets that had been created by giving false fronts and new profiles to the old sets of *King Kong* and *Little Lord Fauntleroy* in order to simulate buildings of the American Civil War period. Selznick knew he was about to take a tremendous gamble. Over the past two and one half years he had, after all, sent out to every hamlet in the South the best talent scouts in the country, dispatched director George Cukor and a whole crew to follow, and had personally seen hundreds of young women who were untrained actresses and an equal number who were trained and who read and tested for the part. In fact, he had done everything conceivable, and yet there was still no Scarlett. There was the possibility that Margaret Mitchell's world-famous heroine with her seventeen-inch waist—the smallest in three Georgia counties—would never be found.

But Selznick was a gambler by nature and he knew his financial backers would not wait. Either he was to begin work or abandon the project. Never had he felt so excited at the start of a film. Like Sherman himself he paced back and forth on the high-railed observation platform from which he was to watch the spectacle of Atlanta burning. But still he would not give the signal for the crew to turn on the gas jets to start the blaze for the cameras to photograph. The crew waited impatiently. The three pairs of Scarlett and Rhett doubles, the three identical buckboards—each with a Melanie, her newborn baby, and the servant Prissy hidden in the back—stood by. But Selznick was waiting for his brother, Myron, and refused to begin without him.

David Selznick was a bear of a man, big and robust and well over six feet tall, and he seemed a positive giant to the crew watching him from below for some sign. Shortsighted, he leaned forward scanning the night for a speck that he might recognize as his brother. Finally, furious at Myron, he gave the go-ahead. As the gas jets were turned on, fire leapt up, devouring the dry wood, and the first set of Scarlett and Rhett doubles jumped on their buckboard and raced alongside the flames. The scene was shot and reshot eight times before Selznick was satisfied. Sweat poured down his face and he had to remove his glasses to wipe them clean. He was exhausted and yet at the same time exhilarated beyond anything in his past experience. The shooting of *Gone With the Wind* had finally begun.

Replacing his glasses, he stood for a moment watching the flames consuming what remained of the set. Every available fire company in the area stood by and the back lot was a maze of men and equipment. Then he spotted his brother, Myron, elbowing his way through, a man and a woman following close at his heels. Myron had mentioned that he was dining with a client, the renowned English actor Laurence Olivier, and as the three came closer he was able to identify Olivier. But who was the woman? Selznick fixed his gaze on her as Myron took her hand and helped her up the precarious steps of the platform. Dressed starkly in black, she held tightly to a wide-brimmed black hat that framed her face as it shadowed it. It was windy at the top of the platform and she turned her head to the side as she approached him, so he could not see her.

"Here, genius," Myron said in greeting to his furious sibling, "meet your Scarlett O'Hara."

The woman tilted her head back and swiftly removed the halo hat so that her dark chestnut hair blew wildly behind her. The reflection of the flames lighted her face and made her green cat-eyes dance. She smiled, her almost childlike mouth turned up at the corners, as she extended her hand.

Selznick stared with stunned disbelief at the young woman who was grasping his hand. Vivien Leigh was indeed Scarlett O'Hara as Margaret Mitchell had described her—"the green eyes in the carefully sweet face turbulent, lusty for life, distinctly at variance with her decorous manner." It was exactly this duality of personality that he had been looking for in every girl he had interviewed for the role: an elusive quality that he now suspected was the chief factor that had caused him to be so slow in reaching a final decision. He had found his star and the world was about to see one of the most famous fictional heroines of all time come alive.

Vivien, like Scarlett, was from her childhood an extraordinary and powerful personality and a desperate and unconquerable survivor. There was about her a wildness that flashed in her eyes, and yet few women had more outward composure, elegance, or style. Even at twenty-five she was a complex, exciting woman who created a world of her own. Hers was a mythical kingdom born of the gleaming palaces of her Indian childhood, the gilded fantasies of her youth, and the glowing pageantry in the pages of Shakespeare that she had devoured throughout her life.

Olivier, young and handsome—England's heir apparent to the crown of the English theatre—stood behind her as she faced Selznick, her back to the charred devastation that had moments before been Atlanta burning. For her he had left his wife and son, and she had deserted her husband and daughter for him. Theirs was a great, an historic love affair, and now she would have a great and historic role. With incredible odds that even a veteran gambler like Selznick would have called impossible, she had traveled halfway around the world to win both.

For the twenty-five years that had led up to that moment high on that windblown platform, Vivien had molded her days from dream and fantasy which never contained defeat, and she had lived in the future where almost anything could happen. Now she was face to face with the role of her life.

In 1905, the time of the British raj, a time when England's young men flocked to India in search of adventure, Ernest Richard Hartley arrived in Calcutta as a clerk in the brokerage offices of Piggott Chapman and Company, not yet twenty and barely able to grow a stubble on his chin. He was the son of a family of moderate good breeding with no fortune to squander, land to inherit, or Court connections to assure his future. He, therefore, considered himself damned lucky to have secured his position. Marriage and children were far from his thoughts.

He had brought to India with him picturesque fantasies founded on Kipling's tales of a life of turbaned sepoys, tiger hunts, and "manly pursuits." It was a great shock to him when he discovered he had come to a city that was virtually a human sewer packed with beggars and lepers, stinking from an overflow of garbage, urine, and excrement, and miles from the exotic life he had imagined. Against his liberal nature but as a means of survival he quickly learned how to live in India as a white Englishman. There were the cricket matches on the spacious lawns of Calcutta's Bengal Club and races and polo games organized by the Calcutta Turf Club. But even more to his liking was the high quality of Calcutta's English-speaking Royal Theatre, for which he was instantly recruited as a performer.

There was no theatrical history in Hartley's background, and no way to explain his extraordinary talent as an amateur actor. Appearances of visiting companies were rare, so the English residents of Calcutta were forced to provide their own entertainments. Several of these amateur productions were presented each year and within a very short time Hartley had progressed to a leading supporting player and collected a respectable box of favorable press clippings. Apparently it caused no conflict of interests, as Piggott Chapman and Company soon made him a junior partner. Hartley, though, had grown into what might be called a "bon vivant." His distant French ancestry had endowed him with a certain irresistible charm toward women. Unfortunately the majority of attractive young Englishwomen in Calcutta were married, and therefore dangerous playmates for a junior partner.

When he returned for a visit to his home in Bridlington, Yorkshire, in 1911, Hartley—who had left six years before as a rather artless lad—was now considered a part of India's romantic legend. The young women of Bridlington were entranced with his "worldly" charm, and their parents were impressed with his patina of success. Certainly he stood apart from other Bridlington bachelors. The intense Indian sun had tanned and weathered his skin; and his theatre training had squared his shoulders, taught him a gallant air, and helped him refine his country speech. It did not take him long to recognize that he could win the charms of even the most beautiful girl in Bridlington. The combination of French-Irish ancestry had endowed Gertrude Robinson Yackje with the fragile look of Sèvres porcelain and the merry nature of a pixie. Hartley fell madly in love, proposed, and with a promise of a life filled with drama and romance won her heart.

They were married in the fall of 1911; and as though he had staged the rising curtain of their life together, his lovely young bride arrived in India on the same date—December 2, 1911—as their imperial majesties George V and Queen Mary. Fireworks exploded over the Bay of Bombay as the city celebrated the monarch's arrival. Gertrude was overwhelmed at the masses of shouting, shoving, unwashed humans. Hartley, sensing her distress, hurried her through the redbrick Neo-Gothic arches of Bombay's Victoria Station and into the first-class carriage of the shiny green and red car with its brown upholstered luxury that would take them to Calcutta and the home he had found in its fashionable suburb of Alipore.

Though their life in those early years was lived a good deal more luxuriously than either had been accustomed to—a staff of several servants and a chauffeured car were at their disposal—neither felt comfortable. Gertrude was a good Catholic and longed for the rituals of her religion; and Hartley could not shut his eyes to the poverty, dirt, and small regard for human life that surrounded him daily. Still, they made the most and the best of it. Ernest continued with his interest in the theatre, helping to raise funds for a larger, more modern building than the one that then housed the Royal Theatre Company. He became quite a good polo player and developed a considerable knowledge of horseflesh. Gertrude remained whenever she could behind the solid white stucco walls and shuttered windows of their palatial home, showing a talent for gardening as she transformed the courtyard into an English garden. She was not unhappy, for she truly loved Ernest and was proud of his achievements. But after two years the monsoon rains and the scorching heat began to test her good nature. To add to these trials she was three months pregnant and by the end of April—only a fortnight away—Alipore would be deserted and only native servants would remain to guard the houses in the unbearable heat of the hot season. She and Ernest planned to follow most of their friends to the cool of the lower mountain regions of the Himalayas, but a house—rather than a hotel room—had to be found, as Gertrude was to remain until the child's birth in November.

By the last week in April, Ernest had located just the right house. He stepped out of his office at 5 Royal Exchange Road and into the unrelenting sun the morning before their departure, not seeming for once to mind the pungent odors. He hurried down the steps and dodged quickly into the rear of his chauffeur-driven limousine. The car swept past the Georgian mansions and offices of trading and brokerage houses, turning off and moving through cluttered lanes and in and out of dark clouds of buzzing flies. He looked down at some papers in his lap, a habit he had acquired to avert the possibility of his eyes meeting a beggar's stare through the car's windows. It was only a short ride until they had passed the figure of the Bengal tiger that surmounted the central gateway of Belvedere, the official residence of the Lieutenant-Governor of Bengal. That meant he was only moments from his home.

They packed that night and by morning were on a train that wound its way north to the breezy mountain resort town of Darjeeling. The house, which belonged to a colleague of Hartley's, more than met their expectations. A two-storied building with the exceptional luxury of two bathrooms and a large bathtub, it stood surrounded by its own thick woods on the side of a hill overlooking the town. Hartley remained there with Gertrude for several weeks before returning to his desk at Piggott Chapman. The summer was almost as hot as it was lonely, but he was kept busy with his work, the building plans for the theatre, and the conversation of his friends at the Turf Club, where he was now involved in breeding racehorses.

In late October he went back to Darjeeling to join Gertrude; and on the evening of November 5,1913, just as the sun went down over the snowcapped peaks of Kanchenjunga and Everest, and the lights of Darjeeling were turned on, the English doctor came downstairs to inform him that he was the father of a fine and exceptionally beautiful baby girl. It was a fitting and dramatic entrance for Vivian Mary Hartley, who would one day become the fabled Vivien Leigh. Gertrude was not surprised that her daughter was beautiful, for she had faced Kanchenjunga just before the child's birth, which the Indian amah had assured her would guarantee her child's perfection of face. Gertrude was happier than she had been since coming to India. Ernest enjoyed being a father, they were both proud of Vivian, and they settled into a most civilized way of life. Then, nine months later, the world was at war.

Hartley was ready to return to England but was persuaded instead to become an officer in the Indian cavalry, for whom his hobby of breeding racehorses now made his services most desirable. Gertrude and little Vivian followed him to Mussoorie, a small hill town near Darjeeling where he trained remounts for Mesopotamia. After two years he was transferred to the military station in Bangalore and his family moved to the suburb of Ootacamund. Vivian thought her father looked especially handsome in shiny boots and uniform. She was ecstatic when she was taken to the racetrack in Bangalore, and though she saw less of Ernest than she wished, she had learned a sure way to capture his attention and admiration.

Ootacamund had an amateur theatre group and the English Army wives took it upon themselves to present children's plays and pantomimes. Gertrude agreed that Vivian should sing Little Bo Peep at one of these performances and costumed the three-year-old as a Dresden shepherdess, replete with sheep crook, flowered bonnet, and rosettes on her shoes and skirt. Standing center stage and with amazing presence, Vivian announced that she would recite, not sing Bo Peep.

Her father was delighted with this and with Vivian's subsequent appearances in Ootacamund, but her mother showed a growing dissatisfaction with Vivian's Indian education. Gertrude, being a devout Catholic, felt strongly that her daughter should not be brought up in a Moslem culture. In the last days before the end of the war she tried to persuade Ernest to return to England so that the child could be reared a Catholic, but peace found him back at Piggott Chapman and Company, the family re-established in the large house in Alipore, and Hartley a senior partner in the firm. His new position made it impossible for him to consider leaving Calcutta. But even though Gertrude's displeasure at remaining was evident, it was doubtful that he would have returned to England under any circumstances. He was enjoying a growing reputation as a ladies' man and thought he was getting away with having the best of both worlds. Gertrude, however, was not as naive as he believed, nor as tolerant as he might wish her to be. One evening she planned a dinner party and invited all the women (and their husbands) whom she suspected of having affairs with Ernest. As she was responsible for the guest lists of their parties, poor Hartley came down to dinner unprepared to face a roomful of women he had bedded and a group of men he had cuckolded. It was an evening he never forgot and one which Gertrude reminded him of often through the succeeding years—but it did not put an end to his infidelity.

Life was thus not too happy in the Hartley household, and Gertrude turned to her religion for solace and soon replaced Vivian's amah—of whom the child was very fond—with an English Catholic governess who saw to it that her daughter was given religious training along with her lessons. Vivian loved stories and reading and devoured any books presented to her. Gertrude introduced her to Hans Christian Andersen, Lewis Carroll, and Charles Kingsley along with the Bible. But Vivian preferred Kipling and Greek mythology and to her father's delight memorized long passages in the *Just So Stories*.

Hartley continued his theatrical endeavors for about a year after his return to Calcutta. But the responsibilities of his new position proved too great, and in 1919 he retired from the stage.

The following year he was given a short leave and the Hartleys boarded an English liner in Bombay with Vivian in tow and her mother intent on leaving her in England at a convent school. Gertrude had been born in Ireland, raised a Roman Catholic, and educated in a convent; and she considered this to be the best of all educations for a young girl. The boarding school that she selected and that Ernest finally agreed upon (he had at the beginning been adamantly against sending Vivian away to school) was the Convent of the Sacred Heart, Roehampton, not far from central London. The nuns and students were from upper-class homes and some of England's finest families were represented. This pleased Gertrude, for though not a snob, she was keenly aware of her new station in life.

When Ernest and Gertrude took Vivian to see Roehampton shortly after they arrived in March she was terrified at the sight of the forbidding medieval stone walls of the convent. They went directly to the office of the Mother General, Mother Ashton Case, a tall, beautiful woman with sharp gray eyes and a regal bearing, and were told that at six and a half Vivian was still too young to be left in the nuns' charge. Vivian was greatly relieved, until she heard her mother say that she would enter her in September then, when she was closer to age seven.

Once outside the convent, Vivian clung to her father and begged him to take her back to India where her memories were of golden sun and warmth, of crowds everywhere, of Gertrude's garden parties with lovely ladies in elegant gowns and high white gloves, of cavalry officers like her father in grand uniforms and polished boots, of sleek, beautiful horses, exotic food and spicy aromas. Ernest was convinced, believing that life in the convent would be too spartan and severe contrasted with the constant attentions of a nurse, a governess, her mother, and the house servants that the child had enjoyed in India. Her doll collection had been enormous, her wardrobe filled with lovely party frocks, and she had always adored dressing up. At Roehampton she would be allowed few personal possessions and would be clothed in a stiff uniform.

But Gertrude remained staunchly insistent that Vivian attend the school come September, and Ernest backed down, finally agreeing to leave Gertrude in England until that time while he returned to India at an earlier date. Vivian was distraught. For weeks she was moody and undemonstrative toward him. After he sailed for India, Gertrude took her to Ernest's parents' home at 14 Belgrave Square in Bridlington. It was meant to be a period of transition, a short, happy interlude before the school term. The house was a bright, cheery place filled inside and out with plants and flowers, the delicious aromas of Grandma Hartley's Irish cooking, the soft and constant purring of eight family cats, and an adoring audience of grandmother, grandfather, Gertrude, Ernest's two sisters, Hilda and Gertrude, a temporary nanny, and Katie the maid, who kept the many hearths glowing and warm. But there was no way that life at 14 Belgrave Square could prepare a child for the convent school at Roehampton.

In September of that year, two months short of her seventh birthday and the youngest child ever to be accepted by the school, Vivian, holding tightly to Gertrude's gloved hand, entered the seventeenth-century main building through massive wooden Gothic doors bearing hand-forged steel crossbars. Inside, the convent grounds were green and well tended but extremely stiff and forbidding. There was a small lake with benches where one could contemplate, but no ducks or geese to feed. There was little color. The nuns wore black, the girls navy blue, and the dormitories could have been a hospital ward in St. George's with their two facing rows of white-curtained cubicles, each containing a small steel bed, a chair, a dresser, and a washbasin.

Vivian used tears and then guile (both of which she possessed in quantity) to reverse her mother's decision, but Gertrude was intractable and left her standing in the courtyard holding Mother Ashton Case's sturdy hand. There was a kitten meowing at the child's feet and she drew away and sat down on the grass hugging the small creature to her. Mother General allowed Vivian to take the kitten to her room and to sleep with it that first night though animals were strictly forbidden. It was difficult not to give the little girl special protection and privilege. Not only was she two years younger than any other girl at the school, one whose parents soon would be thousands of miles away, but she was an exquisite child, with delicate features and incredible grace.

Within a week Gertrude was on the high seas on her way to rejoin Ernest in India. As the distance grew between mother and daughter, she realized it would be at least a year before she would see Vivian again and that two years would lapse before the child would see her father. But she was sincere in her belief that she had made the right and only decision for her daughter's future and that it had been a great sacrifice on her part.

Chapter Two

Vivian was permitted to keep the ginger cat and it mitigated some of her initial loneliness. Mother General took her under her benevolent wing and the sisters and girls soon followed her lead. In Calcutta, Gertrude had impressed upon Vivian that when she was going to a party she must always do what the hostess wanted, to please *her*; and when she was the hostess she must then do what the guests wanted, to please *them*. It obviously never occurred to the child at the time that she might please herself. She was never willful or disobedient. She did exactly what she was told to do. She smiled, the corners of her perfect mouth turned uniquely; she looked people straight in the eye, with wide, interested candor. The nuns made a great fuss over her, but it was in the end the extended friendship of a girl nearly two years her senior, the future film star Maureen O'Sullivan, who helped her to overcome her intense loneliness.

The girls resembled each other—with their large expressive gray-green eyes, their chestnut curly hair, their lithe bodies. But there the likeness appeared to end, for Maureen possessed a budding inferiority complex, caused by a nurse who had constantly put her down, and a rebellious nature. She was straightforward, with a disregard for social prestige, defensively proud of her middle-class Irish background.

"When I leave school, I want to fly," Maureen confessed to her new friend. "I should like to be a pilot."

"I want to be an actress," Vivian, almost seven, replied. "A *great* actress."

Drama and music were stressed at the convent; and Vivian took piano, violin and cello lessons, and played in the school orchestra.

The fact that the only man in the convent was a rather shy young music teacher named Mr. Britten certainly had a good deal to do with the girl's musical interest. Vivian was also enthusiastic about each new theatre production, though in her first year she was given little opportunity to take part.

The girls at the school voted on things like who was the wittiest, the most clever, and the most popular girl in the school. Not long after Vivian arrived they took a vote for the prettiest. Vivian came in first, Maureen second. Vivian accepted the honor with great equanimity and went about her classes. But Maureen returned to her room and cried throughout the day. No one knew what the cause was, but Vivian suspected that her good friend was not as used as she was to extravagant praise, high compliments, and votes of confidence. Far from being resentful that she had not placed first, Maureen had been overwhelmed to come in second to Vivian, whom she considered the most beautiful girl she had ever seen. Vivian's head did not seem to be turned by such flattery. The fact was that there was something extraordinary about Vivian. Mother General noted that she had a curious maturity that set her apart from the other girls, while possessing such an ebullient nature that she was adored by both the sisters and her peers. Her Indian childhood, added to her exotic looks, gave her a charisma not usually attributable to a child her age. She seemed to glide in and out of rooms; her hair was always in place, her uniform impeccable; and she had a way of telling a story that would immediately capture an audience.

But at Roehampton there was little time for childhood games. Students were occupied with their lessons. After English, mathematics, history, and French, there were long hours of religion. Vivian threw herself sincerely into religion, winning ribbons for her achievement at the end of the semester. It was the most meaningful thing in her life, and her short childish notes to Gertrude invariably ended with a scripture quote. There was drama, music, and choir; and Vivian, the only girl to do so, took ballet, a non-credited course given by one sister who had studied dance in her youth. It was an exceptionally brave thing for the child to take on, because at the end of the year the girls had to perform with their classes before the faculty and student body. Since there was no one else in Vivian's ballet class, she had to perform alone, a thing that would have terrified the other girls but excited Vivian.

She missed her father, and wrote him separate letters from her mother's, all about her school adventures, apologizing for what she considered her less-than-brilliant grades and dramatizing everything. She complained about nothing except that she missed her parents and dreamed of returning to India to be with them. She could have voiced her objection to the prudery of the nuns, which she did complain about to the other girls, but she did not.

Looking back, this prudery might seem humorous, but at the time it was a most difficult thing for free-spirited girls to endure. They were forced to take baths wearing long white shifts so that their naked bodies would not be exposed. Maureen, aware that the nuns were too modest to enter the bathroom and check if each girl kept her shift on while bathing, took hers off and bathed naked, after which she would soak the shift in the tub, wring it out, and get back into it. Vivian, who detested the feeling of the cold wet clothes on her body, would shiver in the unheated room, but she never once disobeyed.

Another rule was that no girl could wear patent leather shoes, because somebody might be able to see up her skirts in the reflection. And still another was the nightly edict for each girl to place her neatly folded soiled underclothes, covered by a white nightdress, on a chair in the corridor outside the curtained cubicle so that her personal garments would not be exposed. To top off this curious pile her stockings had to be folded in the form of a cross.

By Easter, Vivian had her first communion. She went to stay with Grandmother and Grandfather Hartley that summer, but both were ailing. Vivian spent the major part of her time playing nurse and rather enjoying the role. But she returned to the school for the second term quite happily. She had adjusted to her new life and felt a sense of security in the care of the nuns. On November 30, 1921, just past her eighth birthday, she was confirmed, an important and solemn occasion for her.

The following March, 1922, Gertrude returned for her first trip home in eighteen months, and she was both stunned and delighted with the changes in Vivian. The child she had left had matured into a charming, gay little girl, who showed Gertrude about the convent as a hostess might show her guests her home. The girls had been taken to pantomimes during the Christmas holidays and Vivian had re-established her keen interest in the theatre. She begged her mother to take her to the London Hippodrome to see *Round in Fifty*. By summer she had managed to coax Mother General and Gertrude into allowing her the privilege of returning to see the show sixteen times. The star was a red-nosed comedian named George Robey.

Hartley joined his family for the summer and they holidayed at a hotel in Keswick in the Lake District. There at the next table one morning at breakfast were Robey and his wife. Vivian stared throughout the meal at him with wide, beautiful disbelieving eyes, confessing when he rose to leave that she was his adoring fan and had seen *Round in Fifty* sixteen times. Robey beamed, took a handful of photographs of himself out of his pocket, and autographed them personally to her. These she pinned up in her locker, as she lived more and more in a world of fantasy.

Yet she was unusually orderly in her habits. Her cubicle was the neatest, her notebooks and papers carefully kept. She was always the leader and organizer of any group activity in which she was involved. Mother General noted that there seemed to be two Vivians, however, for often she would disappear and be found alone by the lake. "Why aren't you with the other girls?" a sister would inquire. "I like to see the trees reflect in the lake," she replied once. "It's a lovely ballet."

To friends she would confide stories of plays and ballets she had made up about golden palaces and golden princesses. India presented exotic images to the girls, but Vivian would seldom discuss it. Nor would she discuss her parents. Private emotions were kept locked away, moods and reverie, sadness or loneliness bottled until she could find time to be alone.

Vivian's group now included Maureen, the lovely Patsy Quinn, Brigit Boland, and Dorothy Ward. They were called the "exquisites" by the other girls. All the group members had beautiful long and luxuriant hair, which meant they had to have their heads frequently scrubbed by the lay sisters. After the hated scouring their hair was laid out to dry under the hot helmet lid of a chimney, with the girls groaning on their knees, heads painfully craned. All the girls wished solemnly that they could shear their tresses.

Therefore, at Christmastime Vivian was quite delighted in being chosen the girl to sacrifice some hair to the life-size wax Christ child in the chapel. The Divine Babe, though very beautiful, unfortunately had no hair. The youngest children were lined up, the predicament explained, and a suggestion put forward that someone with suitable curls be "privileged to give some hair" in order that the wax Christ child be beautified. With great solemnity and little hesitation Vivian was selected as the victim, or honored one, according to one's point of view, it having been decided among them that her tresses were the loveliest of all. However, this could not be done without a parent's approval and the Hartleys were in India.

A cable was dispatched and everyone waited anxiously—but none more than Vivian—for the reply, which came by return cable within a week. Vivian could have her hair cut. So one day with all the girls watching silently, the nun in charge of the youngest children cut off Vivian's curls and placed them on the head of the Holy Child. Then Vivian was taken into the village to a local hairdressers' shop to have her hair "bingled"—a fashionable cut that combined a bob and a shingle. Immediately, as many girls as could gained permission from their parents to have their hair bingled.

For Vivian the new cut not only meant that there would be no more scorched ears, bruised knees, or stiff necks, but that she could now be cast in boys' parts, which she considered the most interesting ones in the school productions. However, she was not allowed to wear trousers, as they were deemed immodest, and wore long cumbersome overcoats in their place. Theatre and plays were taking a great many of her private hours. More than ever she was convinced that she would be a great and famous actress. She wrote her father that perhaps someday when she came back to India they could appear at the Royal Theatre together. He replied that it was a charming idea, but he didn't have much time for theatre anymore.

She did not spend her next holidays with the Hartleys in Bridlington but remained at the convent by herself. She had found that she liked to read, and the nuns allowed her full use of the library. The holidays without her family did not appear on the surface to disconcert her. She was beginning to identify strongly with certain of the sisters and was happy to have the time without the other girls around to cement those relationships. The Hartleys sent her an enormous doll dressed in a crown and ball gown and looking very queenly, which Mother General permitted her to keep on her bed.

The second year at Roehampton passed happily for Vivian, who loved the nuns and the ritual of the religious training. She appeared to be one of the few girls sincerely happy there. Unlike Maureen, who was constantly rebellious and under threat of expulsion, everyone thought Vivian to be the most well adjusted girl at the school. She seldom cried or sulked. She smiled a lot and was genuinely funny, always seeing the humor in situations that the other girls thought disastrous, always fun to be with, and yet no goody-goody. Her friends confided in her with absolute assurance that she would never betray their confidence or criticize them. She was solemnly wise—so much so that no one ever thought about how young she was. "She was," as Maureen later said, "everything you would long to be. We would play silly games—who would you like to be if you could be someone else? Most of us wrote—*Vivian Hartley*."

Gertrude came home to England each summer, Ernest Hartley in alternate summers. Vivian preferred to remain at the convent with the nuns most other holidays, although she usually had invitations to visit with her friends. She continued her reading on her own and for a young girl had surprisingly sophisticated tastes. From Kipling she had gone on with much fervor to Dickens and Shakespeare. There were her lessons, the school orchestra in which she played cello, the choir, her classes in ballet, and the theatrical productions in which she was now an active participant. All the girls thought she was splendid and that someday she would surely be famous.

When her father was home they spent tranquil days in Connemara in the west of Ireland, where she would watch him battle the river trout in the waters that surrounded the village. Hartley was proud of his daughter, and at the same time guilty of the need for them to be separated so much of the time. When she was a child he had always spoiled her with toys. Now, as a growing girl, he indulged her with expensive clothes to wear on holiday and exotic presents of Indian jewelry, pearls, and silk stockings. Often, to brighten the dull convent fare, he would send hampers of delicacies, which Vivian would share generously with the other girls.

Her friends thought her the most glamorous girl in the school. Certainly she did show an unusual flair for fashion, seeming always to know how to assemble the right dress, necklace, and scarf in those rare times she was able to shed her uniform. The girls loved to help her pack and unpack, trying on her clothes and jewelry, and she was exceptionally generous and adored giving presents whenever she could to all her friends. "Oh, you do truly like it," she would comment when a girl would say how lovely something of hers was. "Do keep it. Do!" she would press.

Boys were mysteries, a great excitement. If the plumber came to school they were all thrilled. Yet, in spite of the cloistered nature of their existence, sex, though a special kind of exciting thing, did not seem an impossible fantasy. There were, in fact, two suspected lesbians in the school (older girls), and that created enormous excitement and a lot of whisperings. There were also many older girls who had experimental sex with each other and discussed it with the other girls. Taken as a group, the students at Roehampton were quite worldly and seemed to accept the discovery of sex as part of their education—

though not a part learned in the classroom or under the tutelage of the sisters! Most of them confessed to be waiting for the "real thing" to happen, Vivian Mary Hartley among them.

Suddenly, it seemed, she was thirteen—slim, exquisite, exceptionally bright, and rather disconcertingly "forward" in her thinking. The time seemed right for her parents to return to England. Hartley had made a substantial amount of money, and he and Gertrude were both still young. On July 7, 1927, Vivian left Roehampton on her father's arm, packed and ready for a trip with her parents to the Continent, her head filled with fantasies, her eyes gleaming with anticipation.

Her next four years were spent in Europe's most fashionable resorts—San Remo, Kitzbühel, Dinard, Biarritz—perfecting her French and learning German and Italian. The family took a boat across the English Channel, landing in Dinard at the height of season. The place had been founded by Welsh abbots in the sixth century and looked across the River Rance to Saint-Malo, a rocky peninsula with a fifteenth-century castle and narrow winding streets crowded with Renaissance churches and houses. Her parents rented a villa overlooking the water, with a private beach. She had, of course, taken an ocean journey years before and had often walked the banks of the rivers in western Ireland. But it was in Dinard that she fell in love with water—its tranquillity, its colors, and its peace—and at the same time was conscious of its grasp on her emotions, making her restless and at times depressed. She would sit, her knees bunched up under her, and stare out at the vast blue expanse before her for hours, as she had once stared at the softly rippling surface of the lake at Roehampton. She missed Mother General and the sisters, but she knew it was impossible to go back, that, in fact, she did not really want to.

Hostilities grew between Gertrude and Ernest, making her feel like a curious outsider. For long periods she would withdraw deeper into her own world. Then suddenly she appeared to be bursting with energy and good humor. During these times she seldom slept more than five hours a night and managed to fill every waking moment with activity. Early mornings found her at daily mass, nights she would read for hours in bed. She was wraithlike but seemingly healthy, never appearing to tire.

Her father attributed her fluctuating moods to "boy fever," noting how popular his daughter was with the boys of Dinard. Gertrude, though concerned, was more impressed by her daughter's orderliness—her room immaculately kept, her clothes impeccably tended, her undergarments washed immediately after their removal. Vivian was never late for anything and always ready to do a favor or run an errand. The occasional spells of moodiness that came and went seemed unimportant to Gertrude, and in her opinion were simply signs of her daughter's new "womanliness." The things Gertrude liked about Vivian were her instinctual good manners, her natural intelligence, and her ability to make friends easily.

By the end of the summer both Gertrude and Ernest agreed that plans had to be made for her future education. Since she had seemed so happy at Roehampton they enrolled her in a convent school in Dinard that September and left shortly after for Biarritz on the Bay of Biscay, where the weather was milder in the winter months.

The convent school in Dinard was a difficult adjustment for Vivian. Two factors were involved. First, in this new environment she was no longer the youngest, the pet of the school, and cosseted; nor was she the center of her own group. And after the sense of freedom she had experienced during the summer, she felt that she was being reined in by the school's rules and restrictions. She coaxed and wheedled her parents into meeting her in Paris on school holidays so that she could go to the theatre, but otherwise she felt that she was marking time.

The summer holidays did not come quickly enough for her. She met Gertrude in Paris and they joined her father in Biarritz. He was delighted to see her and took her everywhere they were invited. She wrote her Roehampton friends that she was madly in love and that several boys were madly in love with her. She sent everyone presents and begged them not to forget her. But her days at Biarritz—with its seven miles of sandy beach, the glistening golden bodies of the international set sprawled upon them—came to an end with the approach of September.

The Convent of the Sacred Heart in San Remo, on the Italian Riviera off the Ligurian Sea and close to Monte Carlo and Nice, was now selected as the next school for her to attend. It was a direct affiliate of Roehampton, and some of the girls Vivian knew were enrolled there. Also, since Vivian had done so well in French, Gertrude reasoned that Italian would make an excellent third language. Vivian, now nearly fifteen, abhorred the stiff, unflattering navy blue convent uniform and shed it whenever she could. The clothes she was forced to wear were not her only complaint about San Remo. There was the Victorianism and hypocritical prudery of the nuns.

The school was in the old upper town near the twelfth-century Romanesque church of San Siro and overlooked the sea. The girls would have to dress in black bathing costumes with high necklines, long sleeves, and skirts that reached their ankles, then march single file down the steep hillside and through the modern town to the beach, where they would then dash across the narrow strip of sand and submerge immediately to their necks in the water. Vivian buried herself in religious fervor as well, collecting peonies and scattering the petals at the feet of the robed priests from San Siro as they walked on the ancient cobblestone roads in solemn procession at the feast of Corpus Christi. And she never missed early mass.

But she was beginning to question a good many things about Catholicism, and whereas at Roehampton she had dearly loved and respected the nuns, such was not the case at San Remo. There were far too many hints that sexual liaisons existed between certain nuns and the priests at San Siro. More upsetting were the blatant hints of lesbianism among the sisters. It was not the sexual promiscuity of the convent staff that disturbed Vivian so much as the religious hypocrisy involved. For the first time her grades were poor. Always marvelous with language, she even did badly in Italian. Her father was amused, but not Gertrude, when the Reverend Mother wrote that Vivian had become "unruly" and that her conduct had been reprehensible. Enclosed was a note containing a few words, undeniably in Vivian's handwriting and apparently confiscated, that said "Reverend Mother is a . . ." Alongside this was a sketch of an angry, bristling cat.

The Hartleys summered in Ireland in the wilds of Galway, and Patsy Quinn came up to visit. The two girls spent their time acting out plays together, making them up as they went along. Both were fresh from reading *The Light That Failed*, and so Patsy would be an artist going blind and Vivian the loving heroine. They soon found themselves crying broken-heartedly, so moved were they by their own performances, at which point they broke up with hysterical laughter. By the end of the summer and with a great deal of persuasion on the part of both Vivian and Ernest, Gertrude agreed that she could attend a fashionable school in Paris in the residential district of Auteuil, along with another friend Molly McGreachin. Vivian was ecstatic. Paris was the magic city, and she would be there without the restrictions of a convent school. Her happiness was increased when an actress from the Comédie Française joined the faculty, and Vivian and a few other special students were given speech, deportment, and drama under her tutelage. There were only twenty girls of Vivian's age in the school and the headmistress was young and progressive-minded and permitted them midnight feasts, the use of makeup, and cared very little if any of them attended mass or church services.

On their return to Zurich from a ski trip in the Bavarian Alps, Gertrude and Ernest ran into a friend who had seen Vivian at a theatre in Paris on a free afternoon and informed them that she had looked strikingly beautiful as always, but to their surprise was wearing rouge and lipstick and a rather revealing frock. The Hartleys wasted no time in hurrying back to Paris and pulled Vivian out of the school to her great and dramatic objections. They then drove across France and Switzerland to a school near Bad Reichenhall near the Austrian border which Gertrude had previously investigated.

Vivian was entered in mid-term, and despite her gloom at having been forced to leave Paris she adored the school from the beginning. The original plan was for her to complete only that term before finding still another school. But when Vivian joined her parents in Kitzbühel for the spring holiday, she begged to be allowed to continue, and, pleased at her progress in German, Gertrude agreed.

Those last semesters of her education on the Continent were her happiest. Salzburg was less than an hour away, and she attended the music festivals. Vienna was near, and she was permitted to go there to the opera, which she loved, particularly the dramatic Wagnerian works. Christmas was spent with her parents for a second time in Kitzbühel. She was never a good skier, since she suffered from a balance problem, which also made riding a bicycle difficult; but she adored the mountains and the hikes in the snow and felt, she wrote to her Roehampton friends, that she was closer to God on the peak of an Alp than she had ever been in the front pew of a church.

At Easter 1931 Vivian was seventeen, her studies completed. Gertrude came to collect her and they spent ten days together in Munich, visiting the opera nightly. Gertrude sat in the opera box each night staring at her daughter much of the time instead of watching the performances. The young woman suddenly seemed a stranger to her. There was an intensity about her that she did not recognize as Vivian strained forward to study the movement on stage; and there was her ability to so totally involve herself (which Gertrude could not) that she wept, laughed, and appeared wildly distracted. Somehow it unsettled Gertrude and made her feel truly protective toward Vivian for the first time, and when they left the Continent to join Ernest in London after the ten days were past, she did so with a curious feeling of apprehension.

Chapter Three

By 1931 D. H. Lawrence's controversial book *Lady Chatterley's Lover* had gained notoriety, and Vivian read it from cover to cover and then reread it. She was a romantic young woman, blossoming with a new sexuality and possessing a rare, breathtaking beauty that caused strangers on the street to turn and stare. The grace of her slim, delicate body, the chiseled perfection of her oval face, the startling vividness of her gray-green-blue eyes, the dazzling whiteness of her skin, and the long graceful curve of her neck gave her the look of a Modigliani sculpture. Her one imperfection was her hands. They were curiously oversized for her arms and body and she was self-conscious of them, making a point of pocketing, gloving, or folding them away out of sight.

Although her peers thought she was the most beautiful girl they knew, Vivian had little vanity. The combination of Gertrude's training and that of the nuns at Roehampton had imposed a kind of selflessness upon her that was to remain with her all of her life. She would nervously dismiss any compliment and was the first to notice something special about the other person.

Reading was still one of her passions, as were art (she seemed never to tire of museum trips), music, theatre, and parties; and she continued to sleep less than six hours a night without appearing weary-eyed the next day.

Gertrude and Vivian had met Ernest in London, where the three of them had seen several plays before traveling to Aasleagh in County Mayo, Ireland, where they spent the summer. In October they returned to a bleak London in the throes of a depression. Ernest, with his usual optimism, was confident that Great Britain would overcome the severe economic slump. But in London the Hartleys saw hunger marchers, listened to talk about the distressing rise of Fascism in Germany and Italy, and read headlines about the Japanese invading Manchuria. Hartley was inclined to believe Prime Minister Ramsay MacDonald's statements of optimism, yet the family was experiencing a "pinch" as his investments began to decline in value.

A formal coming out party for Vivian was out of the question, and as the Hartleys were living in a London hotel a series of smaller parties could not be considered. They chose instead to lease a house for the winter in the West Country near Teignmouth, where living would be a good deal less expensive, and where Ernest's good friend and former associate at Piggott Chapman, Geoffrey Martin, his wife, and daughter Hilary lived nearby. The two girls were friends and spent a gala holiday season as belles of all the local festivities. But by the New Year the Hartleys could see that country life would be no advantage to Vivian. More important, she seemed restless and somewhat "wrought up."

There was serious talk about sending her back to India for a year to stay with good friends, but Vivian put an end to that. She had for weeks been thinking about the possibility of an acting career. To everyone's astonishment Maureen O'Sullivan, who was only two years older, was out in Hollywood, and a film in which she was a star was opening in the West End. Gathering her courage, Vivian announced to her parents that she wanted to study to become an actress. Hartley was openly pleased and immediately made plans to enroll her at the Royal Academy of Dramatic Art in London. It was February and she had to wait until the first of May, when the next term began.

One of the last galas she attended in the West Country was the South Devon Hunt Ball held on Torquay Pier. There she was introduced to a rather attractive man with pale, serious eyes and blond wavy hair. His name was Herbert Leigh Holman, but his friends called him Leigh and his family had a country place in the next village, Holcombe Down. Vivian was taken with him. At thirty-one he was the oldest bachelor she had met, which in itself attached a bit of extra glamour to the meeting, as all the young men Vivian had known were no more than a few years her senior. He also resembled one of her favorite actors, Leslie Howard, had attended Harrow and

Cambridge, and was a barrister at law with chambers in the Middle Temple in London. She blurted out to him that she would soon be in London herself. Plans were made for them to meet again at that future time and he confessed before they parted that he had seen her on the street of Holcombe Down a few days before and inquired who the girl with the beautiful profile dressed in black might be. Upon hearing that she was to attend the South Devon Hunt Ball, he also decided to attend, though such affairs generally did not take his fancy.

For days thereafter Vivian went about the house in a daze. She was certain she was in love and confided to her friends that she was positive Leigh was the man of her dreams. Alerted when Vivian suggested they allow her to go to London earlier than originally planned to stay with one of her Roehampton friends, Gertrude promptly packed her off to Grandmother and Grandfather Hartley in Bridlington, using the true pretext that they were not well and that her visit would be a great boon to their spirits.

Many weeks of daily correspondence between Bridlington and the Middle Temple followed, and Grandmother Hartley made sure that Gertrude and Ernest were apprised, voicing her own opinion that Vivian should not be permitted to be alone in London. The Hartleys, therefore, preceded Vivian to London and took a flat in Cornwall Gardens, where Vivian joined them about a week before she was to begin her new course of study.

Vivian suspected that Leigh did not think highly of theatre people, so she neglected to discuss with him the extent of her ambitions. On his part Leigh assumed that her interest in theatre was a hobby and that her parents regarded the Royal Academy of Dramatic Art as a finishing school. "Although no more enchanting girl than Vivian could have existed," Leigh Holman says today, "she did not seem to me *at that time* to have ambition or those qualities that brought her fame. I was taken by surprise as it happened."

At that time Vivian was trying desperately to juggle the two loves of her life—Leigh and the work she was doing at the Academy on their new premises on Gower Street. She wanted more than anything to please Leigh, and so she was always ready when he called upon her to go someplace with him and would make up her work at the Academy by studying through the nights, often with only an hour or two of sleep.

Sir Kenneth Barnes, who had heard her entrance audition (Lydia's love scene in *The Rivals*), had been most impressed; and her Shakespeare class teacher, Ethel Carrington, felt she was decidedly gifted, although her voice was feared to be too high-pitched and frail for the theatre.

When she wasn't with Leigh she spent time with her good friend Patsy Quinn and new friends Rachel Kempson and Leueen Mac-Grath. She took the role of Starveling in her old favorite *Midsummer Night's Dream*, blacking out her teeth to secure the best comic effect. And she was delightful as Rosalind in *As You Like It*.

Vivian was well aware that Leigh was not a man to dally with a young woman's affections. He made it apparent almost from the time she arrived in London that he would eventually propose marriage. And, indeed, she was in hopes that the day would soon come, but it seemed to her there would be plenty of time to discuss her stage aspirations. After all, it was rather premature and conceited to believe a career might even exist, since she was still an untried neophyte.

On Sunday, June 19, Leigh and Vivian motored down to Brede in Sussex to visit with Leigh's good friend Oswald Frewen, who was first cousin to both Winston Churchill and Shane Leslie. Leigh privately told Frewen, "I might marry Viv," and his friend was most enthusiastic about the possibility. "They'll make another nice couple to come here in the future," he wrote in his diary that night after supper when Vivian and Leigh had departed.

A month later, Leigh bought a ring with a green stone in it for thirty-five pounds at Mappin and Webb and presented it to Vivian, who was delirious with happiness as she dashed into the flat in Cornwall Gardens to show it to her mother. Trying to be as tactful as possible, Gertrude said that green simply would not do, as it was unlucky, and that she was certain Leigh would understand and exchange it. If his pride was injured Leigh did not expose it, and the ring was returned and a small diamond one bought in its place.

A round of parties followed. Leigh's birthday was November 3, just two days before Vivian's, and they celebrated them together. Vivian was nineteen, Leigh thirty-two. That next weekend they motored down to Brede and had dinner with Oswald Frewen and his sister, Clare Sheridan, the sculptor. Saturday was bitter cold and Leigh went into Dell Head to do some wood-cutting. Vivian took a chill and Frewen put her to work in the sheephouse to get warm.

In truth, Vivian and Leigh did not share the same interests. If she wanted to attend the theatre, she went with one of her friends, because he seemed to grow restless; and though she was proud of his chambers in the Middle Temple, she found any discussions of his briefs a bore. But she felt well protected when he was by her side. It was comfortable and safe. Gertrude, with some belated insight, spoke to her about the possibility that she and Leigh might not be perfectly mated, underscoring the fact that marriage for a Catholic was for *life*, and she suggested that Vivian speak to a priest. Vivian would have none of it. She was in love with Leigh and that was the end of it.

They were married on December 20, 1932, at a Roman Catholic church, St. James's, Spanish Place. Patsy Quinn and the other brides-maids wore peach satin dresses with puffed sleeves and were thrilled to be part of a wedding, as Vivian was the first of the group to marry. There was a stir when she walked down the aisle on Ernest's arm, looking pale and nervous. Her hair was drawn back from her face by a crocheted white Juliet cap, and she wore a simple white satin gown. She appeared younger than her nineteen years as she faced Leigh at the altar and stared up at him with more childlike obedience than wifely admiration. After their vows were exchanged, she clung to his arm.

Patsy and Gertrude went with her when it was time for her to change into her going-away outfit—a blue suit trimmed with silver fox fur. Her wedding band was an eternal ring of diamonds, and when she went to wash her hands before rejoining her guests, she took it off. Gertrude flew into a rage. "Vivian you should not have done that," she cried. "It's so unlucky, so terribly unlucky!"

The newlyweds honeymooned in Kitzbühel and Vivian took Leigh on a side trip to Bad Reichenhall to meet her former principal. She was proud of Leigh and of her new status. If she formerly harbored any fears about their compatibility, walks in the Bavarian Alps together, the shared delight of viewing picturesque spots and discovering small shops and cafes, and the mutual need for companionship stilled them. After three weeks they returned to Leigh's bachelor flat in Eyre Court in St. John's Wood.

Reality set in fast. The flat was small and household tasks were competently managed by Leigh's maid. On his request Vivian had given up her studies at the Royal Academy before their wedding. There were rounds of weekend parties, but the days seemed interminable. She simply had not learned how to cope with idleness, for from her first days at Roehampton each hour of her life had been programmed and accounted for. Not putting time to good use was a serious character defect. The flat consisted of two fairly good-sized rooms, a tiny one, and a kitchen and bath; and it made her feel unbearably claustrophobic. Leigh was gone all day; her friends were at the Royal Academy or other schools. She was bored and wanted desperately to return to the Academy. Leigh vehemently disapproved.

However, he was a promising barrister at law, and anything she did to enhance their social prestige met with his immediate approval. His cousin was married to Alwyn Boot, the daughter of Sir Jesse Boot (later Lord Trent), founder of Boot's Cash Chemists, who took a great fancy to Vivian and agreed to present her at Court. Vivian was delighted and threw herself wholeheartedly into preparations. It was as though she were preparing herself for an opening night. *Everything had to be perfect.* There was the gown that had been designed and made for her, the ostrich feathers for her hair, the rehearsal of the walk, the curtsy, the proper hand gesture, the position of the head, and finally the makeup (sparing amounts for the best advantage) and hairstyle (simple and swept back so that her face would be visible at all times).

At last June 13, the awaited day, arrived. Leigh was not able to go to the palace with her and she was a bit saddened by this, for she would have liked him to share the experience. As she entered the state room she was pleased she had decided upon a dress with a train as it imbued her with an inner regal sense that allowed her to act the part of a Shakespearean lady for the entire spectacle.

She memorized each small detail, planning to re-enact it for Leigh that evening. There were the scarlet and gold uniforms and the fanciful white-plumed hats of the elegant gentlemen at arms, the awesome shimmering crystal chandeliers, and the plush flowers and velvets and brocades. Never had she seen such an enormous room, never had she been so close to royalty. She recalled Gertrude's story of the royal couple's arrival in India. She stared across the room at their majesties King George and Queen Mary seated beneath the durbar canopy they had brought back from that 1911 trip to India. An orchestra was concealed and the rich sound of many violins punctuated the clipped speech of the participants.

Vivian stepped forward as if in a dream. The gown was taffeta with huge puffed sleeves and it crackled as she moved. She had the feeling all eyes, even their majesties', were upon her. She tilted her head to get a better look, conscious that her throat was bare and that the simple pearls she wore reflected her warm flesh tones. She curt-sied deeply, smiled demurely. "What a lovely child," the Queen was heard to say before Vivian had backed away.

It was an experience she could not, would not, ever forget, and it was a momentous day in her life. As she went back through the palace gates and stepped into the rear of the chauffeured car that was waiting for them, she knew she must go back to the Royal Academy and that there was only one life for her—the stage.

She immediately talked to Leigh about returning, perhaps to take the French classes, as he knew how much she enjoyed working with the teacher, Madame Gachet. Leigh agreed, believing it was better for her to be kept occupied and that she should maintain her fine fluency in French. But he was not aware of her deep inner conviction that nothing would now stop her from being the *great* actress she had confided to Maureen O'Sullivan at age six she would one day be-come. In fact, Leigh did not consider this a possibility. He had not, for that matter, seen her perform any part except that of the comedic Starveling in A *Midsummer Night's Dream*; and as she was a wonder-ful mimic and adored parties where they played games like charades, he thought it was great fun for her and little else.

She began the weekly lessons under Madame Gachet and then added other classes. Her hands were causing her a great deal of anxi-ety. She had become especially aware of their size and considered them ugly, developing mannerisms to keep them hidden. Finally, in exasperation, one of her teachers gave her a copy of Ellen Terry's *Memoirs*, and she discovered that the great lady of the English stage had also had a complex about her hands and that years of self-con-sciousness had only been overcome when she forced herself to use them constantly and to develop special ways of turning the "defect" into an asset.

Vivian took heed and practiced gestures for hours before a mir-ror. She also lengthened the cuffs on most of her dresses, added wrist frills, and was seldom seen on the street or at rehearsal without gloves or at a party without bracelets and bangles that fell loosely onto the back of her hands.

Shortly after her presentation and her return to the Academy she became pregnant. Two decisions had to be made. The first was when she would have to postpone her studies and the second was whether she and Leigh could continue on at Eyre Court. She remained at school until June, even appearing in Shaw's *St. Joan* in chain-mail armor and heavy boots. At that time, since Leigh had agreed that they would have to find a larger, more suitable place for them, she searched London daily and was ecstatic to locate a house with a theatrical history. Lynn Fontanne had once lived there. It was a rather unsafe structure with a bulging front wall at 6 Little Stanhope Street in Shepherd Market, but to its advantage was the fact that it was the first house they had seen that Leigh could afford. Built in about 1700, the small, narrow house might have been unsafe, but it was rather enchanting, having wide hearths and pitched ceilings. Their good friend Hamish Hamilton took over their flat in Eyre Court, and they moved in at Little Stanhope Street surrounded by painters and carpenters and plumbers. All the rooms were thirteen and a half feet square and looked up Pitt's Head Mews or back onto the seventeenth-century Shepherd's Cottage. Venetian windows faced the front.

As the decoration began, their first true mutual involvement came into focus. Leigh had a long-standing and deep interest in old furniture; and although their tastes were not the same, Vivian, spurred by Leigh's initiative, became caught up in the search for paintings, fabrics, fittings, and furniture. It was, unfortunately, only a short time before Leigh drew back somewhat and, as he says, "I became a spectator with growing wonderment." Her knowledge and expertise seemed to be instinctive, and yet she would always manage to purchase the most exquisite pieces at bargain prices and without ever wheedling a merchant. She loved motoring out to the country to find antiques and often discovered some seemingly worthless piece of furniture, hidden under years of dust and tons of heavy hardware, that Leigh would insist was quite hopeless, then bring it home to discover it was worth at least ten times the price they had paid.

The household now consisted of Mrs. Adamson, the cook; Aide, the maid; and Nanny Oake, who had been hired to move in after the baby's birth. The little house was crowded, although there were enough rooms for everyone and even a small library where Leigh could work on his briefs.

Little Suzanne Holman was born at a nursing home at 8 Bulstrode Street on October 12, 1933, and her mother recorded the occasion in pencil in her delicate blue diary with a single sentence, "Had a baby—a girl." Suzanne was born a month prematurely and the delivery was not an easy one. It was several weeks before mother and daughter came home, but once there it did not take Vivian long to become bored, as the household was being run -quite adequately by the staff, and baby Suzanne was well tended by the nurse-nanny.

Yet, returning to the Academy did not seem the right thing to do either. Harboring a growing restlessness, Vivian began to test herself and her talent, giving frequent parties that sparkled and lasted till late at night. The "enchanting Vivian Holman and her nice husband" were the new couple on everyone's guest list, and Vivian was always the last to leave. Leigh did not enter happily into the pace such a social life created, but he was aware of Vivian's disquiet; and, therefore, when she said she was going to pose for a fashion photographer he did not object, although he did not encourage her either.

Actually, many of the young ladies in her set were modeling and also took small roles in films as a means to make some extra money, and also because it was then "the thing to do." "Vivling," as some of her new friends called her, was the center of a bright group of independent young women who could not conceive of being chained to a husband, a house, or children.

By summer the original excitement of the social whirl began to pall. On August 5, a Sunday, Oswald Frewen visited them for tea at Little Stanhope Street and, sensing a new "skittishness" about Vivling, suggested she and Leigh might enjoy going off on a yachting trip together. Leigh thought that a good idea and arranged passage for them on a cruise in the Baltic.

Vivian entered into the plans with some enthusiasm until a friend suggested that there might be a small part for her in a film that was scheduled to star Cicely Courtneidge. Vivian spoke to the casting director, who was encouraging. Leigh did not believe she was serious when she said she wanted him to put off the trip until she found out if she had the role. The film was to be called *Things Are Looking Up*, and as the ingenue had been cast all Vivian could hope for was a few moments on the screen as one of a group of schoolgirls. It did not seem to Leigh that a "lark" paying thirty shillings a day should intrude upon their proposed holiday. For the first time he was rather forceful in his wishes, and together they went to Gothenburg, where they boarded the boat and sailed to Aarhus and then past Elsinore to Copenhagen.

A cable waited for Vivian in Copenhagen informing her she was to report August 12 to begin work on the film. There were unpleasant words exchanged, and in the end Vivian returned to London while Leigh continued with the cruise. Directly after she had left he had read of a fatal accident where a young woman had been electrocuted by the faulty wiring of a bathroom heater. Vivian was always chilly and just before the trip Leigh had installed a similar heater in their bathroom. He was beside himself with concern and cabled her not to use it, but there was no reply.

When she returned home, Vivian was told there was to be a delay in the shooting of her scenes. Worried that Leigh would now understand even less the urgency of her flying trip back to London, she went down to Sussex to spend a few days with Clare Sheridan. She discussed her decision to follow a stage career and her fear of Leigh's disapproval with Clare, who was a sensible woman. By the time Leigh came home Vivian knew she had to confront him with the truth, but in spite of Clare's prodding she was unable to do so.

Leigh had been so tormented during their brief separation that he assured her that of course it would be all right for her to do the film. He added that it had been selfish of him not to realize that she was too young and beautiful to devote herself only to her child and her home. He did not include himself, and it was perhaps this kind of selflessness that made Vivian hold her tongue.

Chapter Four

Vivian was now a professional actress and it did not seem possible to her that she could ever achieve anything more that she wanted unless it was to appear in a West End stage production.

For three weeks she rose at five in the morning to be at Lime Grove, Shepherd's Bush, by half past six, where the film was being shot. It was dark outside, the fires cold, the household asleep. September was unusually damp that year, and she shivered in the early morning chill as she heated water for tea and dressed in front of the open door of the lighted oven for warmth. She wrote notes to Aide, notes to Nanny Oake, and finally a short message to Leigh, which she would put on his dresser. The streets were deserted as she motored to her acting job in her small two-seater car. Once at the studio, she would dress in the summery white gym uniform she wore in her role as a schoolgirl, close to an electric fire in a drafty dressing room along with the other "schoolgirls," Judy Kelly, Hazel Terry, and Gillian Maude among them. All the girls were exuberant with excitement. The film was a low-budget comedy destined only to fill a programming bill, but it was cinema and they were star-struck.

The last week they checked in at Lime Grove and then were transported by private car to Lord Darnley's Elizabethan house, Cobham Hall, which was being leased and used for exterior location shots of the fictional girls' school. Vivian had one line to speak: "If you are not made headmistress, I shan't come back next term!" But the camera singled her out a number of times for close-ups, and caught her in some comedic interplay with the other girls. She had learned something from film that she had not learned at the Academy—the value of facial reaction when you were in the background. During the long delays between takes she would talk to the technicians. In the close-up, she was told, eyes and brows were the most important features, for facial reaction could save yards of film.

Her work on *Things Are Looking Up* had not been a great hardship on Leigh. To the contrary, she was home for dinner and had refused all party invitations, wanting to look her best in the morning. He was reconciled to this new interest of hers, though he did not take it seriously and assumed it would eventually pass.

But Vivian spent long hours pressed close to her dressing-room mirror practicing eye expression and learning how to control her eyebrows. Her friend, actress Beryl Samson, recognized her new interest as the commitment it was and suggested she find an agent. That was not an easy task for a girl of twenty who professionally had spoken only one line in a film. Vivian was certain it would be impossible until she had accumulated a list of credits. Then fate intervened.

Beryl was at a party when she overheard John Gliddon, the agent, telling another guest that Hollywood had the right idea in contracting many beautiful young unknowns and training them before the camera with the hopes that at least one might have the makings of a star. Alexander Korda, he was saying, was the only man in Great Britain clever enough to employ such a system. In a two-year span he had signed a number of hopefuls and used them in one film after the other—and look how successful it had been, with Wendy Barrie and Merle Oberon nearing star status in *The Pivate Life of Henry VIII*. Beryl turned to him and agreed, adding that she knew one girl who was bright, spectacularly beautiful, had attended the Royal Academy of Dramatic Art and appeared in one film. She added, "If you are looking for star potential, Vivian Holman has it." Gliddon was interested, and the next day Beryl and Vivian went to see him in his Regent Street office.

Vivian wore a lovely wide-brimmed hat that framed her face. She looked up at Gliddon with eloquent eyes. "Beryl says you are the only man who knows how to make a girl a star." She smiled, the perfect sycophant. Gliddon replied rather modestly that he could not work miracles but that he was convinced she had a good chance if she let him manage her for a year.

"But your name—Vivian Holman—must go," he insisted.

"How about Vivian Hartley?" she asked.

"No good either," he replied. "You need something more memorable." After concentrating for a time he suggested April Morn.

On the ride back to Little Stanhope Street, Vivian was troubled. "Leigh would never accept my being called April Morn," she said.

Beryl said she would have to agree with Leigh if he thought it was a vulgar name.

The two women rode in silence for a time, and as Vivian pulled the car up to her front door, Beryl said, "How about Vivian Leigh? He's bound to approve that."

For several weeks thereafter the newly christened Vivian Leigh was escorted by Gliddon on a daily round of luncheon, tea, and cocktail dates at such posh places as the Ivy, the Ritz, and the Savoy Grill, where she was bound to be seen by the titans of Wardour Street—those men and women who controlled Britain's film industry. With Vivian wearing a different outfit at each meeting, being seated so that her extraordinary beauty was shown to its best advantage, Gliddon was successful in his campaign. Korda's office rang for an interview with Vivian, and Gliddon hastened to accept.

The financial success and the international critical acclaim of *The Private Life of Henry VIII* had made Alexander Korda the undisputed king of Great Britain's film industry. Adding to the luster of his crown was his kingly manner and his glamorous past. From the time he was a young man in Budapest, Sándor Korda (as he was originally named) had been devastatingly attractive to women. He had a leonine head, strong bones, and eyes that were at once hypnotic, slanting, and sensitive. His first film was made in his native Hungary in 1914, when he was twenty-one years old, and from the beginning he had lived with and dispensed luxury on a royal scale.

One of the earliest and youngest of Hungary's film elite, he soon built his own studio with a suite of his own impressive offices. Five years later his empire crumbled as the fearful purge known as the White Terror gripped the nation. The Communist regime that had held Korda in high esteem had fallen. Admiral Horthy, an enemy of Bolshevism and a German sympathizer, was now in control; a direct attack was made against intellectuals, Jews, and film makers, and Korda was all three. He moved his headquarters to Vienna, where he continued living the grand life and began to build a new empire.

The building of that empire had taken eleven years and had transported him from Vienna to Berlin, Hollywood, Paris, and finally London, where he opened the grandiose offices of London Films on

Grosvenor Street in Mayfair. *The Private Life of Henry VIII* had not only made Korda both internationally famous and rich, but had catapulted the British film industry into the world market for the first time. Without question Alexander Korda was the most important man in British films, and Vivian Leigh was not unaware of his power. Yet their meeting seemed somehow fated to her. She had known in her heart for over two years that Korda would one day single her out, as he had Maureen O'Sullivan. While making films in Hollywood in 1930, Korda had given Maureen (then only eighteen) her first starring role in *The Princess and the Plumber* opposite Charles Farrell. Vivian, on her return from the Continent, had seen it three times; and since she and Maureen had always looked alike and often for a giggle had exchanged places to fool a casual acquaintance, it was not difficult for Vivian to fantasize herself in her place.

Korda's offices were like one of his own lavish sets, and they were staffed with Continentals who spoke a polyglot of eight languages, which greatly added to the glamour. One journalist had called the offices "International House."

Vivian and Gliddon were greeted in the anteroom by a fräulein, ushered into a waiting room by a mademoiselle, escorted into Korda's private office by a señorita, and greeted finally by an elegant, tall, slim, commanding man with a charming Hungarian accent. His appearance was most impressive. His manners were impeccable. He rose, came around his desk, took her hand in his, and through the glasses he had only just begun to wear, held her in a riveting glance. The interview that followed was not at all what she had expected. He asked her questions about her background, her family, and her ambitions; but he also wanted to know what books she liked to read and which plays and films she had liked. She commented on a painting he had hanging in the office, and he got up and went over to it to discuss its merits with her.

Vivian was enthralled and certain the meeting had been a tremendous success. However, when Gliddon rang later, Korda said she was exquisite, *yes*, charming, *yes*, but that she did not fall into any type that would stamp her as unique. He explained that his current list of contract players consisted of Merle Oberon, who was *exotic*, Wendy Barrie, who was a *pure English girl*, and Diana Napier—*a beetch*. It was this one identifiable character projection that made a girl a candidate for stardom, he claimed, and at this point he did not think Vivian Leigh had it.

Vivian was badly disappointed, but Gliddon did not allow her to languish in self-pity. He managed to get her a part in a quickie film to be made by British and Dominion called *The Village Squire*. She was the leading lady, and the film—for which her pay was five guineas a day—was made in six days. A month later she was cast as a typist in another quickie titled *Gentleman's Agreement*. Both films were dreadful and received poor reviews.

But David Horne, who had also appeared in them, rang to tell her that he had been cast as an elderly man in a play set in fifteenth-century Florence called *The Green Sash*. They were having difficulty casting the role of the flirtatious young wife. John Gliddon spoke to Matthew Forsyth, the producer, and with only a few weeks' rehearsal time before the scheduled opening at the Q Theatre, Vivian was engaged to play the role of the wife, Giusta.

The Green Sash opened on February 25, 1935, and was reviewed the next morning in *The Times:* ". . . The dramatists have given so vague a sketch of Giusta that Miss Vivian Leigh has little opportunity for portraiture, but her acting has a precision and lightness which should serve her well when her material is of more substance."

It was not a very auspicious stage debut, but Vivian was heartened by the review and thrilled that she had now made a professional stage appearance. The play lasted for two weeks, and she reveled in every moment of its run. Leigh was not nearly so ecstatic, for their home life was considerably turned about. He hardly saw her, as she went to the theatre about the time he came home from chambers and was generally sleeping when he left in the morning, not having got to bed until dawn. He was not what one might call "good humored" about his wife's new stage career and being a practical fellow could see no reason she should continue. And, considering the pale reviews of *The Green Sash*, the discouragement of her interview with Korda, and the lack of any notice of her appearance in the Cicely Courtneidge film, *Things Are Looking Up*, it was understandable that Leigh thought she should see the handwriting on the wall.

The Green Sash closed on Saturday, March 9. The next morning, although it was freezing cold, she and Leigh motored down to Brede to visit Oswald Frewen. "Despite Arctic weather we were all happy and kept ourselves warm with risqué stories except old Leigh who assiduously dug the first trench of my new Kitchen Garden," Frewen wrote in his diary.

One night Vivian confessed to Patsy Quinn, "Oh, Pat, I feel so tied. I'm so young and I do so love the gay life, and Leigh—though I adore him—is not very social." Attending theatre was her greatest pleasure, and so if Leigh was not available as an escort she would go with Patsy or Beryl or her parents. She yearned for something more than she had, but she was not sure what it was, except that somehow the theatre was a part of it. She was always weaving magical and glamorous stories in her head. At Roehampton she had been able to see dancers and a queen swan on the small lake; at Dinard she could sit on the sand and imagine glittering ships filled with partying passengers and a queen of the festivities. Always now her daydreams contained a masked king or prince, an elusive suitor who could not reveal his identity.

Never in Vivian's maturing years had she suffered the pain or the ecstasy of an unrequited crush. If she decided she must have a young man's attention she had always received it. There was no more adoring husband than Leigh in their set. Still, Vivian flirted outrageously and had wild fantasies that she would confide to her closest friends, shocking them. ("If the Prince of Wales asked me, I would become his mistress." Then she would elaborate on how she would behave in this role.) There were several young, handsome matinee idols of film and theatre at the time—Ivor Novello, Noël Coward, and the young Laurence Olivier. Of the three, Olivier held the greatest sexual charisma and an aura of assurance that gave him a commanding, a regal presence. He was far more than a fine performer. He was a star on the rise, a prince among players, and from the first moment Vivian had set eyes upon him he had been the romantic figure in all her fantasies—the man behind the mask.

She had first seen Olivier the previous year as Richard Kurt in *Biography*, then as Bothwell in *Queen of Scots*, and as the dashing, eccentric Tony Cavendish in *Theatre Royal*. This last thrilling and theatrically superb performance had totally mesmerized her. There was the handsome young Olivier, his dark eyes flashing, his slim hips tightly trousered, a white shirt gashed open at the throat to reveal a portion of his manly chest, speaking the most outlandish and suggestive dialogue and leaping over a balcony in a virile Douglas Fairbanks fashion.

Olivier's stage presence affected Vivian on many levels. Certainly she had a great admiration for his talent, but he also aroused in her a sexuality that she had previously not known existed. Finally one night she was introduced to him in the Savoy Grill, where he was dining with his wife, the lovely and well-known actress Jill Esmond. Vivian had been escorted by a young man who was a friend of both Leigh and herself, and she had insisted they go to the Savoy Grill because she knew Olivier often dined there. Olivier greeted her casually, but she caught his unguarded reaction as she grasped his hand tightly and smiled that devastating smile that was so uniquely her own. Perhaps out of pique, her escort said some disparaging things about both Olivier's appearance and his acting ability, and Vivian savagely defended him, to her companion's dismay. Having now met Olivier, she was fully convinced she was in love with him and that he was as deeply in love with her.

From that evening on, all she could think about was Olivier. Her feelings toward Leigh turned to a detached fondness. He was dear, he was sweet, but she had been too young, too inexperienced when they had married to know or desire a grand passion. It had been Leigh's maturity and accomplishment and his life in London that had originally drawn her to him. They never truly had found much in common, and she could not speak to him of those things which seemed the most important at the time—her growing passions as an actress and as a woman. She was positive that a man like Olivier would not only understand but help her to fulfill herself.

Gertrude was well aware of her daughter's dilemma. She had always been disturbed with Vivian's restlessness, and she was fearful her daughter might do something (she was not sure *what*) that would violate the laws of the Church. She tried to get Vivian to attend mass but did not succeed. As often as possible she reminded her that marriage was a sacred vow. Vivian assured her mother there was nothing and no one for her to worry about. But Gertrude now knew her daughter too well to be deceived.

On the other hand, Laurence Olivier was not yet truly aware of Vivian's existence.

Chapter Five

Laurence Olivier was born on May 22, 1907, in a small red-brick house on Wathen Road in the town of Dorking, where his father, the Reverend Gerard Kerr Olivier, was an assistant at St. Martin's. In the sixteenth century the Oliviers or de Oliviers were Huguenots who lived at Nay in Gascony, a village south of Pau in the Basses-Pyrénées. The Reverend Jourdain Olivier emigrated to England in 1688 as chaplain to William of Orange. For generations the English branch of the Oliviers had followed church tradition and sired future Anglo-Catholic (High Episcopalian in the States) ministers. There were three children in Laurence's family: his brother Richard, his sister Sybille, and himself. At a very early age he assumed he would follow family tradition and would someday become a clergyman.

Laurence's childhood had not been an easy one, with the Oliviers having to move constantly from one parish to another. His father was a stern, cold Victorian man; his mother the center of his world. She died when he was thirteen. "I spent most of my stupid youth being terrified of my father," Olivier admits. "Then my mother died and I was nearly destroyed."

But he had survived, and his father had taken over the running of the family not truly knowing any of his children well at the time. But the Reverend Olivier had been more of a maverick than his younger son suspected, and in his youth had done a bit of acting with the Oxford University Dramatic Society when he was up at Merton. And there was no doubt that he was very dramatic in the pulpit, using wide gestures and a thunderous voice, with great yawning pauses.

Laurence had not been a strong child. He himself says, "I was born a weakling. As a child I was a shrimp, as a youth I was a weed. I was a miserably thin creature and my arms hung like wires from my shoulders." His mother had encouraged him to act in an effort to overcome his awkwardness, and he had appeared in school plays from the age of ten. He was also a choirboy at All Saints, Margaret Street, where the precentor, Geoffrey Heald, was a superb actor. But after his mother's death Laurence was sent to St. Edward's, Oxford, where he did not do well and where he acted only once—as Puck.

"I was a muddled kind of a boy," Olivier confesses. "I liked acting. I adored the theatre, but part of me wanted to go into the mercantile marine, and I was very keen on the idea of being a farmer."

But when he was seventeen his older brother went to India to be a rubber planter, and Laurence's life—to use a play on words—took a dramatic turn.

"The night Dickie went," Olivier recalls, "I was very miserable—my mother had been dead four years—and I went up to the bathroom. I always had my bath after my father had his and got into his bathwater to save water. My father came in and sat on the edge of the bath. He was missing Dickie as well. I said, 'When can I follow Dickie out to India?' He said, 'Don't be a fool, Kim'—that was my family nickname. 'You're going on the stage.' "

And that was exactly what he did. He began to study with the extraordinary Elsie Fogerty in 1924 and was her favorite pupil. But when he finally went to look for work he had no idea what kind of actor he wanted to be, though he did have a burning ambition. But, as he puts it, "I think possibly one of the most strongly contributing facts toward such an ambition was my upbringing. The atmosphere of genteel poverty is probably almost the most fertile ground for ambition that there can be, because you seem to say, 'I want to get out. I'm going to get out. When I get out of this, I will show them!' without having the faintest idea how or what you're going to show them. I simply had this driving feeling—I'm going to be a smashing actor!"

Yet even with Elsie Fogerty's fine training and the fire of ambition, success did not come immediately. He played walk-ons in numerous productions and then minor parts with the Birmingham Repertory Company for two years. His last season with them was from January to May 1928 at the Royal Court Theatre, London, where he was the Young Man in Elmer Rice's *The Adding Machine*, Malcolm in *Macbeth*, and the lead in Tennyson's *Harold*.

In his first play away from the Birmingham Repertory Company, *Bird in Hand*, which ran at the Royalty Theatre for seven months, he appeared with a beautiful, slender dark-haired girl named Jill Esmond Moore (she soon dropped the last name), who was the daughter of Eva Moore, the famous actress, and H. V. Esmond, the even more illustrious playwright and actor-manager. The two young hopefuls fell in love and on July 25, 1930, at All Saints, in Marylebone, were married. Olivier by this time had played in a long string of co-starring roles (*Journey's End, Beau Geste, The Circle of Chalk*) and went almost directly after the ceremony into the cast of *Private Lives* with Noël Coward.

Roles in New York and Hollywood followed, and by the time he returned to London's West End and Vivian's attention he was well on his way to becoming a matinee idol, and had been signed by Korda to a remunerative film contract. He was young, famous, handsome, a successful actor—and he was quite happily married to one of the prettiest young actresses in England.

In Hollywood, New York, and London women had been throwing themselves at the dashing Laurence Olivier to no avail. If Vivian harbored fantasies of a grand affair with him, it hardly seemed possible.

Shortly after her first play had closed in March 1935, Vivian was cast by Associated British Film Distributors at Ealing as the ingenue in a film to star Gracie Fields. It was called *Look Up and Laugh* and was to be directed by Basil Dean.

Her former work in films had not prepared her for working with Dean. A tough director, he was a martinet who seldom humored his players and never mollycoddled them. He would tear her scenes apart, shout invective at her before the entire cast and crew, dissolving her into tears. "Don't worry, love," Gracie Fields assured her, "you've got something."

But neither Dean nor his cameraman gave her any sense of assurance that Gracie Fields might be right. One of their main complaints was her neck, which they claimed was too long. Unlike her experience in *Things Are Looking Up*, she was not singled out for many close-ups, and though she sang pleasantly in the film and when allowed a chance on camera was quite charming and certainly believable, once again *The Times* overlooked her, although the picture was considered "skillful and entertaining." Aubrey Blackburn, the Ealing casting director, tried to get the studio to sign her, but Basil Dean was influential in putting an end to that possibility.

Look Up and Laugh had taken only four weeks of Vivian's time, but Leigh was glad when it was completed and hoped they could finally settle down. But the very next day after the film's end, John Gliddon called Vivian to meet him in Sydney Carroll's offices on Charing Cross Road for an interview for a part in his new production, *The Mask of Virtue*, to be directed by Maxwell Wray, who had been Korda's dialogue director in the past. Gliddon told her very little about the play or the role, as he did not want to raise her hopes. The part was that of Henriette Duquesnoy, a young woman of the streets being masqueraded as an innocent girl to lure the Marquis d'Arcy into a marriage that would disgrace him. The role was not easy and it was the pivotal one of the production. Wray had already tried to get Peggy Ashcroft, Diana Churchill, and Anna Neagle, but none of these well-known actresses was available. Frantic as the opening date drew nearer, Wray rang his old friend Aubrey Blackburn and asked if he could suggest an actress who might be suitable. Blackburn was not too helpful until Wray mentioned that "this girl has to be spectacularly beautiful."

"Vivian Leigh," was Blackburn's immediate reply.

She met Gliddon in a stark black dress that emphasized her slimness and the whiteness of her skin; her chestnut hair and oval face were framed perfectly by a wide-brimmed black hat. They went together to Sydney Carroll's offices. Carroll (whose real name was George Frederick Carl Whiteman) held a special niche in the English theatre. For many years he had been a most revered drama critic for *The Sunday Times*; and now, as well as heading his own theatre management company, he wrote a powerful theatre column for the *Daily Telegraph* every Thursday, was the film critic for *The Sunday Times*, and the author of many books. He had been a successful actor as a young man, having made his first appearance in 1896 at nineteen in *The Sign of the Cross* at the old Standard Theatre.

There were about ten other girls sitting in the anteroom. Leaving Vivian waiting there with the other aspirants, Gliddon went in to speak privately to Wray and Carroll. He admitted she had only made one former appearance on stage but that since beauty was the main requisite for the role Vivian certainly had it.

Wray left the office for a few minutes and then came back. "If Vivian Leigh is the girl dressed in black sitting at the end of the table in the outer room, then as far as I am concerned, the part is cast," he said.

She was engaged at a salary of ten pounds a week. Carroll also asked her to alter the spelling of her name to Vivien, as he thought it was more feminine, and she agreed.

This time she had a director who was determined for the success of the play to give her every advantage. He studied her for a long time during rehearsals and decided her best qualities were her extraordinary grace when sitting or moving and her great beauty in repose. He worked with the lighting director to make the most of these attributes. She also had one extremely difficult scene at the end of the play, when on Henriette's wedding night the Marquis discovers her duplicity and threatens her with his pistol. She throws herself at his feet begging his forgiveness and declaring her true love. Wray took her through this scene over and over, assuring her that her own natural intelligence and sincerity would come through to make the scene believable.

The other members of the cast—Frank Cellier, Jeanne de Casalis, Lady Tree, and Douglas Matthews—were marvelous to her. On opening night Leigh escorted her to her dressing room (he had not attended the first night of *The Green Sash*), where presents from all her co-workers were waiting for her bearing little notes of good wishes. Maxwell Wray came in to tell her it was a full house and that she was not to be nervous. Then he left her alone, taking Leigh out of the dressing room with him. He did not tell her that on his insistence his friend the great Alexander Korda was in the audience.

Korda, occupying a center aisle seat in the stalls of the Ambassadors' Theatre that night (May 15, 1935), expected to see an intelligent interpretation of a German comedy that he was already familiar with, and fine performances by the well-known members of the cast. He was as certain that newcomer Miss Vivien Leigh would give an adequate but rather stereotyped performance as the prostitute. Leigh Holman, seated only a few seats away, expected little more.

The houselights darkened, the curtain rose. From the first moment of Vivien's entrance, Korda and the rest of the audience were enthralled. Vivien possessed a kind of radiance that transcended the footlights. There was magic in her performance, an intangible electricity that sparked her audience. No matter what else was happening on stage, it was difficult to tear one's eyes away from her. She was lighted and costumed so that, with the magnificence of her classic long neck and her ivory skin and perfect face, she looked in repose like a Florentine painting. There was a lilting beauty to her voice even if it lacked range, and she had a curious vulnerability that brought instant sympathy to her role.

Korda headed for her dressing room as soon as the last bravos echoed in the house. He had been able to see in her performance that stamp of uniqueness that he had missed previously. She was the passionate street girl who could be a great lady at the same time or, in reverse, the great lady who could be a street girl. There was, he observed, a complex and mesmerizing duality to her personality. (Korda was right, and Vivien's most successful roles were to be portrayals of either of those two aspects of the "dual" woman.) Korda met Gliddon at her dressing-room door and told him to come and see him the next day. Then he went in and congratulated Vivien. "Even a Hungarian can make a mistake," he said suavely.

Vivien was in a whirl, but she tried to keep her head. She dressed and went with Leigh and her parents to a small cast party at the Savoy and then to the Florida to dance. At four in the morning she and Leigh taxied to Fleet Street to buy the morning papers; and they stood in the gray light, Vivien shivering in her evening gown in the dampness of the early morning, and read the headlines on the theatre pages:

VIVIEN LEIGH SHINES IN NEW PLAY
YOUNG ACTRESS A TRIUMPH
ACTRESS IS A DISCOVERY
NEW STAR TO WIN ALL LONDON

She was ecstatic with happiness as she got back into the taxi with Leigh. On the way home they passed the Whitehall Theatre. The marquee lights were out, but she had already memorized the names: Laurence Olivier, Cecil Parker, and Greer Garson in *Golden Arrow*.

It seemed anything was possible for her now, even her name on the same marquee with Olivier's—or even Olivier himself. Later that day, when Beryl Samson came over to Little Stanhope Street to congratulate her, to her friend's astonishment Vivien confided, "Someday I am going to marry Laurence Olivier."

Beryl was too taken aback to remind her that they were both already married to other people.

Chapter Six

All the evening papers carried front-page stories about "the fame-in-one-night girl." She was now Vivien Leigh and her new identity was indelibly etched in printer's ink. When she saw Leigh's puzzled and unhappy face as he returned from chambers that night after having had to push aside the reporters to enter his own house, she knew what she dared to lose. The need for love and security had always been the motivating powers in her life. She loved Leigh and yet was not in love with him, and the security he gave her made her terrifyingly insecure in the end, because with it she lost the comfort of her own identity.

Even having shared her opening night, Leigh was mystified by the clamor she had created. He did not think fame had much meaning to her. Only a short time after the opening they had motored to Brede, and when they had entered, Frewen had walked a circle around her and looked her up and down and then had said, "Well, I don't *see* any change."

Vivien had nearly burst into tears. "There *isn't* any change and there never *will* be, Oswald," she had said.

Gliddon had kept his appointment with Korda for the day following the opening, and Korda had offered a contract paying Vivien £750 for the first year. Gliddon, feeling in a strong position for once, protested, but Korda, the charming voice suddenly becoming rapier-edged, refused to bargain. Gliddon pressed his case further and at the end of the meeting Korda agreed to give her a five-year contract starting at £1300 for the first year and rising with the standard options to £18,000 in the fifth year. She would have to be available to make two films a year, but she could use the time between for appearances on the stage.

Gliddon was delighted, but when he discussed it with Vivien and Leigh, Leigh did not think it at all equitable, since, in his opinion, Korda had all the options and Vivien none. Vivien overrode his advice not to sign, and three days later the newspapers carried headlines like £50,000 FILM CONTRACT FOR LAST WEEK'S UNKNOWN ACTRESS!

Feeling that Vivien's newfound stardom could fill a much larger theatre, Carroll transferred the play to the St. James's so that his discovery could be seen by twice as many theatregoers. It was a poor error in judgment. Vivien's voice did not carry in the immense St. James's, and her great beauty seemed lost on the cavernous stage. The play lasted only ten weeks after the transfer. Then Carroll sent it on the road, planning to bring it back into a smaller theatre. But by that time there was no smaller theatre available.

Vivien was not unhappy about her sudden inactivity, since Korda had just announced that she was to play Roxanne to Charles Laughton's Cyrano de Bergerac. But Laughton did not like the script, the putty nose created for him, or Vivien as Roxanne, and Korda refused to let him film the production simultaneously in French and English. Plans were therefore abandoned.

Days for Vivien were now filled with housewifely duties, and she had no time to take the two-year-old Suzanne to play by the Serpentine. The taste of fame had spurred her ambition. All she could think about was the theatre. She read everything she could, seeing if she couldn't find a role for herself. Staying in the public eye in whatever way she could manage occupied much of her time. She lunched at the Savoy and the Ivy. She posed for Cecil Beaton and Vogue magazine, and she gave interviews whenever asked. Almost every night she dragged Leigh to parties, remaining very often after he had gone home, sometimes even until dawn.

Leigh viewed it all as a whim. Her success and instant fame after Mask of Virtue had surprised him, but he still had not taken it seriously. She was spoiled and beautiful and easily bored. She was either wildly excited or cool and detached. It was enough to drive Leigh to distraction, but he also found her bright, exhilarating, and quite irresistible. He had led an ordered life before he had met Vivien, but her mercurial presence brought him a vitality he did not possess himself, and he truly loved her.

The big theatrical event that autumn was the Olivier-Gielgud production of *Romeo and Juliet* at the New Theatre. The two men alternated playing Romeo and Mercutio. It was a grand theatrical stunt on its own, but also Olivier introduced to the stage a new interpretation of Romeo, bringing to the role a sexuality that had not been portrayed previously. It was a bold and fearless thing for him to do, and it was obvious that nothing could have kept Vivien away from seeing the play.

She chose a matinee performance and went by herself. Olivier's sheer animal magnetism leaped across the stage lights as he stood against the balcony in an extraordinarily insinuating pose, and Vivien had much the same reaction as she had when she had seen him in *Theatre Royal*. She decided to go backstage to congratulate him on his performance. There were a few people in his dressing room when she arrived, but he was aware of her presence as soon as she entered. "I'm Vivien Leigh," she said, "and I just had to tell you how marvelous you were."

Olivier thought her the most beautiful woman he had ever seen. He asked her courteously if she had any theatre plans after telling her that he had seen her in *The Mask of Virtue* and had been impressed with her ability. She replied that she had been offered the part of Jenny Mere in Clemence Dane's stage adaptation of Max Beerbohm's story *The Happy Hypocrite* opposite Ivor Novello. "That sounds a good project," he told her, and then suggested that perhaps they could meet for lunch and talk about it before she went into rehearsals.

Olivier had taken the initial step in helping to guide her career, though he was not aware of it. Vivien signed for *The Happy Hypocrite*. Directly after she did so, it was postponed for several months, but Korda now decided to exercise his option and cast her opposite Conrad Veidt in *Dark Journey*, a spy story that was to go immediately before the cameras. Vivien managed time to meet Olivier for lunch, however. They ate at the Ivy, but it was not the rendezvous Vivien had hoped it might be. Gielgud was with them. Olivier was charming and wittier than she expected. His dark eyes flashed with merriment as he told some funny anecdotes about himself. Vivien was dazzled and now more drawn to him than ever. He suggested she audition at the New Theatre one afternoon for a role in a production Gielgud was preparing of *Richard II* to be given by the Oxford University

Drama Society. Gielgud agreed. Theatre and the classics seemed to be all that mattered to Olivier, and though he found films necessary to support himself and Jill he had a low opinion of them.

The luncheon literally changed Vivien's thinking. Of course she must play in the classics. Nothing else would be an achievement. She found time out from the filming of *Dark Journey* to audition at the New Theatre. Olivier sat down front as she read a scene from the play to Gielgud. Standing, looking out into the audience of one, Vivien began: "This way the king will come . . ." Gielgud invited her to participate in the play, casting her as the Queen. Rehearsals began directly upon the completion of the Korda film.

On January 20, 1936, King George V died. Vivien had never forgotten the image of the aging but still imperious and handsome monarch at her presentation. She wept at the news and was quite affected by his death. She was, and would remain, in awe of royalty, and perhaps that is why she loved her first experience with the classics.

Florence Kahn, who was Sir Max Beerbohm's wife, and Vivien were the only professionals in the undergraduate cast, and the young people included them in all their festivities. The last night there was an Oxford University Drama Society supper and Beerbohm spoke. It was three A.M. before the party broke up. Vivien had her little two-seater car with her and she piled John Gielgud, his brother Val, and four others in with her and started driving to Burford in the Cotswolds to continue the party. They were traveling forty miles an hour along the Burford road, Vivien dozing at the wheel in spite of John's dramatic recitations to keep her awake, when the car hit the grass verge, swerved, and almost turned over. They had all been saved by Gielgud's fast thinking, for he seized the wheel and straightened it. Vivien was badly shaken and quite sober by the time she returned to London and Leigh the following day. But if Leigh expected her to be high spirited on her return, he was wrong. Immediately before leaving Oxford Vivien had heard that Jill Esmond Olivier was pregnant.

She attended the preview of *Dark Journey* with Gielgud. Her role in that film was of such a mysterious nature and the script so complex that Vivien did not understand what the film was about or what the character she was playing in it was doing. "What am I doing that for?" she whispered to Gielgud. He just threw up his hands. "Why did I say that?" Gielgud obviously had no idea. "Where am I supposed to be?" Gielgud was as confused as she. *Dark Journey* was indeed a complicated spy story, set in Sweden, with Vivien playing a French double agent masquerading as Swiss. The film was seldom convincing, but Vivien photographed exquisitely, a fact that no reviewer could overlook. But vanity was not one of her character traits, and she despised the idea that she was being commended only for her beauty. No matter how successful the film was, *Dark Journey* would remain a failure to her. It had been no test of her acting ability. Olivier was right. Theatre and the classics were the most valuable training.

Disappointed in her first venture with Korda, she threw herself into rehearsals of *The Happy Hypocrite*. Ivor Novello was one of the best-looking men in the English theatre. His coal black hair covered a magnificent head, and his profile could only be rivaled by John Barrymore's, with the high forehead, large luminous eyes under sweeping lashes, regal nose, and determined chin. He was a prodigious playwright and actor and was often compared, to his disadvantage, to Noël Coward. Novello, defending himself, claimed he wanted to be associated only with commercially successful plays, so he wrote what he thought were guaranteed profit makers and acted roles below his true ability. But it was clear that it was a thorn in his side to be considered a second-rate Coward.

The Happy Hypocrite was Novello's departure from that pattern. In it he played a bloated, fat, dissolute, raucous-voiced rake, who by the miracle of finding true love (Vivien) reverses both his looks and his personality. The production was marked by good taste, and the reviews were laudatory. (James Agate, Vivien's former severest critic, even wrote, "Miss Vivien Leigh as Jenny might have stepped out of a poem by Tom Moore. She is artless without artifice, and no simper mars this freshness and this charm.") But *The Happy Hypocrite* was Novello's least successful play since he had become a star, and in three months it closed.

Vivien then accepted an offer of Sydney Carroll's to appear as Anne Boleyn in a production of *Henry VIII* in Regent's Park. It was a particularly soggy month of June and she had to walk back and forth on the thick wet grass to go from her dressing room to the stage. A few days after the production ended and during which she had felt ill, she came down with a bad case of influenza. Leigh and Gertrude and Ernest were all concerned about her health. She was rail-thin at the time and she was left with a cough that seemed to hang on. Still she continued to smoke incessantly, using a long black ebony holder.

Korda arranged a meeting with her one afternoon and warned

her about the way she was destroying her health. A man who overindulged, smoked to excess, and took no exercise himself, he believed strongly in a sensible regime for others. But what was really on his mind was her film career. They talked about many things that day, and Olivier was one of them. "He's married and apparently very happy," Korda warned her. A few days later he rang to tell her he was starting work on *Fire Over England* with Flora Robson starred as Queen Elizabeth, Leslie Banks as the Earl of Leicester, and Vivien and Larry as the two young lovers—Michael Ingolby and Lady Cynthia.

Vivien and Larry were now thrown into daily contact and began spending all the time between takes in each other's company away from cast and crew. It did not go unobserved by Korda, who was often on the set to see how things were progressing. But he did not interfere. European film makers took a more realistic view of the private lives of their players than their American colleagues.

On August 21, during the filming of the picture, Jill gave birth to a son, whom they named Tarquin. It was a curious name to bestow on a child. Years later, as explanation of the choice of such an unusual name, Tarquin was told that shortly before his birth his father and mother had been entertaining luncheon guests in their home in Cheyne Walk, and as Olivier carved the meat, he sliced the air with the knife dramatically and said, apropos of nothing in particular, "I am going to have a son and call him Tarquin!" Tarquin was the name of an Etruscan family which ruled Rome circa 600 B.C. The name translated from Etruscan meant "Lord." The first Tarquin subdued the Sabines, laid out the Circus Maximus, and built the Forum where the first gladiatorial games were held. His reign was splendid, but he was murdered after thirty-eight years and all the other Tarquins who followed were despots and finally rooted out. The last and most infamous Tarquin (and the one Jill and Olivier would have known best) was the Tarquin immortalized by Shakespeare in *The Rape of Lucrece*.

After the fourteen weeks it had taken to shoot *Fire Over England*, Olivier and Vivien had become dependent upon each other. He had never before met a woman quite like her. She was the extreme opposite of Jill, who was cool and calm at all times, dispassionate, a good friend more than a lover. Vivien was exciting, unpredictable. She had a great sense of humor, was daring, intensely passionate, and at the same time thoughtful, loving, and considerate. She made him feel he was her entire world, that she lived for him.

Yet she was the most intelligent woman he had personally known, far brighter by his own admission and better-read than he. And he was certain she was one of the most beautiful women in the world.

Shortly after Tarquin's birth Vivien once again came down with the flu, and when Oswald Frewen came by to see how she was, he found Olivier at the house ministering to her. It was the first time Frewen had seen them together. Olivier suggested some hot rum as a cure.

> Olivier opined rum [Frewen writes], and I popped over to the Pitt's Head and amused them by asking them to give me some in the tumbler I brought with me . . . we pumped it into the Vivling with hot water added and sugar and she hated it. . . . Larry was amusing. He couldn't make out what I was doing in the house . . . nor least of all why I should sit on her bed and propose to "talk her to sleep" after he was gone. He tried and tried and tried again to establish the fact that we both leave her. I said I had a voice *calculated* to put anyone to sleep in 10 minutes; Vivling agreed (with a seraphic smile), Larry was not amused.

It was a difficult time for Olivier. He had fallen in love with a married woman, meeting her at home while her husband was in chambers and her young daughter in the care of a silent but disapproving staff. Personally he liked Leigh, though the two men shared little in common. And Jill, who could not be accused of any wifely indiscretion, had just gone through a pregnancy which had brought her own career to a standstill to present him with the son he had wanted. The fact was that until the filming of *Fire Over England* he had considered himself a happy man. He now was in a terrible quandary. To deliberately hurt Jill, whom he greatly admired and respected, was unthinkable. To turn away from Vivien, who made him feel so wondrously alive, was equally impossible.

By the last day of shooting, plagued by indecision and exhaustion, they parted, each planning individual holidays—Larry to Capri, and Vivien with Leigh to the Continent—hoping that this time with their respective mates would ease their inner turmoil and perhaps prove to them that their attraction was not truly love. At the last minute Leigh could not leave chambers. Vivien talked Oswald Frewen into accompanying her on a holiday to Sicily and Capri. ("She was so natural that sex didn't obtrude and I was never once conscious of a defensive action on her part," Frewen entered in his diary.) It was also obvious that since she chose Capri she was as desperate for the sight of Olivier as she was for the scenic distractions.

Their first stop was Taormina, Sicily, and on October 29 Vivien wrote Leigh:

Darling, I wish you were here—it is a heavenly day and we are sitting out on the balcony overlooking everything—and we think Etna is choking and are hoping for an eruption any minute. But apparently he often smokes for want of something better to do, and it never comes to anything really big.

Yesterday we had a very funny time—we hired a car and were going to drive up Etna in the *beautiful* sun. As it happened, half an hour after we started it all clouded over and got freezinger and freezinger and foggier and foggier. We saw nothing and felt frightful but occasnally (no—can't spell it) thought it quite funny that this was what we had left England for! The lava fields were very interesting at *first*, but began to pall as we got more miserable. The hotel at the top was nice tho and we drank a lot of red wine and felt rather tight and fortified for our downward trip. The silly ass of a hotel-keeper never told us we would be going up 3,000 feet.

However—

Tomorrow we drive to Syracuse and catch the plane to Naples and on to Capri where we'll be Thursday and Friday. Then one night in Naples or Rome and back to you my darling. I would hate coming back if I didn't think you were lonely and I want to see you so much. It would be lovely to come back to a warm sunny place like this together some time.

There was no mention to Leigh of her plans to meet Jill and Larry at the Hotel Quisisana in Capri.

Oswald Frewen was not yet alerted to the depth of Vivien's feelings for Olivier and except for that one meeting on Little Stanhope Street had not seen them together. Being a bit of an outsider to film and theatre gossip, rumor had not yet reached him. Surprisingly, it had not reached Jill either.

Frewen's description of the meeting of Jill, Larry, and Vivien in the Hotel Quisisana lobby indicates his lack of awareness:

Larry, on the other side of the hall, cried loudly, "Darling!" and Jill uttered further love-cries, as all three met in the middle of what could only be described as a joint passionate embrace; the while I smiled agedly and with benignity! The three broke away and both Larry and Viv at the same moment made an advance on me and introduced Jill. I was given a room one side of the Oliviers and Viv the other, so we were three in line and all on a communal basis—nobody ever knocked to enter and we all used all three rooms at will and Viv confided to me she thought it was "alright" and that we were not unwelcome. It was a great surprise not because I *need* have been surprised at Viv behaving like that or her friends, but just because it is rather outside my earlier experience of "the Young."

Frewen and Vivien left the Oliviers after a few days and went on to Rome. The Oliviers stopped in Naples, where Larry rang Vivien, creating quite a stir. Frewen begged her to give herself time and not to do anything impetuous.

Later Vivien would confess to Frewen that it was in Capri that Larry knew he was really in love with her and she knew she was in love with him. Capri was no doubt the point in their relationship where Larry, seeing Vivien and Jill together for an extended time, was able to weigh his emotions. And in Capri Vivien's fantasy came to an end. Shortly after she had returned to London, Laurence Olivier became—in reality—her lover.

Chapter Seven

Leigh Holman was not aware of his wife's liaison with Olivier. He was not a naive man, nor was he one to probe deeply beneath the surface, and Vivien was an intensely complex woman. The years as a child in India and her life in convent schools had polished and refined the exterior woman so that she possessed exquisite manners. Impoliteness was a cardinal sin, as were vanity and inconsiderateness. She was humble and appreciative of any small service done for her and still showered those close to her with tokens of her affection, Leigh included. Her personal fastidiousness edged on being a fetish. Dozens and dozens of white gloves (at one time about seventy-five pairs), freshly cleaned and individually wrapped in tissue, occupied her top bureau drawer, and she always tucked a clean pair in her purse to avoid having to suffer the embarrassment of wearing one that might be smudged. She carried perfume at all times, using it as a personal deodorant, room deodorant, and breath freshener, fearing she might offend someone with her natural body odors. And each night—if at home, visiting, or in a hotel—she would carefully fold her soiled clothes, place them on a chair, and cover them with a lovely pale peach satin and lace square that she had had specially made.

She was so burdened by secret guilt that it is surprising she did not falter under the weight. Her defection from the Catholic Church created disturbing confusions. She had been deeply affected by what she felt to be Church hypocrisy at San Remo and no longer attended mass. Yet she was besieged with requests from Catholic charities, which she was never able to refuse.

Her training had been to please everyone. Why then could she not feel the maternal love for Suzanne, the sexual desire for Leigh, and the religious dedication so important to her mother? Jill and Tarquin had their place in her private guilts as well. She could only accept their presence by continually telling herself (and later all her confidants) that Larry and she were destined for a great love.

The lovers would meet as often as they could and as discreetly as they were able. They were so wildly in love, so passionate in their need for each other, that they found it impossible to contain their feelings in front of others. Vivien began more and more to turn to Olivier for all advice. He quickly became not only her lover but her confidant, her adviser, her god. She was at the studio almost every day while Olivier made a film for Korda called *Conquest of the Air,* a feature documentary about the history of aviation. On Olivier's advice she was studying with Elsie Fogerty, who was working hard to lower her voice, insisting she throw out all of her high heels for a start, as she claimed they caused Vivien's back to go out of alignment and cramped her lungs. She was always pumping Olivier's old friend and teacher about Olivier's philosophies and probing for any anecdotes that Elsie Fogerty might recall. At home with Leigh she was sweet and charming, the perfect companion.

Frewen writes about that trip to Capri:

> . . . so ended one of the happiest episodes of my life. It is not only that Viv is beautiful to look at, gracious in manner, and quick on the uptake, but that she is extraordinarily *considerate* and you never seem to find her "off her guard" whether it is early morning after a bumpy train-night, or draggle-tailed evening after a wet weary day, whether you're the only friend with her in the whole province, or whether it's a party including the Young, and all the Distinguished and all the Amusing, she remains just the same, always treating me as though I were the best friend she has ever had and whom she has just met after months and is going to be parted from in a short half-hour. I've never known anything like it; she is the Perfect Companion.

Once she knew she had Olivier's love, Vivien was capable of being the Perfect Companion to Leigh, too. He was relieved to see her restlessness gone, that curious erratic bit of her that perhaps had been attributable to youth. She still did not sleep much, but she had given up parties, and she seemed content to read until dawn. The long ebony cigarette holder that she had used was not so much in evidence, as she smoked less, and with few parties to attend she drank very little. Leigh wished many things—that she would look up to him with the same childish delight she had early in their marriage, that she would show a more maternal interest in Suzanne, that she would give up her career. But he had to remember that she was only twenty-three. With all the problems, he considered himself a lucky man. She was beautiful, charming, well-mannered, loving—if not passionate— witty, a marvelous hostess, and well loved by all their friends.

But the genteel exterior was a mask for ruthlessness. She possessed a single-mindedness that was startling in one so young. Leigh did not see this side of her; nor did he recognize that at this time Larry and only Larry was in her thoughts—how to win him, how to please him, how to hold him.

There was no question that an open rivalry existed between Vivien and Jill. Jill was deeply and desperately in love with her husband, but she was conscious that she was losing him and she had known Vivien was the cause since Capri. Yet, curiously, despite the fact that Vivien threatened to break up her home and take away her adored Larry, Jill was able to tolerate Vivien's company and, in fact, was fascinated by her.

Vivien wooed Jill for luncheon dates where they could talk privately, and Jill seemed incapable of refusing. She was completely aware that Vivien was probing her mind for ideas on what to do in order to improve herself in Larry's eyes and to discover all she could about him.

What books mean the most to Larry? she would ask Jill casually.

He doesn't read much. But . . . Wuthering Heights, *perhaps, and of course Shakespeare*—a reply equally casual.

Why do you think Larry hates Hollywood so?

It has no sense of history.

Vivien was doing all she could to make Jill fond of her, and she was succeeding. Not only was Jill seeing Vivien at lunch, she quite often accepted her presence with Larry at dinner and would watch as Vivien used much of the information she had given her about Larry to her best advantage.

Oswald Frewen saw the Oliviers and Vivien together at the Moulin d'Or for supper one evening and escorted her home. He sat up with her until two-thirty in the morning begging her not to run away with Larry—"anyway not for a year." She was quiet for a moment and then thanked him for his "good advice." But on the subject of Olivier she never asked for it again.

She had convinced herself that she could never run off with Larry; her guilts toward Leigh and Jill and the two children, Suzanne and Tarquin, were too strong. Another factor was Gertrude, who was not as blind as Leigh as to what was happening in her daughter's life. They had lively discussions that dissolved into arguments. Gertrude seemed less concerned with Vivien conducting an affair than with her instigating a divorce. But with each passing day Vivien's need for Larry only deepened, and the chasm widened between those needs and her other loyalties.

The year 1936 was a vintage one for romance, as all the world watched and waited as the uncrowned King Edward VIII fought for his throne and for the woman he loved. Early in the year, directly after the death of Edward's father, King George V, Wallis Simpson was only a dim shadow to the English public, appearing first with her husband, Ernest Simpson, and then alone on guest lists for dinner parties at which the King was present. By spring not only Great Britain but the entire world knew that Edward VIII was in love with an American woman, once-divorced and now remarried. Dinner conversation centered on speculation as to whether Ernest Simpson would give his wife a divorce and if the King's mistress would then become his morganatic wife.

Vivien adored gossip and read every printed word she could about the King and Mrs. Simpson, and in conversation she always championed Mrs. Simpson's cause. In Capri it had been a main topic of discussion. On her return she had cornered Noël Coward and made him tell her about the dinner party she knew he had attended at Lady Colefax's when the King and Mrs. Simpson were present. She could not help but identify with Mrs. Simpson, for in her eyes there was a parallel between the royal affair and her own. Olivier was the Prince of Players on his way to becoming King, was he not?

On December 4, 1936, shortly after Wallis Simpson received her divorce decree, it was announced that the King had been told he could not marry her. Vivien took this to heart and discussed with Noël Coward the fear that if Larry was named by Leigh as corespondent in a divorce action, or in the reverse she was named by Jill, the scandal might be ruinous to his career. One week later the King had abdicated, telling his subjects he could not discharge his duties without the help and support of the woman he loved. No one wept more tears than Vivien at that decision.

The discussion of the King and Mrs. Simpson at Capri shared

equal time with Larry's plans for the next season at the Old Vic. *Hamlet* was to be the first production, and Olivier had come to Capri with a suitcase crammed with books of criticism and commentaries. The director, Tyrone Guthrie, had decided on a new interpretation of the role; but after the critics' cool views on his Romeo, Olivier was uncertain if Guthrie was right.

Before rehearsals had begun, the two men, at Guthrie's insistence, had been to see Ernest Jones, a Freudian analyst and the biographer of Freud, who had published some theories based on the interpretations of his master of the true motivations of Shakespearean heroes and villains. Guthrie followed Dr. Jones's thesis. The Hamlet he directed and Olivier portrayed delayed the revenge of his father's death because he was in love with his mother.

Vivien went to see the play fourteen times. Her worship of Olivier's theatre talent grew fourteenfold. She was in awe of his "greatness" and of the steely body and fiery mind he brought to the poetry and pathos of Shakespeare, and she harbored the deep feelings that until she had achieved some measure of that "greatness" on stage herself she was not worthy of his love, even though she was confident by this time that she did indeed possess it. But her intent was to do something concrete about it, which made the guilt tolerable.

Inactivity was her nemesis, forcing her to think about things she did not want to recall, and so she was thankful when Gliddon secured a part for her in a play going immediately into rehearsals. *Because We Must* was a light effort by playwright Ingaret Giffard, and Vivien's role was the only dimensional and theatrical one in the play. Need overbalanced judgment, for it is doubtful that she would have accepted the part in view of her lack of belief in the play's merits if she thought there was another choice.

Because of Olivier's performance in *Hamlet* and the demands of his personal life, Vivien was spending a good deal of time alone when Leigh was at his chambers. Nights were more difficult than ever. They loved each other passionately, yet Larry went home after the theatre to Jill, and she lay sleepless beside Leigh. Eclectically, voraciously, she read Shaw and Shakespeare, biographies and art histories, Lawrence, Lewis, and Joyce until dawn.

Although the American best seller *Gone With the Wind* had already been purchased by Selznick for films, the book had just been published in England. Vivien was enthralled by it. She had known little about American history and found the Civil War a heart-wrenching saga. Olivier was fascinated by human conflicts in war, and his taste leaned toward Shakespeare's histories. She made notes on the North and South to discuss with him. But most of all she was immediately drawn to Margaret Mitchell's heroine Scarlett O'Hara.

On opening night of *Because We Must* she gave each member of the cast a copy of the book and told John Gliddon that she felt she was ideal to play Scarlett in Selznick's planned film version. Gliddon, used to the enthusiasms of his acting clients, patiently tried to explain to her that the part was as American as Tom Sawyer. "Ridiculous," Vivien replied. "Scarlett's parentage was French-Irish, just like mine, and the South was still mostly first- or second-generation English in the mid-eighteen hundreds!" Gliddon then reminded her that since Selznick owned the rights and she was under contract to Korda, her interest would come to naught.

Vivien became obsessed with Scarlett. She went back and reread the book cover to cover and dog-eared passage after passage that she particularly liked. Then she spoke to Gliddon again. It was impossible to say no to Vivien. "Dear John," she cajoled, "I know I am right for Scarlett and that you can help me convince Mr. Selznick." He noted that she smiled gently but that there was a note of intensity in her request that he had not been conscious of previously. Certain that he was only appeasing her, he sent some photographs and press clippings on her to Selznick's New York office and promised them some film as soon as *Fire Over England* was ready for release.

He received only a cursory thank you, but apparently someone in New York had been sufficiently impressed to show the material to Kay Brown, Selznick's New York representative, who in turn sent him a telegram urging him to consider her, and Selznick wired her back:

FEBRUARY 3, 1937

TO: KATHARINE BROWN
     AND OSCAR SERLIN
CORRECTING ON MATTER IN TELETYPE, I HAVE NO ENTHUSI-
ASM FOR VIVIEN LEIGH. MAYBE I WILL HAVE, BUT AS YET HAVE
NEVER EVEN SEEN PHOTOGRAPH OF HER. WILL BE SEEING
"FIRE OVER ENGLAND" SHORTLY, AT WHICH TIME WILL OF
COURSE SEE LEIGH.

In May of 1936, one month before its American publication, Selznick had hesitated in paying $50,000 for *Gone With the Wind*, but his associate John Hay Whitney had wired him that if he didn't buy it for Selznick International (Selznick's film company, in which Whitney had a financial interest), he, Whitney, would purchase it and hold it for the company. Selznick capitulated and paid the asking price (the largest amount they ever paid for a book that was not yet an established success) and read it for the first time on board a boat to Hawaii.

MGM, in exchange for a half interest in the film, had loaned Selznick $1,250,000 (the film cost $4,250,000) and Clark Gable's services as Rhett, applying pressure for him to cast Joan Crawford as Scarlett, Maureen O'Sullivan as Melanie, and Melvyn Douglas as Ashley—all Metro performers. But Selznick felt that these good actors would be miscast and thereupon launched the most publicized talent search in the history of film.

By the time Vivien had read the book and pressed Gliddon to enter her name in the sweepstakes, Bette Davis, Joan Fontaine, Tallulah Bankhead, and many other top actresses had been tested or considered. Vivien was virtually unknown to Hollywood and her chances seemed even less than slim. She did not drop the idea, however, and brought it up from time to time. There is no doubt that Scarlett held a fascination for her, but she was also astute enough to realize that the winning of the part would bring her international stardom, an accomplishment she felt could place her on a more equal footing with Olivier and enable her to obtain better stage roles.

Because We Must closed within a month, and Korda exercised his option by casting her in the film *Storm in a Teacup*, a funny but inconsequential comedy adapted from the Bruno Frank play *Storm im Wasserglas*, which had had a fairly successful Broadway run as *Storm Over Patsy*. She co-starred with Rex Harrison and Scruffy the dog, and her role could not have given her much pride of accomplishment, though she gave a witty and warm performance.

In early 1937, Sydney Carroll was putting a slim farce called *Bats in the Belfry* into rehearsal at the Ambassadors' Theatre, where Vivien had so captivated London in *The Mask of Virtue*. She accepted a part he offered her in it, but it was a mistake. The play was indeed very light and slipped away almost unnoticed in a matter of weeks.

Vivien's career seemed to be slipping away from her as well. She knew Olivier did not think her a good actress yet, and the parts she had just played had done little to bolster her image. It had been two years since she had swept London by storm, and she had not appeared in one good play since. Nor since signing with Korda had a top film role come her way. She was quietly disturbed when Jill played opposite Larry in *Twelfth Night*, which followed *Hamlet* at the Old Vic.

Yet Olivier believed that she had a unique quality and that she had to work hard at some of her inadequacies. He found her rather thin and high-pitched voice still her greatest failing as a stage performer and began to work with her to overcome this and other problems. More and more their relationship was moving out into the open.

In March they were assigned co-starring roles by Korda in a film based on Galsworthy's *The First and the Last*, which Graham Greene had scripted under the title *Twenty-one Days*. Basil Dean was the director, and Olivier's work with him in the past on two plays had not been much happier than Vivien's film experience in *Look Up and Laugh*. Korda stepped in himself to direct some sequences when he saw that his director and his stars were at such odds with each other. He also thought the film needed the Continental touch, and the scene he contributed—a court scene—had a Brechtian quality.

Korda's decision to make the film had been stimulated by his belief in Vivien's star potential, and in *Twenty-one Days* she had a chance to be sensual and a lady—exactly the combination of traits he thought would work for her. He was also a romantic, and a film co-starring two young lovers appealed to him (by now there were few in London's theatre and film circles who did not know of the affair). He took Larry and Vivien's side throughout the making of the film and had an active part in helping them finally to run off together, as, coincidentally, the two characters they portrayed in the film also did. Korda, whose first marriage to Maria Corda (a well-known silent screen star) dissolved in 1932, directed most of his attention to being the head of his male-dominated family (all three of the Korda brothers—Alex, Zoltan, and Vincent—had sons). He enjoyed men relating to him paternally, perhaps because of his problems with his own son, and he easily "adopted" younger men like Olivier. Becoming the benevolent father, he arranged the shooting schedules so that Larry and Vivien could take a week off to appear together in *Hamlet* in Elsinore (Denmark), Vivien to play Ophelia.

Before the two lovers left, Jill, pent up with desperation, arranged a meeting with Vivien, intent on pleading with her not to go away with Larry. She arrived at Little Stanhope Street late in the afternoon when Vivien had just returned from the studio and while Leigh was still at the Middle Temple. Waiting nervously in the small sitting room surrounded by evidences of Vivien's exquisite taste, she rehearsed what she planned to say. Vivien swept into the room impeccably dressed, showing no sign of anxiety at the rather dreadful audience ahead of her.

"Hello, Jill darling." She smiled, one hand grasping Jill's hand warmly as with the other she pulled the cord for the maid.

"Champagne," she ordered when Aide appeared.

And Jill was never able to speak what she had come to say. When she left the house she knew she had waited too long and that she had lost Olivier.

The trip to Elsinore was a memorable one for Vivien. Her love for Olivier seemed boundless, her pride enormous. Never in her life had she wanted anything more than to be the object of his devotion. Once London was behind them the restrictions were off, decorum could be ignored. The cast and crew of *Hamlet* became their confidants. By the time they reached Denmark, the lovers knew they would never be able to turn back.

From Elsinore, Vivien wrote Leigh that she begged his forgiveness but she had gone off with Larry and would not return to Little Stanhope Street. Oswald Frewen tried to intercede and get them to reconsider their decision, to which Olivier replied that it was to Vivien's benefit to live with a man who shared her artistry and her life and not with Leigh, whose opinion on *drama* was by Olivier's standards contemptible.

Drama was the most important thing in young Olivier's mind. Vivien understood this and worshiped at the same shrine. She also was aware that to share the experience of his portraying Hamlet, a role that had more meaning to him than any other, would bind them even closer together. John Gielgud had already been acclaimed as the Hamlet of their generation, and after *Romeo and Juliet* a distinct rivalry existed between him and Larry. Olivier did not think of himself as the same sort of actor as Gielgud. He felt they were different faces of the same coin, with Gielgud the top half—all spirituality, beauty, and abstract things—and himself all earth, blood, and perhaps the baser part of humanity. When he played Romeo he was fighting for his own conception of great theatre, trying to sell realism in Shakespeare. The part of Hamlet, because of its enormous length and depth, seemed ideal to make his point.

They were to play *Hamlet* in the courtyard of the ancient Kronborg Castle in Elsinore with its pinnacled towers and the thick stone walls against which the sea crashed endlessly. It was a cold June week, wind and rain constant, and Vivien had to rehearse beneath an umbrella, but still she shivered and froze for two days and two nights while Larry fed her coffee and schnapps to keep her going.

The day before the opening the sky was darker than usual, with thick, coiling black clouds and a tempest wind that made it impossible for lines to be heard. Guthrie made the decision to transfer the production to the nearby Merienlyst Hotel, where they were all staying. It was a disappointment to the entire company, except for Vivien, who felt more relaxed and confident of her voice in the smaller "theatre."

It is difficult to assess if the onstage or offstage drama being played was the more intense. Having made a decision to leave their mates and children and live together, they now had only a few days to arrange this most difficult crisis. Jill and Leigh had to be told before the press got wind. Her parents and several friends needed to be notified, and although Korda's office would be helpful in writing a press release, there would still be reporters to face upon their return. It was a delicate situation. Tarquin was an infant; they had fallen in love while Jill was pregnant. Then there was Suzanne. Vivien was not sure what to do about the child in the future, but she knew the four-year-old would be better off until their plans were set to remain with her father and in her nursery at Little Stanhope Street in the care of Nanny Oake. The press might not react well to that either.

In spite of all the problems, Vivien was happy in Elsinore in 1937. Sharing all of Larry's private and public hours made her completely oblivious to the poor working conditions and the long hours. The Times sent a reviewer up to cover the opening, and the next morning she and Larry had the review read to them over the telephone. Olivier's Hamlet was superlative, it said, and Vivien Leigh's Ophelia showed real promise.

The sun broke through the shifting black clouds, and that night they moved back to the courtyard of Kronborg. Darkness covered the town of Elsinore, the Swedish coast was lost, and only the lights of a cargo vessel flickered on the waters. Two thousand people sat silently waiting for Hamlet's ghost to pass through the turreted courtyard. The production had triumphed twice. To Vivien and Olivier it seemed a good and special omen.

Chapter Eight

Aide, the maid at Little Stanhope Street, was pretty and young and proceeded to get married during the time Vivien was in Denmark. Leigh's old friend Beryl Samson came to his rescue and sent Daisy Yoguel over to take Aide's place. Just after moving in with Olivier, Vivien returned to the house when Leigh was at the Middle Temple to collect her personal effects and was met at the door by an unknown maid. Before she was able to enter the house, two elderly neighbor ladies, visibly disturbed, came rushing up to announce that they had just seen Nanny Oake angrily smack Suzanne in the park.

Shaking badly and on the verge of tears, Vivien went inside and waited for Nanny Oake and Suzanne to return. But as she gathered together the things she had come for, she could not help having mixed and anxious emotions. She was a stranger in the home that she herself had so lovingly put together. But, of course, that was not the most painful cross she must bear. If Nanny Oake was in fact mistreating Suzanne, what right had she to fire Nanny? After walking out on Leigh and, yes, her child for the man she loved, what rights did she have? And unless she was prepared to fight for Suzanne's custody, did she have the right to intervene at all in the child's care? It was a scene directly out of the just-released American film *Stella Dallas*.

Nanny Oake and her charge finally returned. It seemed that Suzanne had tossed her bonnet for Nanny to retrieve one too many times for Nanny's considerable patience. The explanation did not ease Vivien's anxiety and she left the house in a state.

Whatever wounds Leigh Holman suffered he bore with incredible good grace and with a politely indifferent facade. In the early months of the separation he was certain that Vivien would return home to him and treated the matter much in the way one might a child's tantrum or a juvenile's escapade. His law practice and the running of a motherless household kept him busy. He remained on good terms with Gertrude and Ernest, and he never spoke bitterly about Vivien or with self-pity about his own plight. He merely carried on with his life in a dignified, self-possessed fashion. There was no question of his love for Vivien; and he refused to accept the undeniable truth that Vivien and he were simply not well mated, that their needs and desires had been worlds apart even when they were together.

Olivier had bought Durham Cottage at 4 Christchurch Street in Chelsea. It was a charming but modest seventeenth-century house with a lovely walled garden, near Burton Court and the Chelsea Hospital. Being small, its care would be minimal and decoration not too big an undertaking. Conscious of Vivien's state of anxiety, Larry decided they should first have a brief vacation in Venice.

They stayed at a comfortable hotel along the Grand Canal. It was July and the city glittered in the sun. The water shimmered, buildings shone, and there were so many marvelous impressions to seize and to hold. St. Mark's Basilica with its eight hundred marble columns, the Campanile, and the interior of St. Mark's, where at every turn there was a vision of marvels—such a profusion of gold and precious stones, such works of great and beautiful art.

They fed the pigeons in the Piazza, held hands in the Chiesa della Salute, put on their sunglasses to gaze at the brilliant facade of the Ca' d'Oro, and strolled in the clear moonlight along the Molo. Vivien was radiant. Life took on a new, deeper meaning for her. Olivier noted with relief the disappearance of her anxieties.

No sooner had they returned to Durham Cottage than she was cast as the second lead in A Yank at Oxford, which was the first film Metro-Goldwyn-Mayer was to make in England. Korda had loaned her out for the small but showy part—that of the adulterous young wife of an Oxford bookseller—certain that the American exposure would greatly enhance her career. Louis B. Mayer was not pleased at the idea of casting an "unknown," but British producer Michael Balcon persuasively appealed to Mayer's financial acumen. Vivien was in London, which meant no traveling expenses, and in addition her loan-out fee to Korda was far less than the salary of a known American actress. This knowledge of why she was finally cast as flirty Elsa Craddock was disturbing to Vivien, more so, perhaps, because Maureen O'Sullivan had been cast in the lead.

It was the first time the girls had met since their Roehampton days; and though it should have been a happy reunion, it was in fact a most difficult one for Vivien. In their childhood friendship Vivien had always been the leader. Now Maureen was the star. Yet Vivien was a true professional, quite used to repertory companies where actors and actresses considered the play first and their egos last. And actually, though a secondary role, Vivien's was the most interesting. But there was a deeper and more painful reason for Vivien to be stand-offish with Maureen. It was quite impossible for her to explain to a contemporary who had shared her convent schooling how she could have left her husband and child to take up a life with a married man who was a recent father. (At this time Tarquin was only one year old.) The situation was made somewhat easier for Vivien because they had few scenes together. Most of her scenes were with Robert Taylor, Griffith Jones, and Lionel Barrymore.

Jack Conway, who had previously directed Arsène Lupin, Red Headed Woman, Viva Villa! and A Tale of Two Cities, did an admirable job on a trite script. But even so, Vivien felt that his notions of English character were somewhat one-sided. She leaned heavily in her portrayal on Olivier's home advice, and her independent interpretation did not ease tension on the set. She did, however, contribute strongly to the final credibility of the film; and though she was not aware of it, Maureen viewed her with even greater admiration, for she was always early on the set, always prepared, and never flagged in her energy. And in spite of the ghastly makeup and the frizzy hairdo chosen for her, Maureen thought Vivien more beautiful than ever.

Her life at Durham Cottage could not have been more of a contrast to her life on Little Stanhope Street. Olivier was filming The Divorce of Lady X (a remake of the 1932 film Counsel's Opinion) opposite Merle Oberon and with Ralph Richardson at the same time as Vivien was filming for Metro. Both were up early and off to the studio at the same time, returning home tired but happy and able to discuss their days. They read lines together and discussed interpretations. Vivien hated to see that time come to an end, for when it did Larry went back to the Old Vic as Macbeth while she waited for Korda to pick up (or perhaps drop) the option he held on her services.

It had been almost six months since they had run off to Denmark. Larry decided it was time to ask Jill for a divorce, and Vivien in turn to ask Leigh for one, so that they could marry. Leigh replied that he would do nothing to release her unless forced to (meaning, it seemed, that he would refuse unless she became pregnant with Olivier's child), and he confessed to Oswald Frewen that he still hoped to win her back. The second blow came when Jill refused to divorce Larry.

It was a dismal situation, but Vivien would not accept the facts. She was convinced they would find a way to marry, and her love for Olivier grew each day. Friends were constantly remarking that it was almost impossible for her to keep her eyes off him when they were in public.

On December 27, after spending a private, happy Christmas together—their first—Vivien appeared as Titania at the Old Vic under Tyrone Guthrie's direction in A Midsummer Night's Dream with Robert Helpmann, Anthony Quayle, Ralph Richardson, and Alexander Knox. She was enchanting, as indeed was the entire production. The stage ceased altogether to be self-consciously theatrical, a spell descended upon it, and the illusion was complete.

Vivien deeply believed Olivier was the greatest actor alive, and during this period she was his most devout and devoted pupil. His entire life revolved around his acting experience. They might be riding on top of a bus and he would single out a fellow passenger and begin to discuss him with Vivien, noting the man's gestures and reactions. "Why do you think he did that?" he would ask. And then would proceed to analyze the man's action with an imaginative explanation. Much later, in a performance, Vivien would note that he was using the man's gesture as a bit of business and that it worked mainly because it seemed true and real. He also identified so greatly with each role he was playing that she could expect him to be some of that character off stage.

His advice to her was always to anticipate what the audience expected—and then not to do it. Working on her phrasing with her, he reached back to Chaliapin's teaching and warned her never to take a breath when the audience expected, thus they would not notice when a breath was taken and believe a whole phrase had been sung on one breath.

"You have to feel it to do it," he would explain about a part. "If you do it right you feel it. The suffering, the passion, the bitterness, you've got to feel them. And it takes something out of you and puts something in, as all emotional experiences do."

For the next few months she watched him do exactly what he preached as Iago in *Othello*, Vivaldi in *King of Nowhere*, and in the title role of *Coriolanus*. This last portrayal was considered his greatest performance in his thirteen years on the stage. His voice was deeper and stronger than ever, and the role required a patrician quality and a pride of nature that made the man too proud to accept praise. Olivier confessed that it was quite easy to get into the role. "Getting into" his role was, of course, the prime thing for him, and to do that with Iago (to Ralph Richardson's Othello) he returned to the eminent psychoanalyst Ernest Jones. As in his analysis of *Hamlet*, the doctor insisted that homosexuality was Shakespeare's theme. There followed several hours of discussion about the interpretation of each scene taken in this new light.

Olivier portrayed Iago as a man possessed of a subconscious affection. Therefore, the great climax in Act III, when Iago and Othello kneel together planning the death of Cassio, virtually became a love scene, with Othello's "Now art thou my lieutenant" and Iago's reply "I am your own for ever" taking on a new significance. It might have worked if Richardson's Othello had been played with an understanding of this new Iago. When Olivier and Tyrone Guthrie left Dr. Jones, Olivier confessed, "I don't think we dare tell Ralphy." Any overtones of sexual perversion, however unconscious, would immediately gain Richardson's disapproval, so they never did come right out and confront him with what they were attempting to convey. Rehearsals therefore went forward with Richardson quite unaware of why Olivier was playing Iago in what he could not help but think was *a curious manner*. "Never mind your psychology!" he would exclaim whenever the subconscious was even mentioned. "The beauty of the play to me is the magnificence of its rhetoric. Leave me my 'monumental alabaster,' " he would insist. And they did sincerely believe that perhaps Othello would *not* have been aware of Iago's perversion, in which case their character study might be the more powerful. But if Richardson had known, the critics might have reacted better than they did. As it was, they missed the point entirely.

Vivien was at the theatre nearly every night learning, as she confessed, by just watching Olivier perform. Olivier might seem her Professor Henry Higgins, but Vivien was no Eliza Doolittle. On her own she was terribly funny, and very witty. And, not unlike their good friend Noël Coward, shrewd and intelligent. Olivier had never felt himself to be much of an intellectual. Noël, as he said, "made him use his silly little brain," pointing out to him when he talked nonsense. Vivien was in her way just as taxing, just as thrilling to be with, and most of all she carried on what Coward had begun. She made him read. He had read very little early in his life except for scripts of plays and films in which he appeared or thought he might appear. However, he never kept pace with Vivien's intellectual interests. The pursuit of anything other than acting always took second place, but he was stimulated and excited by this side of Vivien.

In the meantime her love and appreciation of opera and music and art grew. She had learned a great deal about art and artists from Korda, and she loved museums and auctions, and bought art selectively and with great insight and sensitivity. Two years before she had, for instance, purchased an early Boudin for two hundred pounds that had already risen dramatically in value.

During the spring of 1938, Korda loaned her to Charles Laughton's newly formed independent Mayflower Productions for the lead in St. Martin's Lane (Sidewalks of London in the U.S.A.). This meant Vivien and Olivier (who was having one of his most stellar seasons at the Old Vic, where he gave a quartet of great performances) were on different schedules. She would come home from the studio at Denham, study her lines for the next day, meet Larry at the theatre, return home late, and rise at five A.M. after no more than three to four hours' sleep for what was certainly her most strenuous role to date, involving not only a highly dramatic part but one demanding an ability to dance and sing. It was trying and exhausting, and it was made more difficult by her poor rapport with Laughton.

The filming was fraught with hostility. Vivien and Laughton did not get along any better now than when he had refused to star opposite her in the abandoned Cyrano. He felt she was tremendously gifted and capable physically and emotionally of being a great film star, but she somehow unnerved him. Vivien, on her part, admired Laughton as an actor, but was terrified he would make a physical advance which she would be forced to reject. Therefore she kept to her dressing room as much as she could. Curiously, though sensitive to things of this nature, she was not aware of Laughton's homosexuality.

A rather interesting sidenote is that Vivien had recently added a few four-letter words to her vocabulary. Though still (and always) almost painfully polite, she would curse quite venomously at inanimate objects or at herself. Laughton could not bear to hear these profanities spoken by her, and it became a considerable issue between them.

By summer 1938 four of Vivien's films—*Fire Over England*, *Storm in a Teacup*, *Dark Journey*, and *A Yank at Oxford*—had opened in New York with an extremely good press. However, only *A Yank at Oxford* received a general release. Outside of New York and a few major cities, if Americans thought of her at all they thought of her as a frizzy-haired flighty young woman who almost got Robert Taylor kicked out of Oxford.

Chapter Nine

The summer of 1938 was to be the last season of peace England was to have for a long time. But Vivien and Larry did not know that then. Exhausted by the tense days of filming St. Martin's Lane, Vivien was thrilled when Olivier decided they should take a holiday. Where to was not an easy question, as the threat of war hung over the Continent. Her beloved Austria was out. Only three months earlier truckloads of young men wearing swastika armbands had paraded in the streets of Vienna defying the police as they hauled down the Austrian flag and raised the blood-red banner with the swastika. Austria had been swallowed up by Hitler. It horrified Vivien, as did the thought that Hitler might not stop at Austria. Surely there would be war then. But three months had passed since the Anschluss, and there had been no further threat from the Reich.

They decided on the South of France because many of their friends were spending the summer there—dropping in and out of the villa that John Gielgud and Hugh Beaumont had rented in Vence—and because they were desperate for sun, London having been depressingly cold and dreary the entire spring. Vivien also liked the fact that the Duke and Duchess of Windsor, now having married, were in Antibes, though she had had many heated discussions with Noël Coward (who saw the royal couple occasionally) on the trip they had just made to see Hitler, which she thought ill-advised, if not simply stupid. Still, royalty intrigued her as much as it always had, and privately she longed to be invited to one of the Windsors' intimate parties.

Vivien and Olivier drove down through France to the Riviera in her trusty but rather weary old Ford V-8 two-seater. The threat of Hitler, the terror of the bloody civil war so close in Spain, the rise of Fascism under Mussolini seemed unreal beneath the comforting warmth of the southern sun. First they stopped at St. Paul, a fortified town built in the twelfth century and set high up in terraces on a spur of rock. Vence, where Gielgud was staying, was only a fifteen-minute drive. Their hotel, La Colombe d'Or, was charming. In their early years Picasso, Dufy, Modigliani, Bracque, Matisse, and Chagall had often stayed there, trading paintings for food and lodging. These great works were hung in all the public areas of the hotel. Vivien adored eating lunch facing a Modigliani or a Dufy, and she walked happily along the old ramparts looking down at a view that could have been a scene from any of the Impressionists' paintings. But both she and Larry missed the sea, so after a few days they drove down along the coast to the small village of Agay, which had a sheltered bay where they could swim and sun-splashed beaches for them to stretch out on. They stopped at the Calanque d'Or, a little hotel not nearly so grand as the hotel in St. Paul, but with an irresistible plus for Vivien: the patron had eighteen Siamese cats.

Life was an idyllic day-to-day existence—swimming, sunning, sightseeing and occasionally visiting with Gielgud and Hugh Beaumont, or Peggy Ashcroft, or Glen Byam Shaw and his wife Angela Baddeley, who were also on the Riviera that summer. June melted with a curious unreality into July, when on the first Monday, Olivier received a cable from his London agent:

ARE YOU INTERESTED GOLDWYN IDEA FOR SEPTEMBER FIRST
FOR VIVIEN YOURSELF AND OBERON IN WUTHERING HEIGHTS
STOP ANSWER AS SOON AS POSSIBLE STOP

They discussed this for several hours before sending an ambiguous cable stating that they would discuss it on their return to London.

In the past Hollywood had been an unhappy experience for Olivier. Once, after a flurry of just such cables, he had gone to do a film with Garbo, only to be replaced soon after he arrived by John Gilbert. Nor had he been happy there with Jill on a succeeding trip. He harbored, as well, a lack of respect for films, especially those made in Hollywood. In addition, Vivien was being offered the secondary and, in her opinion, rather dull role of Isabella. *Wuthering Heights* had always been a favorite of hers, and she felt a closer affinity to Cathy— a part it seemed Merle Oberon was to play.

One week later the script arrived following several more cables begging them to read it before their return, as the director, William Wyler, was to be in London. The script was a literate and good rendering of the book. The role of Heathcliff had been adapted exceptionally well. Isabella, however, remained for Vivien uninteresting, and after her experience in A Yank At Oxford she did not feel she should accept a supporting role in an American film when she had, after all, starred in four recent English films. Since they did not want to be parted and Olivier was not that keen to do a Hollywood film, they sent back a cable stating that they were not interested.

Toward the middle of July they drove back up through France, stopping as they had planned at Roanne on the Loire. A letter from Olivier's agent waited for him there. He hoped, the agent wrote, that because of the importance of the film, and the standing of William Wyler (Counsellor at Law, Dodsworth, These Three, Dead End, and Jezebel), Olivier might be persuaded to change his mind. Olivier again read the script, this time liking the role sufficiently so that the first thing they did upon their return to London was to see Jezebel. The film, starring Bette Davis, had been made by Warner Brothers to beat out Selznick's Gone With the Wind, which was still, after more than a year, uncast. Vivien was particularly impressed with the performance Wyler got from Bette Davis, and knowing in her heart that Larry now wanted to play Heathcliff, insisted they at least meet with Wyler.

In Hollywood, Samuel Goldwyn, who was the producer of Wuthering Heights, and Wyler, had decided Olivier was the best choice for Heathcliff. Wyler, considering the role a "plum for any actor—particularly one relatively unknown in America," was puzzled at Olivier's original lack of enthusiasm and had assumed (somewhat rightly) that it was due to a previous unpleasant experience in Hollywood. But Wyler, a deeply perceptive man, knew the moment he entered the small walled garden of Durham Cottage to greet her as she stood by a late-blooming trellis of roses that Vivien was the real reason.

He had tea with them in front of the open fire of the modest sitting room, a Siamese cat Vivien had brought back from Agay purring at his feet before it settled itself in the corner of Vivien's chair. There were small bowls of flowers on either end of the mantel and on all available tables, as well as lovely porcelain figurines. Bookcases flanking the hearth were crammed with beautifully bound book sets, and over the hearth was a good oil that Vivien had recently bought at auction. The room strongly bore Vivien's signature. She talked animatedly and persistently, leaning most carefully forward so as not to disturb the cat as she poured tea from a fragile Limoges pot, setting it back again on a glass-topped white wrought-iron Victorian cocktail table. Olivier sat on a straight cane chair, his eyes following her every gesture.

They discussed Wyler's native Alsace, Bette Davis, and *Gone With the Wind*. Wyler had recently fallen in love with Margaret Tallichet, a pretty twenty-one-year-old redhead who had come to Hollywood from Austin, Texas, with film aspirations and who was working as a secretary in Paramount's publicity department to finance acting and singing lessons. A chance meeting with Carole Lombard brought her to the attention of Selznick's publicity man Russell Birdwell. Through Birdwell's efforts she was put under contract as a Scarlett possibility. Vivien was intrigued with all the machinations of Hollywood, Selznick, and the search for Scarlett and asked Wyler a million questions. *Was Gable truly signed to play Rhett? Was Margaret Mitchell doing the screenplay? What sort of man was Selznick? Who was to direct?*

Toward the end of tea, Olivier mentioned that there was to be a showing of Vivien's new film, *St. Martin's Lane*, and that perhaps Wyler might like to join them. He accepted, knowing instinctively that the two hoped that after viewing the film he would be convinced Vivien should be signed as Cathy in *Wuthering Heights.* Wyler *was* impressed and moved by her performance and agreed that she was not only excellent but had a tremendous film presence and could very well play Cathy, but—*and here it was*—he could not offer her any role but that of Isabella.

"I will play Cathy," she said, smiling nervously.

"Merle Oberon has already been cast," he replied, "and she is under contract to Sam Goldwyn."

"I will play Cathy or nothing," she insisted.

"It's impossible and I assure you that you will never get a better part than Isabella for an American debut," Wyler urged.

They parted with Wyler knowing Vivien would not accept a secondary role and doubting that Olivier would sign for Heathcliff in view of this fact. But with all his sensitivity, Wyler had not perceived the depth of Vivien's understanding of the man she loved. Having met Wyler, Olivier now wanted to play Heathcliff desperately, and he had refused because he had not wanted to leave her behind. Fearing that self-sacrifice of this nature could destroy them more quickly than separation, she insisted he go to Hollywood to do the film, reasoning that she would be well occupied for the three months of the projected separation, as she had been offered the title role in *Serena Blandish*, to open shortly at the little Gate Theatre; and then, at Christmastime, she had a commitment to appear in the revival at the Old Vic of *A Midsummer Night's Dream.*

Olivier was not convinced that she should be left behind to fend for herself in what he knew would be a difficult situation, and he put off making an immediate acceptance of Wyler's now exceptionally generous offer. He was co-starring with Ralph Richardson in *Q Planes* (*Clouds Over Europe* in the U.S.A.) for Korda, and he discussed this dilemma with both men. Korda, now in love with Merle Oberon and facing a similar separation, felt the two lovers had to adapt their lives to the demands of their careers and not the other way around. And Richardson advised him to go to Hollywood to do the film because the fame attached would do him no harm.

Q Planes was completed by the end of October, and on November 5, Vivien's twenty-fifth birthday, she drove with him to Southampton to see him sail for America on the *Normandie* and then returned that evening for a performance of *Serena Blandish*, which had opened on September 13 and was closing that week after an unsuccessful run.

Vivien was idle until Tyrone Guthrie summoned her to begin rehearsals on *A Midsummer Night's Dream*. Meantime, Olivier sent her a cable from New York: Goldwyn had called from Hollywood as soon as the *Normandie* had docked to ask if Vivien might still be available, as they were having problems with Merle Oberon. But no sooner had Vivien had her hopes raised than Larry cabled her back from Hollywood that Oberon was going on with the role as agreed.

Daily letters began arriving at little Durham Cottage. Olivier was not getting on well with Merle Oberon, and open war had developed during a love scene because Oberon claimed he had spat on her as he spoke his lines. They replayed the scene. "You spat again!" Olivier's leading lady accused. At which point Olivier let loose an abusive reply and Merle Oberon walked off the set.

Then there was the problem of Olivier's makeup. Used to the theatricality of the stage, he had insisted on heavy makeup. After viewing the first rushes, Goldwyn followed Wyler onto the set screaming in his famous accented voice, "This actor is the ugliest actor in pictures! This actor will ruin me!"

Olivier's going to Hollywood now seemed a terrible mistake; and to add to the difficulties of their separation, the production problems and his own insecurity in his performance, he had developed a terrible case of athlete's foot and had to walk around on crutches which were removed only when the cameras were ready to roll.

Vivien was lonely and despondent. What she could withstand with Olivier she found quite impossible alone. There were her parents, who felt this a good opportunity to discuss her situation with her, attempting to convince her to return to Leigh; and there was Leigh and little Suzanne and the motherless house on Little Stanhope Street. Her awesome, frightening restlessness returned. Her heartbeat accelerated wildly. She felt she might be drowning and had used up all the air in her lungs. She smoked incessantly and never seemed able to satisfy her hunger. The nights became terrifying, and she slept less than ever.

Once again she picked up her dog-eared copy of *Gone With the Wind* and reread it and then called John Gliddon. "You know," she said, "the passage where Scarlett voices her happiness that her mother is dead, so that she can't see what a bad girl Scarlett has become? Well—that's me."

Scarlett had still not been cast, and everyone knew a final decision had to be made soon or Selznick would never get the film before the cameras. As fate would have it, Olivier's Hollywood agent, Myron Selznick, was David's trusted brother.

Vivien wrote Olivier asking him to speak to Myron, but no sooner had she posted the letter than she cabled she was sailing on the *Queen Mary* the next day and then would fly from New York to Los Angeles, where she could only spend five days before having to return to the Old Vic. It seemed a mad and reckless expenditure for a five-day visit with Larry, but Vivien was convinced she must do it.

Act Two

And all my fortunes at thy foot I'll lay
And follow thee my lord throughout the world.

—Juliet
in Shakespeare's
Romeo and Juliet

Chapter Ten

Dawn usually found Vivien a lonely figure on a deserted deck wrapped mummylike in woolens to protect her from the freezing December sea winds. Yet, with all the discomfort of an unseasonal and rough Atlantic crossing, she was exuberantly happy. Soon she would see Larry. There was little else she thought about, unless it was her intense wish to be cast as Scarlett O'Hara in *Gone With the Wind*. Olivier was to remain in Hollywood until the beginning of March. It seemed perfectly sensible to her that if she were to get the role they could remain together.

She saw nothing of New York when they docked, rushing as soon as she was through customs to the airport for the next scheduled flight to Los Angeles. Having never flown before, she was not sure what her reaction to it would be. It was terror, and had she not been so desperate to see Larry, and if their time to be together was not so precious and short, she never would have boarded. She had a sleeping berth, as the trip took fifteen and a half hours and required three stops for refueling, but she was unable to close her eyes. To pass the time she worked on "Scarlett expressions" in her makeup mirror. In her description of Scarlett in the book, Margaret Mitchell kept comparing her to a cat. So Vivien practiced "a Cheshire cat smile," "eyes of a hungry cat," and "clawlike gestures of her hands."

Olivier met her at the airport, but it was a restrained meeting, for they were not alone. Hollywood morality, he explained to her later, was set on a double standard. Residents did not have private lives. They had public and *secret* lives, and he had been well warned by

Myron Selznick, his agent, that careers had been ruined for less reason than a public affair being conducted by two people legally married to other mates. Vivien was driven to the Beverly Hills Hotel, where a room had been reserved for her by Larry. But Vivien's great joy at being reunited with him overcame any quarrel she might have with this arrangement. She was giddy with happiness and bubbling over with ideas and schemes. Somehow she would have to meet and make an immediate impression on David Selznick. Somehow she would have to get an immediate test. Somehow things would work out so that she and Larry would not have to be parted.

First, Myron Selznick had to be convinced that no one but she should be cast as Scarlett. On the morning of December 10, the third day of her stay, they met briefly. "My God, you are Scarlett!" he said. "And if I know my brother as well as I think I do, he is going to agree." They planned to meet for dinner after Larry was through filming that night.

It had been almost two and a half years since David Selznick had purchased the film rights to *Gone With the Wind*, a period fraught with script, casting, and financial problems. Many of the best writers in Hollywood had worked on the script, including John Van Druten, Jo Swerling, Oliver H. P. Garrett, novelist F. Scott Fitzgerald, and Sidney Howard, who perhaps contributed the most to the final shooting script. (As scenes were written and rewritten during the entire production, there was no actual final screenplay per se until the last day of shooting.)

David Selznick's original choice for Rhett Butler had been Gary Cooper, but that had been quickly set aside for Clark Gable. Leading contenders had also been Ronald Colman, Basil Rathbone, and Errol Flynn; but Selznick never wavered in his enthusiasm for Gable, who was the people's choice in every public poll.

Leslie Howard uniquely represented the brooding, poetic intellectual hero to film audiences (*The Petrified Forest, Of Human Bondage*), and Selznick had thought if he offered Howard the part that, at least with the role of Ashley Wilkes, there would be no casting problem. To his dismay, the actor was not keen to accept. Melvyn Douglas, Jeffrey Lynn, Ray Milland, and Shepperd Strudwick were then considered, none of whom Selznick thought right. Finally he succeeded in persuading Howard to accept the role, and then, seeing his first costume tests, he became duly alarmed. Howard looked his forty-five years, and Ashley in the opening sequences of the film was a man of twenty-five.

Before Olivia de Havilland was cast as Melanie Hamilton Wilkes, Frances Dee, Andrea Leeds, and Anne Shirley had been tested. For a time Selznick considered Joan Fontaine, planning it for her major film debut. But Joan, holding out for the plum role of Scarlett, suggested her sister, Olivia, who was under contract to Warner Brothers.

It was Scarlett, though, who was the major concern; and in the search for the actress to portray her, girls flocked to Hollywood hoping to secure a test, talent scouts combed the South for possibilities, and almost all of Hollywood's glamorous leading ladies were considered and many of them tested. Yet the cameras were set to roll after two and a half years without a Scarlett. There were many candidates— among them Joan Fontaine, Paulette Goddard (who seemed in the lead), Susan Hayward, Norma Shearer, Lana Turner, Miriam Hopkins, Loretta Young, Joan Crawford, Katharine Hepburn, Bette Davis, Jean Arthur, Joan Bennett, Lucille Ball, Tallulah Bankhead, and unknowns Margaret Tallichet, Mary Anderson (who played Maybelle Merriweather in the film), Alicia Rhett (finally cast as India Wilkes), and Catherine Campbell (an Atlanta belle now Mrs. Randolph Hearst).

Selznick was a man under fire. Shooting could not begin without Scarlett O'Hara, and his financial backers were snapping uncomfortably at his heels. Then William Cameron Menzies, the film's production designer—who had a fine record of screen direction as well, including Korda's *Things to Come* and portions of *Conquest of the Air*—came up with a stroke of genius.

Construction of the interior sets—Tara, Twelve Oaks, and the Atlanta Bazaar—was already begun on Stage Sixteen but in order to build exteriors, space had to be cleared on the Selznick back lot, which was now piled high and wide with the sets and building facades of films dating back to the days of the silents. Clearing the back lot for a set the size required to re-create ante-bellum Atlanta would cost dearly, but to burn the old sets and then to film that fire as the burning of Atlanta would satisfy John Hay Whitney, Metro-Goldwyn-Mayer, and all the money people who threatened to withdraw further support if more time was lost. With Menzies' plan the film would be under way, and literally in a blaze of publicity and with a design beneficial to the budget.

Originally conceiving Sherman's sacking and burning of Atlanta as a final shooting sequence in the production, Selznick was quick to see the advantages of Menzies' plan and gave the order to proceed immediately.

Myron Selznick, astute showman that he was, had prolonged dinner with Vivien and Olivier at Chasen's as late as he could so that her entrance would not go unnoticed in all the excitement of the blaze-setting. And Vivien delayed him with question after question about David, the search for Scarlett, and the casting of the other roles in the film. Her beautiful face was alive with feverish excitement by the time dinner ended. Carefully she put on her wide-brimmed black picture hat. Her eyes were lined with deep green shadow, making them seem more catlike than usual, and the dress she wore cinched her waist so that it appeared as small as Scarlett's. Myron had been struck by Vivien's rightness for the role of Scarlett from the moment they had met, but the dinner that night convinced him.

When they pulled out of the restaurant's parking lot and turned the corner looking south from Beverly Hills, the sky was glowing red over neighboring Culver City and the Selznick studio. David had set fire to Atlanta.

Selznick later commented on that historic moment when Vivien faced him on the raised platform overlooking the devastation of Atlanta: "When he [Myron] introduced me to her, the flames were lighting up her face . . . I took one look and knew she was right—at least right as far as . . . my conception of how Scarlett O'Hara looked. . . . I'll never recover from that first look."

Though he had seen her in A *Yank at Oxford* and *Fire Over England*, at that startling moment Selznick had not made the connection. Vivien talked animatedly to him, her wide green eyes so intent on him that she seemed unaware of even Olivier standing at her shoulder. A remark of Selznick's sent her into peals of merry laughter. When she glanced past him, staring at the dying flames, her eyes appeared wild with anger and her delicately molded chin was set, hard and determined. Selznick caught his breath as he stood watching her. Only moments later tears welled in her eyes, as though she was mourning the death of her own civilization.

A screen test was set up for her almost immediately with George Cukor, who was to direct. Cukor had been in England that year, just before the British release of *St. Martin's Lane*, and when asked by interviewer Max Breen if he had seen Vivien Leigh, who Breen thought would be a marvelous Scarlett O'Hara, Cukor had replied, "I saw her in A *Yank at Oxford*, and she seems to be a little static, not quite sufficiently fiery for the role." But he made no mention of this to Selznick and agreed to see her the next day, which was a Sunday.

He was almost as taken with her as Selznick had been and arranged the test for the following week. Vivien cabled Tyrone Guthrie that her return would be delayed, adding that she hoped it would not make things difficult for him and the company.

Monday morning David wrote his wife, Irene, who was in New York at the Sherry-Netherland Hotel:

Darling:
Saturday night I was greatly exhilarated by the Fire Sequence. It was one of the biggest thrills I have had out of making pictures—first, because of the scene itself, and second, because of the frightening but exciting knowledge that *Gone With the Wind* was finally in work. Myron rolled in just exactly too late, arriving about a minute and a half after the last building had fallen and burned and after the shots were completed. With him were Larry Olivier and Vivien Leigh. Shhhhh: she's the Scarlett dark horse, and looks damned good. (Not for anybody's ears but your own: it's narrowed down to Paulette, Jean Arthur, Joan Bennett, and Vivien Leigh.)

That same day he wrote his general manager, Henry Ginsberg:

. . . Scarlett will definitely be decided upon as the result of this next group of tests, which I hope we will be able to see by Monday or Tuesday of next week. . . .
The girls to be tested in these scenes are Miss Goddard, Joan Bennett, Jean Arthur, and Vivien Leigh.

Myron gave her the script pages of the test scenes (the same as the other actresses were to perform) as soon as he could, and she went over them, with Olivier feeding her the lines. Cukor was to direct the tests himself. The plan was that each actress was to do three scenes which when viewed by Selznick would be intercut so that each of the four would appear consecutively in each of the scenes. Vivien's test was to be the last shot on the following Wednesday, December 21.

She cabled Guthrie again to say she now could not return in time to appear as Titania. He cabled that he had already replaced her, guessing as much. Then she wrote Leigh:

Darling Leigh, I do hope that the sweaters arrived all right and that they fit. It's a bit silly that they were made in Scotland, but I hope that that means you won't have to pay duty on them.
You will never guess what has happened—and no one is more surprised than me—you know how I only came out here for a week—well,

just two days before I was supposed to leave, the people who are making *Gone With the Wind* saw me and said would I make a test—so what could I do?—and so now I am working frantically hard rehearsing, and studying a southern accent which I don't find difficult anyway. These are the final tests they are making and there are just four of us—they seem to be very pleased with me—and I don't know what I think or what I hope—I am so afraid it will mean my staying here (*if* I get it) for a long time and *that* I know I don't want to do.

The part has now become the biggest responsibility one can imagine—and yet it would be absurd not to do it, given the chance. I will not know definitely till the end of the week.

I do hope you will have a nice time at Hyes, and that Suzanne is well. I hope all the right books arrive for her Xmas present . . . Darling Leigh I do hope you are well. I will write and let you know what is happening. With dearest love. Vivien.

It was a completely truthful letter, except in the barest essentials, and if Leigh Holman hoped someday she might return to him, it was this curious kind of attitude in letters and conversations that kindled his hope. Remaining in the States meant she would not see Suzanne for many months, and she was fearful of both Leigh's and her parents' censure of such an apparent lack of maternal feelings.

Cukor decided she should not worry about the Southern accent in the tests. The scene she played with Mammy lacing up her corsets was deliciously funny, loving, and yet showed Scarlett to be an arrogant young girl; while the confrontation with Ashley at Twelve Oaks was sensual, moving, and brilliant. There was no doubt in anyone's mind as soon as the tests were completed that Vivien was Scarlett O'Hara. Vivien, however, found out she had the role in a rather casual manner.

The Sunday following the tests was Christmas, and Cukor invited Vivien and Larry to a cocktail party he was having that afternoon. Toward the end he took Vivien aside. "A decision has finally been made," he told her, his expression serious, his voice controlled.

Vivien, thinking the worst, interpreted this as meaning someone else had been cast. Cukor eased her fears.

The announcement was not immediately made, as Selznick now had to get Korda to agree to loan her services to his company. Korda was in Hollywood pursuing his romance with Merle Oberon (they were married six months later in Antibes), and at first was quite difficult to deal with, not being convinced that the American public would accept an English actress as Scarlett, and concerned that it might end disastrously for Vivien. But he was also a good enough businessman to make sure he would benefit in some way if he was wrong.

Selznick in a confidential letter to John Hay Whitney (his major private investor) on January 4, 1939, writes:

> Korda is going to wind up with the choice of having the second picture beyond *Gone With the Wind*—in other words we would have *Gone With the Wind* and one picture, then one to Korda, then one to us. The lucky Hungarian has fallen into something, and we're going to make a fortune for him. However, if she is really as good as we hope, I suppose we're lucky too, and shouldn't be greedy that someone else gets something out of it.

But before they could make an announcement to the press, another problem presented itself. It was thought Vivien needed Leigh's permission before she could file for an American work permit. Vivien cabled him right away, and to her dismay he refused. His consent turned out to be unnecessary. She could, after all, file for a permit and remain in the country without his approval. She cabled him back that she was glad he had said no, explaining in a letter that followed that she now had a better deal, which she was certain had been made because of his refusal, adding in the letter:

> You know I understand your reasons for not consenting entirely, Leigh, but cannot help hoping also that it may mean you are beginning to feel a little more reconciled to the thought of a divorce later on. But I am sorry for having put you in such an awkward position.

And then she goes on about how she "loathes" Hollywood and how

> one hears terrible rumors of war all the time here, and the Americans are very vehement about the cowardice of the English and do nothing but show films full of anti-British propaganda—it is quite infuriating. With my loveliest love to you Leigh darling. Vivien.

Makeup tests, costume fittings, and lessons in Southern diction were begun, but it was three weeks after Christmas before Selznick finally was able to issue a release to the press saying that Vivien Leigh had been signed to play Scarlett O'Hara. Typical of Selznick, it was 750 words long and cleverly avoided all the issues by referring to her "recent screen work in England," her "French father and Irish mother," and her education in England, France, Austria, and Italy.

Nowhere did the release mention she was English. Nor was her relationship with Olivier even hinted at. Selznick referred to her as "Mrs. Leigh Holman, the wife of a London barrister."

But it was not the public release that disturbed Vivien. As soon as she had signed her contract, David Selznick met with her and Olivier. He explained to them that one of the reasons Paulette Goddard's casting had been held up (she was very close to being signed for the film before Vivien entered the contest) was her ambiguous relationship with Charles Chaplin (no one knew if they were or were not married) and that the American public was sensitive to such unorthodox arrangements. He went on endlessly, stressing that the reason he had taken so long to notify her that she had been chosen (meaning the five days between the test and her meeting with Cukor at his cocktail party) was the company's fear that her love affair with Olivier could present a difficult problem if the public learned about it. He recognized that theirs was a deep and genuine love, but they were still married to other mates, and there was a child involved on each side. Both of them were famous now, he reminded them, and though their liaison was common knowledge in England, it was not in the United States. He impressed upon her that scandal at this time—particularly a sensational divorce suit on either side—would ruin him, her career in the States, and the chances of a grand success with the film.

To bring the point home to them he added that Gable and Lombard were having an affair and Gable was married, though they did not share a house. But before he announced that Gable would portray Rhett Butler, he (Selznick) and his father-in-law, Louis B. Mayer, had made an arrangement with Rhea Gable to file suit for a divorce of an amicable nature against Clark.

Then, before they left his office, he begged them not to be seen alone together in public and to use discretion at all times.

Chapter Eleven

The Sunday morning after the burning of Atlanta, Vivien and Cukor met for the first time in his office. The famous director reacted instantly to what he called "something exciting in her presence." There was a tenseness about her, a glow in her eyes—just as Scarlett would have possessed. He handed her a scene to read to him. A quizzical smile spread across her face. "Hail Mary, full of grace!" she said to his surprise and then glanced down and quickly thumbed through the loose pages. It was the scene at Twelve Oaks when Scarlett waits for Ashley in the darkened library to tell him that she loves him and wants to marry him, knowing that he is already betrothed to Melanie. For a moment there was silence in the room, and then Vivien began in a very clipped, self-conscious manner.

Cukor stopped her. "You sound like someone's got their finger up your ass," he said rudely.

She roared with laughter and then, glancing away, fell silent for a few moments. Suddenly she appeared to be trembling.

"What is it?" Cukor asked, his words happening to be the opening lines of the scene.

She seemed suddenly charged with electricity, possessed of the devil, as her declaration burst from her mouth. "I love you!"

Cukor immediately answered her with Ashley's next speech. "Isn't it enough that you've collected every other man's heart here today? Do you want to make it unanimous? Well, you've always had my heart, you know. You cut your teeth on it."

Vivien's eyes left the paper and she stared passionately, somewhat wildly at him. She appeared to have memorized the scene in-stantaneously, never once having to refer to the script. "Ashley, Ash-ley, tell me—you must. Oh, don't tease me now! Have I your heart? Oh, my dear, I love you. I tell you I love you and I know you must care about me because . . ." She paused, and a look of abandon leaped into her eyes. "Ashley, do you care? You do, don't you?"

Cukor was more than impressed. For months he had listened to girls read those lines, but this was the first time he had ever been moved by them. He sat back and studied Vivien as she continued. On the outside she was exquisite, graceful, and perfectly mannered; un-derneath there was something neurotic, something driven—two women, really, and he doubted if she was even conscious of it.

When she had finished the reading he apologized for the early hour of the meeting when he knew she had been up late the previous night.

"That's all right." She smiled sweetly. "I've never slept much, ever. Since I was born, I haven't slept much."

They parted without him giving her any idea of how he had reacted to her reading, but he noted that her nervousness seemed to have left her and that she appeared quite sure of herself as she po-litely thanked him for his time. She immediately confided to Myron Selznick that she trusted Cukor instinctively and felt they were on the same wavelength. He was after all, like Olivier—first of the theatre. He had directed Florence Eldridge in *The Great Gatsby*, Ethel Barry-more in *The Constant Wife*, Laurette Taylor in *Her Cardboard Lover* and *The Furies*, Dorothy Gish in *Young Love*, and Bette Davis in *Broadway*. Not to mention films like *The Royal Family*, *A Bill of Divorcement*, *Dinner at Eight*, *Little Women*, and *Camille*, all films with great women's roles. But quite apart from his impressive credits, Vivien was mesmerized by his instant and great magnetism, for he was a man charged with contained but constantly flowing energy. His movements and gestures were sure and quick, and as he spoke his eyes probed, his hands struck out at the air, he was in constant motion.

Vivien spent the next week working on her interpretation of the three scenes that were to constitute her film test. It was not an easy week, as Olivier was having his own problems on *Wuthering Heights*. By Wyler's own admission, there was a lack of communication and articulation on his part. On Olivier's part, he was still not ready to leave behind his theatre technique, which Wyler knew would be dis-astrous to the final outcome of the film. The days were long and

ABOVE: Vivian's stage debut, age three, Ootacamund, India.
BELOW LEFT: With her mother, Gertrude, in Calcutta, 1915.
BELOW RIGHT: Grandmother Yackje in Bridlington.

ABOVE: Calcutta Turf Club, circa 1913. Photograph was taken by Vivian's father, Ernest.
BELOW: Vivian's parents in India, circa 1913.

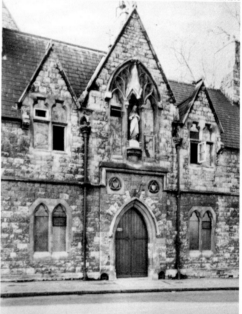

ABOVE: Class photograph taken at the Convent of the Sacred Heart at Roehampton, 1925. Vivian is in the middle row, third from right.
RIGHT: Convent of the Sacred Heart at Roehampton, 1925.
BELOW: The school orchestra, Vivian with cello, 1925.

ABOVE: An outing with friends in London, 1931. Vivian is at the far right.
OPPOSITE: As a model for Vogue magazine, 1933.
BELOW: Mr. and Mrs. Leigh Holman, December 20, 1932, St. James's Church, Spanish Place, London.

ST. JAMES' THEATRE
KING STREET, ST. JAMES', S.W.1

Lessee and Manager · · Gilbert Miller
Licensed by the Lord Chamberlain to Thomas H. Bostock

Evenings, 8.30   Mats. Tuesdays & Fridays, 2.30

VIVIEN LEIGH
IN
"The Mask of Virtue"

IT is an agreeable task to be able to welcome a new actress with unrestrained praise. "The Mask of Virtue" obtained a personal triumph for Vivien Leigh, a discovery of Sydney Carroll. Miss Leigh is ravishingly pretty which might not matter but that her talent equals her beauty. She moves with grace. She is lovely in repose. Her voice is most attractive, and warmth, ardour and sincerity are not wanting in her acting. Vivien Leigh gave genuine life to the part of the girl enchantingly reconciling her conflicting qualities. Her quiet dignity in the acceptance of a repugnant task, the growth of affection, and the awakening to the sense of a triumph odious to her, were beautifully expressed and composed a performance that grew in loveliness and interest.

A. E. WILSON, *The Star.*
May 16th, 1935.

Vivien Leigh
now appearing in
"THE MASK OF VIRTUE"
THE "FAME IN A NIGHT GIRL"

ABOVE: The "fame in a night" girl, newly christened Vivien with an *e*, 1935.
OPPOSITE: The lovers in their first film together, *Fire Over England*, 1936.
BELOW LEFT: With Ivor Novello in *The Happy Hypocrite*, 1936.
BELOW RIGHT: *Storm in a Teacup* with Rex Harrison, 1937.

MANDER AND MITCHENSON THEATRE COLLECTION   NATIONAL FILM ARCHIVE

NATIONAL FILM ARCHIVE

ABOVE: The runaway lovers in Denmark at Elsinore during rehearsals for *Hamlet*, 1937. From left, Vivien, Tyrone Guthrie, Olivier, Mrs. Guthrie.
BELOW: *Hamlet* performed by the Old Vic Company, 1937. Left, Vivien and Olivier as Ophelia and Hamlet. Top right, Elsinore. Bottom, courtyard of Elsinore with production in progress.

ABOVE: Mrs. Laurence Olivier, the actress Jill Esmond, 1937.
RIGHT: Olivier and the woman he loved, London, 1937.

OPPOSITE ABOVE: Vivien as a counterspy in *Dark Journey*, 1937.
OPPOSITE BELOW: As a street entertainer with Charles Laughton in *St. Martin's Lane*.
RIGHT: Vivien's father, Ernest, right, with a friend at Ascot.
BELOW: The romantic couple taking a studio break during shooting of *Twenty-one Days Together*.

ABOVE: Scarlett O'Hara becomes a bride, a scene from *Gone With the Wind*. From left, Thomas Mitchell, Barbara O'Neil, Vivien, and Rand Brooks.

BELOW: The Atlanta premiere of *Gone With the Wind*, December 1939. From left, Vivien, Gable, Margaret Mitchell, David O. Selznick, Olivia de Havilland.

Scarlett has a nightmare on her honeymoon with Rhett. *Gone With the Wind*.

CULVER

ABOVE: *That Hamilton Woman* with Alan Mowbray as her deceived husband, Lord Hamilton.

OPPOSITE: Unmarried lovers on screen now wedded in private life, Vivien as Lady Hamilton and Olivier as Lord Nelson. *That Hamilton Woman*, 1941.

RIGHT: With Robert Taylor in *Waterloo Bridge*, 1940.

Between acts of *The Doctor's Dilemma*. On tour, with bombers overhead, Olivier in uniform, and Britain at war.

difficult, still Olivier found time nights to work with Vivien on her scenes (two were to be with Ashley, a third with Mammy). Since he was filming, she was alone much during the day. The old guilts returned to haunt her. She had sent Leigh sweaters from on board the *Queen Mary* and purchased books for Suzanne for Christmas as soon as she arrived in Los Angeles. The truth was she had never intended to remain five days, and that truth was gnawing uncomfortably at her.

She noted (and told Olivier that night) that when she put on her costume for the test, it was still warm and "there could hardly have been time for the previous actress to get out of it."

Cukor adjusted his glasses and stood looking at her with amazement as she began her scene with Leslie Howard, deciding she should not attempt a Southern accent. That morning he had put Joan Bennett through the same scene. She had been sentimental and tearful. In contrast Vivien was striking in her passion. "There was an indescribable wildness about her," Cukor thought. She was never coy, never a young girl with a crush; she was instead a young girl with a fully matured sensuality, direct in her desire, and dangerously—*threateningly*—impatient. She was Scarlett as Margaret Mitchell conceived her and as he had always hoped she could be played. She ended the scene with a high hysterical laugh that was so effective that Leslie Howard flinched as if struck hard emotionally.

The rushes were shown to Selznick that night, and he agreed with Cukor that Vivien was absolutely startling in her likeness to the character as they envisioned her. He was only concerned about her ability to master the Southern accent.

The following morning Vivien was called in to meet Susan Myrick (the film's expert on Southern speech and manners), who was to work with her on acquiring the accent. Three days later Vivien was called back to shoot the third test scene—Scarlett and Ashley toward the end of the war. She was quite disappointed that Leslie Howard, whom she admired greatly, was not available to do the final test with her. She had to play it with a rather wooden Douglas Montgomery, but it hardly seemed to matter. Cukor held the camera on her, and the underlying panic and desperation, the fierceness of her disturbing appeal to Ashley, were even more striking than the earlier reactions between the same two characters. More impressive, though not yet perfected, was her accent, which was natural-sounding and convincing, not one trace of the English inflection marring its believability.

Vivien signed a seven-year contract with Selznick (she was paid about $30,000 for *Gone With the Wind*, but her salary was to rise yearly). Her commitment was to one picture a year. The first (as in his letter to Whitney) to follow *Gone With the Wind* for Selznick, the second to Korda, and then the third back to Selznick, and she was also permitted stage appearances but with Selznick's approval only. It appears it was never her intent to honor the contract, though, for she wrote Leigh after signing it:

> My agent here [Myron Selznick] assures me that if the picture is a success I can make demands to get my contract altered. . . . I will never make a fuss about the financial side but am determined to ask for more time for the theatre, etc. I know perfectly well, I could not stay here half the year.

Korda, who knew her a great deal better than Selznick, was positive this was the truth. That she would, in fact, not stay anywhere six months without Olivier. He spoke to Vivien about it; and facetiously quoting Scarlett and smiling like a Cheshire cat, she replied, "Dear Alex, I will think about that tomorrow."

Principal photography began January 26, 1939, with the opening scene of Scarlett as a young girl flirting coquettishly on the front porch of Tara. She wore a low-necked flowered muslin dress designed by Walter Plunkett. (Later the scene was reshot because Selznick preferred a white high-necked ruffled dress, which was to make Scarlett look more virginal.)

In the next two weeks Cukor filmed the birth of Melanie's child, Scarlett's shooting of the Union deserter at a sacked Tara, and Rhett's gift of a Parisian hat to Scarlett. Vivien was deliriously happy with Cukor's direction and also his loyalty to the original book, dialogue from which he would often substitute on the set for that on the script pages given to him by Selznick. Had Vivien known of the battle being waged off the set and in Selznick's executive offices, there is little doubt that she would have entered it herself, for there were now heated discussions and strong pressure on Selznick to have Cukor replaced on the film.

Clark Gable lacked confidence in himself as a dramatic actor, although he was quite aware of his impact as a great screen personality. As each day passed, his own fears mounted that Cukor was devoting too much attention to Scarlett's and Melanie's roles and not enough to his own, and that his performance would therefore suffer appreciably. He wanted a director who understood his film appeal and could get the most from it, and it did not seem to him that Cukor was that man. He had his agent call Selznick with daily complaints and threats, and when that did not work he brought Louis B. Mayer into it. Selznick could hardly ignore this. It did not help Cukor that though Selznick liked Cukor's work it had been done with script pages he had not authorized. He began to come down on the set, a thing he had never done before, to oversee Cukor.

On February 8, exactly two weeks after the commencement of photography, he dictated the following memo to Cukor:

Dear George:

You will recall that before we started the picture we had a long discussion concerning my anxiety to discuss with you in advance the points that I personally saw in each scene. We had both hoped that we would have a . . . chance to see the whole script rehearsed. This, for many reasons, was impossible. Then we discussed seeing each scene rehearsed, and this idea was in turn lost sight of in the pressure of many things.

Now the idea becomes more important than ever, because we have little or no opportunity in most cases even to discuss each rewritten scene before you go into it. I therefore would like to go back to what we discussed, and to try to work out a system whereby I see each block scene rehearsed in full before you start shooting it.

Cukor never would abide such an arrangement, and the two men continued their argument for several days, Cukor steadfastly fighting for the right to be his own man and admitting to Selznick that he might make mistakes but insisting that if the film was to carry his name it must be his work.

Selznick replied, "If this picture is going to fail, it must fail on *my* mistakes, not yours."

And on February 13 he issued the following statement to the press:

As a result of a series of disagreements between us over many of the individual scenes of *Gone With the Wind*, we have mutually decided that the only solution is for a new director to be selected at as early a date as is practicable. . . . Mr. Cukor's withdrawal . . . is the most regrettable incident of my rather long producing career, the more so because I consider Mr. Cukor one of the very finest directors it has ever been the good fortune of this business to claim.

I can only hope that we will be so fortunate as to be able to replace him with a man of comparable talents.

Cukor was almost as shocked by this as Vivien was, and all the cast speculated that it had been Gable's doings, but Cukor felt that might or might not be true. "Perhaps Gable mistakenly thought that because I was supposed to be a 'woman's director' I would throw the story to Vivien—but if that's so, it was very naive of him and not the reaction of a very good or professional actor. It's not the director who throws 'things' and puts the emphasis the wrong way. That would be like singing a song and singing certain notes very loudly or heavily to divert attention from the others."

It seemed more likely to Cukor that his removal from the film had to do with Selznick's overwhelming need to identify himself with *Gone With the Wind*, which he considered the supreme effort of his career.

Vivien was stunned when the news of Cukor's dismissal reached her, and deciding to take matters in her own hands, she persuaded Olivia de Havilland to go with her to see Selznick in his office. Costumed in their "widow's weeds," they begged and pleaded with Selznick to retain Cukor, to no avail. Vivien contemplated refusing to go back on the set until he reversed his decision, but that night Myron and Olivier convinced her that she would risk harsh legal consequences if she did so.

Shooting was suspended for several days, during which time Robert Z. Leonard, Jack Conway, King Vidor, and Victor Fleming (all MGM contract directors) were mentioned as possibilities, but there obviously had been no doubt in Selznick's mind who Cukor's replacement was to be, because the day following Cukor's exit (the final scene being the Atlanta Bazaar sequence), Victor Fleming, Gable's old friend, and his choice to take over for Cukor, was taken off the completion of *The Wizard of Oz* and signed to direct *Gone With the Wind*.

On February 20, Selznick sent a memo to his production manager, Raymond Klune, that read:

> We will start shooting again on Monday. Please get together with Mr. Fleming immediately in connection with the opening scene. We should start with the twins [Tarleton] and then go to Gerald [Scarlett's father] and Scarlett to permit you to change the condition of Tara. It would be my preference, if there is no reason against it, and if Fleming is agreeable, to then jump into retakes in the Bazaar, followed by Rhett and Scarlett on the McDonough road.

The last being the scene where Rhett leaves Scarlett to continue on to Tara with Melanie, Prissy, and baby Beau after the burning of Atlanta.

On March 1, they resumed shooting. Vivien did not like Fleming personally, and liked him even less as a director. She began to visit Cukor at his home every available moment, working with him on her scenes. Selznick never got wind of this, though she did it through the entire production. Nor did he discover that Olivia de Havilland was doing the same thing (unbeknown to Vivien), which meant Cukor's influence on the end result of the film was considerable.

Vivien was most concerned with the delay in the shooting schedule caused by all these machinations, which meant she would have to remain longer than anticipated in Hollywood. While waiting for Fleming to take the helm, she had moved into a house at 520 North Crescent Drive. The lovers were as discreet as possible, still they managed to achieve some semblance of domestic life.

But Olivier was soon to finish *Wuthering Heights* and would have to spend one week on the road and then return to Broadway to appear opposite Katharine Cornell in S. N. Behrman's *No Time for Comedy*. She had come all this distance and gone to extreme lengths to be with Olivier, and now they would once again be separated. She was not happy that he had accepted the role, but she was unable to deter him. And Olivier, seeing Vivien settled in a house with a good staff, removed from their English pressures, and with the greatest female role in film history to occupy her time, felt convinced she could manage alone. To Vivien's credit, she understood that Larry had to return to the stage after a long, trying film experience like *Wuthering Heights*, as the stage for him was like air to a long-distance swimmer.

She appeared at the studio each morning after his departure earlier than her call, hoping she could hurry the film along and feeling more disdain than ever for film making and the role of being a film actress. No one else, however, possessed her dedication, and her eagerness was to no avail.

Fleming considered himself a man's man. He had been a cameraman, big game hunter, and an air force pilot before becoming a director, and he always spoke about giving up the industry to return to shooting tigers. He regarded Cukor's sensibility and deep involvement in his work as effeminate and from the start treated Vivien in a chauvinistic manner. He named her "Fiddle-dee-dee" (a line Scarlett used frequently in the film) and told Walter Plunkett, the costume designer, "For Christ's sake, let's get a good look at the girl's boobs!" directly in front of Vivien. Plunkett was coerced into forcing Vivien to have her breasts taped to press them closer together and thrust them forward and upward, resulting in deeper cleavage. She was furious about the entire incident.

She regarded Gable as lazy, not too bright, and an unresponsive performer (though she was always laudatory about his kindness and good manners to her). She could not understand how he could leave the set promptly each day at six P.M. as though he held an office job. She seldom left the studio until eight or nine at night and worked six, often seven days a week. "What are you fucking about for?" she would complain to Gable and Fleming when Gable took time out to rest. Gable admired his leading lady's vocabulary, as did Fleming, but otherwise he was a bit put off by her intellect and her dedication to work. Nonetheless he took it upon himself to teach her the game of backgammon. She proceeded to beat him each time they played. She then taught him a naval war game of strategy using graph paper, but Gable did not stand a chance. A sense of competition grew between the two that carried over into their scenes together.

But it was Gable's bad breath caused by his false teeth that was the most unpleasant aspect of their working together for Vivien. Vivien's good manners held her back from mentioning it to him, while at the same time it kindled her hostilities.

Her primary hostility was to Selznick, who she was convinced had engineered Olivier's role in No Time for Comedy in order to separate them and avoid any grist for Hollywood's gossip mill. Vivien felt desperately lonely, but also found it emotionally difficult to achieve consistency in her film character's psychological development.

Owing to the episodic method of film making, scenes were seldom shot in chronological order, and Vivien was faced daily with having to skip from a sixteen-year-old Scarlett to Scarlett at twenty-seven within a matter of hours. In one case she worked twenty-two hours without rest, filming the famous scene when Scarlett falls to her knees in the fields of Tara vowing never to be hungry again. She then slept four hours and returned to the studio to portray a giddy Scarlett visiting Aunt Pitty at the start of the war. Unlike any of the other characters, she was in a good percentage of the footage and seldom had a day when her services were not required.

The occasional few hours she was able to escape to George Cukor's house for a swim and a rest in the sun by his pool offered her short periods free from the tensions of the film. Cukor had grown very fond of Vivien and became quite concerned about her state of health as the film progressed. One day she had been so exhausted that she had fallen asleep in her wet suit by the pool, and hating to wake her—so exhausted had she seemed to him—he had tossed a blanket over her when the sun went down and let her sleep. He was relieved when Olivier managed to fly back to Los Angeles for one day directly before his play was to open in New York.

Vivien was ecstatic to see him and Selznick and Fleming agreed not to interfere with the twenty-four hours the lovers had together.

"I'm quite shocked to find how exaggerated stage acting is after the films," Olivier told her. "I simply didn't notice it before, but now it seems to me that in the theatre audiences swallow dialogue and acting conventions which on the screen would draw howls of derisive laughter."

It seemed to her that Larry was gone almost as soon as he had arrived, and she was once again back at war with Fleming. Days on the set would often end with Vivien in tears and Fleming in a rage. Vivien felt he was attempting to reduce Scarlett to a one-dimensional character—a bitch-shrew without any motivating forces. She had Margaret Mitchell's book with her on the set at all times and would argue against changes in Scarlett's original characterization. Fleming felt the film should be a melodrama and concentrated on the spectacle rather than the characters. One day she inquired how she should play a scene. "Ham it up," Fleming answered. She retorted sharply and began quoting Cukor's advice.

"Miss Leigh, you can stick this script up your royal British ass!" he shouted at her and walked off the set, refusing to return for three days. It was, however, only a short time before they had another confrontation; and Fleming, threatening first to drive his car off a cliff, left for his beach house at Malibu and could not be talked into returning to the studio.

Sam Wood (A Night at the Opera) was called in to replace him, and William Cameron Menzies shot most of the second-unit material, but from the time of Fleming's second walkout, Selznick truly took over the film and it nearly did him in. He was driving himself too hard, gambling too heavily (he was a compulsive gambler and lost huge sums), and watching his marriage disintegrate. On April 14, he wrote his wife, Irene, who was still in New York:

I wish I could just be with you somewhere away from money, habit of work, drive of years' silly hopes. Maybe—oh, I hope so—we can map a program, months, eight or ten of hard work and drive for financial freedom, then some place where there is neither . . . Clover Club nor synopses. I don't think any more my Fate is millions and Leadership. I hope it isn't (as though the hope were not gratuitous!). I'm damned if I know quite what's the alternate hope.

Vivien was torn by the terrible pressures of the film, her need for Olivier's presence, and by her fear of an inevitable war in Europe. In April she wrote Leigh:

It is dreadful being so far away from everything. One only gets such a vague picture of things. The American attitude seems to be changing considerably—two months ago one dared not mention politics—they were so wildly against us—and they're a little cowed now, thank God.

She had made friends with Miriam Hopkins and her husband, director Anatole Litvak, and occasionally visited them at their beach house and saw Ronald Colman and his wife, Benita Hume. She continued her secret meetings with Cukor at his house, but otherwise she kept to herself in her rented house, tended by "two very good German servants. They are so nice—and I have the opportunity of speaking German—also their cooking is a treat after the American food which seems quite tasteless," she wrote Leigh.

Wuthering Heights opened in New York during this time, and Olivier suddenly found himself besieged by fans who mobbed him after every performance. Though they spoke on the telephone often and Vivien wrote him daily, no matter how exhausted she was, both of them feared the separation would give birth to singular experiences such as each was having, experiences that might become some kind of barrier to their mutual understanding. Therefore, as soon as Vivien knew when her last scenes for *Gone With the Wind* were scheduled, Olivier gave notice that he would have to be replaced from that date in *No Time for Comedy*. Part of their plan was to meet in New York, return to England, and remain there about a month, until mid-August, when Vivien had to be available in Hollywood for possible retakes and Olivier was to begin work on *Rebecca* (also to be produced by Selznick and Selznick International). What they hoped was that they could convince Leigh and Jill to give them respective divorces during the time they were in England so that they could marry. And they hoped that they could in the meantime convince Selznick that Vivien should be cast opposite Olivier in *Rebecca* (the lead was still uncast and the major contenders for the role were Anne Baxter and Joan Fontaine).

On June 27, 1939, Selznick telegraphed John Hay Whitney:

SOUND THE SIREN. SCARLETT O'HARA COMPLETED HER PERFORMANCE AT NOON TODAY.

Vivien had gone that same afternoon to another set and tested for *Rebecca*. But it was not a good test and she knew it. She had no time to develop the character before she stepped before the camera and nothing was done to "deglamorize" her. Vivien was too beautiful to play the role without heavy makeup. Selznick followed his telegram to Whitney that evening with a letter:

> Vivien is still anxious to play *Rebecca* for obvious reasons. She really thinks she could knock us dead in another test and that the former test was unfair in that she had to hop right out of Scarlett O'Hara into the girl in *Rebecca* in ten minutes. It is my personal feeling that she could never be right for the girl, but God knows it would solve a lot of problems if she was right, and I have too much respect for her ability as an actress, too much consideration for my own peace of mind during the months of August and September when a certain young man [Laurence Olivier] is in these parts, and too much appreciation of how good it would be for her future with us if she were to play *Rebecca*, to close the door on the possibility of her being right for it. I have therefore said that we would not close with anybody to play the role for a period of ten days from today, during which time she could if she wishes make a test with Larry Olivier in New York.

Six days later Vivien was "secretly" in New York (without the press being alerted) and attended Olivier's last performance of *No Time for Comedy* (he was being replaced by Francis Lederer). That was July 3. They spent the weekend of the fourth with Katharine Cornell at her house at Sneden's Landing. Then Vivien filmed another test for *Rebecca*. She had worked on her concept of the part, but she could not persuade anyone in New York to allow her to go through the test without makeup. On July 11 they sailed on the *Ile de France* and docked in Plymouth five days later. They disembarked and were shocked to find air raid shelters being dug in parks and training in the use of gas masks being announced on large signs outside town halls. People talked of "the state of emergency" that existed, but no one spoke openly about the threat of a war.

The international situation overshadowed their short holiday, which otherwise was an exceptionally happy one. Leigh and Jill had not yet agreed to divorce, but the path was now open. They were certain their love was stronger than ever and they both had high hopes that Vivien would be cast in *Rebecca* so that they could appear together in the film.

On August 17 they boarded the *Ile de France* with Gertrude, who they thought needed a holiday, leaving Suzanne in the total care of Leigh and Nanny Oake. They were only one day out at sea, when the following two radiograms were received:

AUGUST 18, 1939

VIVIEN HOLMAN
ILE DE FRANCE
NEW YORK RADIO

DEAR VIVIEN: WE HAVE TRIED TO SELL OURSELVES RIGHT UP UNTIL TODAY TO CAST YOU IN "REBECCA," BUT I REGRET NE-CESSITY TELLING YOU WE ARE FINALLY CONVINCED YOU ARE AS WRONG FOR ROLE AS ROLE WOULD BE FOR YOU. YOU MUST REALIZE IT IS THIS SAME PATIENCE, CARE, AND STUBBORNNESS ABOUT ACCURATE CASTING THAT RESULTED IN PUTTING YOU IN MOST TALKED-OF ROLE OF ALL TIME IN WHAT EVERYONE WHO HAS SEEN IT AGREES IS GREATEST PICTURE EVER MADE. IT WOULD HAVE BEEN VERY SIMPLE TO CAST BETTE DAVIS AS SCARLETT, THEREBY SATISFYING MILLIONS OF PEOPLE IN-CLUDING EVERYONE IN THE PROFESSION. IT WOULD BE MUCH SIMPLER TO CAST YOU, WHO ARE UNDER CONTRACT TO US, IN "REBECCA" LEAD, AND THEREBY HAVE SAVED US ALL GREAT DEAL OF EXPENSE AND AGONY SEARCHING FOR RIGHT GIRL. AND EVEN THOUGH YOU MUST BE COMPLETELY WRONG CAST-ING, WE MIGHT STILL HAVE PUT YOU IN IT HAD WE THOUGHT IT WAS GOOD FOR YOU, REGARDLESS OF THE PICTURE. BUT I AM POSITIVE YOU WOULD BE BITTERLY CRITICIZED AND YOUR CAREER, WHICH IS NOW OFF TO SUCH A TREMENDOUS START WITH SCARLETT, MATERIALLY DAMAGED. ALTHOUGH HITCH-COCK FEELS EVEN MORE STRONGLY THAN I DO ON THIS QUES-TION, I WAS STILL NOT SATISFIED AND THEREFORE RAN THE TESTS OF ALL THE CANDIDATES FOR [playwright and screenwriter] ROBERT SHERWOOD, WHO IS WORKING ON SCRIPT, WITHOUT GIVING HIM ANY HINT OF OUR FEELINGS. HIS FIRST AND IMME-DIATE REACTION WAS HOW COMPLETELY WRONG YOU WERE FOR IT. STILL NOT SATISFIED, I REPEATED THE PROCEDURE WITH GEORGE CUKOR, KNOWING HIS HIGH REGARD FOR YOU, AND GEORGE'S FIRST AND IMMEDIATE REACTION WAS IDENTI-CAL WITH SHERWOOD'S. AM HOPEFUL OF HAVING SOMETHING SOON FOR YOU THAT WE WILL BOTH BE HAPPY ABOUT, AND ALSO HOPEFUL YOU WILL RECOGNIZE THAT SAME CARE THAT HAS GONE INTO "WIND" AND "REBECCA" WILL GO INTO SELEC-TION AND PRODUCTION OF YOUR FUTURE PICTURES, WHICH IS SOMETHING I HAVE NO HESITANCY IN SAYING DOES NOT EXIST IN MANY STUDIOS. AFFECTIONATELY,

DAVID

LAURENCE OLIVIER
ILE DE FRANCE
NEW YORK RADIO

DEAR LARRY: PLEASE SEE MY WIRE TO VIVIEN. I KNOW YOU MUST BE DISAPPOINTED, BUT VIVIEN'S ANXIETY TO PLAY ROLE HAS, IN MY OPINION, BEEN LARGELY IF NOT ENTIRELY DUE TO HER DESIRE TO DO A PICTURE WITH YOU, WHICH WAS BEST DEMONSTRATED BY HER COMPLETE DISINTEREST IN PART WHEN I FIRST MENTIONED IT TO HER AS POSSIBILITY AND UNTIL SHE KNEW YOU WERE PLAYING MAXIM. YOU WILL, AFTER ALL, BOTH BE WORKING HERE, SO I THINK HER EAGERNESS HAS BECOME EXAGGERATED AND NOT RATIONALIZED. BECAUSE OF MY PERSONAL AFFECTION FOR VIVIEN AND MY HIGH REGARD FOR YOU BOTH, AM HOPEFUL YOU WILL RECOGNIZE THAT MY JUDGMENT HAS BEEN FAIRLY SOUND AND SUCCESSFUL IN THESE MATTERS FOR MANY YEARS. HOPEFUL WE WILL BE ABLE TO FIND SOMETHING FOR THE TWO OF YOU TO DO TOGETHER FOR US AT SOME FUTURE DATE. SCRIPT IS COMING ALONG SPLENDIDLY, AND GLAD BE ABLE TELL YOU ROBERT SHERWOOD IS DOING FINAL DIALOGUE REWRITE. BELIEVE WE ARE ASSEMBLING EXCITING CAST INCLUDING JUDITH ANDERSON AS MRS. DANVERS, GEORGE SANDERS AS FAVELL, REGINALD DENNY AS FRANK, AND NIGEL BRUCE AS GILES. POSSIBLE MAY BE ABLE TO LET YOU HAVE DAY OR TWO IN NEW YORK IF YOU WANT IT AND IF YOU WILL CONTACT US BEFORE LEAVING FOR COAST. CORDIALLY,

DAVID

This meant Vivien might be forced by her contract to accept a film that had to be shot on location (which is what she feared most) and away from Larry. "I simply won't think about it now!" Vivien decided, making the most of the pleasures of the ocean crossing with Larry. Scarlett had a larger claim on her affections than she would have admitted and was, after all, not an easy person to cast off.

Chapter Twelve

Gertrude was now resigned to the fact that Vivien and Leigh would never be reconciled and that a divorce was imminent. No further appeals were made by her for Vivien to honor her marriage vows. She liked and admired Olivier. Yet she could not conceal her disapproval of Vivien's cavalier attitude *before* plunging so headlong and headstrong into such an early marriage with Leigh. She did more than say, "I told you so"; her cry was "You knew divorce was the ultimate sin. You'll have to make your own peace now."

Vivien seldom discussed this situation with Olivier. In spite of her apparent rejection of the Church, she did still think of herself as a Catholic, privately said her prayers, and carried a Bible whenever she traveled. "I'm Catholic in its truest and broadest sense," she told an interviewer. Whatever interpretation one might make of that statement, one thing seemed certain—Vivien still had spiritual and emotional ties to the Church she claimed to reject, and Gertrude stood as an ever-present reminder of her broken vows.

It was not an easy situation and Vivien was more than happy to accept an invitation extended to Larry, Gertrude, and herself to spend the Labor Day weekend with Douglas Fairbanks, Jr., his wife, and friends Nigel Bruce, David Niven, and Robert Coote on the yacht the Fairbankses had chartered to take them to Catalina Island, which lay about fifty miles from Los Angeles.

The week had been filled with speculation and fear for their countrymen as well, for the news from home had not been good. The German-Soviet Pact had been signed on August 24, 1939. Until the time the chartered Fairbanks yacht sailed out on blue Pacific waters that sunny Saturday morning of September 2, the British were hopeful that a miracle would spare them.

Almost all of the yachting party were British. On Sunday morning, September 3, they gathered around the ship's radio to hear that at nine o'clock that morning, British Summer Time (nine hours ahead of California time), Sir Nevile Henderson had delivered the following ultimatum to the German Foreign Office: "If His Majesty's Government has not received satisfactory assurances of the cessation of all aggressive action against Poland and the withdrawal of German troops from that country by 11 o'clock British Summer Time, from that time a state of war will exist between Great Britain and Germany." The ultimatum was refused. Britain and France had been at war with Germany while the Fairbanks party had slept in comfort in the safe, calm waters of Emerald Bay, where the boat was anchored.

Fairbanks switched off the radio. There was a yawning, agonized silence. The slap of the water as they rocked gently at anchor sounded like the ticking of a time bomb. Each was concerned with his own thoughts. Fairbanks, to break the oppression, raised his glass in a victory toast. Larry, quite unlike himself, began to drink heavily. Vivien and Gertrude could only talk about going back as soon as possible to England. Ernest was alone and not well, and she feared he might get it into his head to join the forces. Then there were Suzanne and Leigh. Vivien suggested they all return, but that, of course, was impossible, as Larry's legal commitment for *Rebecca* would mean a delay of three months at least.

Mary Lee Fairbanks came to the cabin looking for Larry. They had all just realized he had slipped out of the lounge, and as he was as "smashed as a hoot owl," they were concerned. Suddenly there was a great commotion in the Yacht Club harbor. Larry had managed to take one of the yacht's dinghies and had rowed himself to the stern of another good-sized anchored yacht. Then, standing unsteadily and shivering in only a pair of swimming trunks, he bellowed in a thunderous Shakespearean voice, "This is the end! You're all washed up! Finished! Enjoy your last moments! You're done for! *Doomed!*" Then he rowed himself to the next boat to shout out the same prophecy.

Ronald Colman's yacht, *Dragoon*, was anchored next to theirs. Somehow the other yacht owners thought it had been Colman who had disrupted the harbor, and they demanded an apology. Fairbanks and his guests immediately returned to the mainland.

Early the next morning Larry and Vivien began work on reservations for Gertrude's return trip. David Niven was the one close friend who they knew would be called up to return to Britain for active service immediately, since he was a former Regular Army officer and in the reserve. Olivier would have liked to have gone with him. He contacted the British Consul in Los Angeles for advice and was told to stay put and not to panic, but at thirty-two, and in good health, he could not conceive of acting in films abroad while his country was at war. He called the British Embassy in Washington and was advised that it was no good returning until his call-up was due.

They managed to book passage home for Gertrude, and she promised to keep them constantly alerted to the true conditions she found and to the safety of the children. Then Olivier reported to the studio for his first scenes as Max de Winter in *Rebecca* and Vivien for the retakes on the opening sequence of *Gone With the Wind*.

The scene with Vivien in the newly designed white gown was first reshot before she and Olivier had left for their holiday. Vivien sat on the porch of Tara, a girl of sixteen, and said, "Everyone is talking of war, war, war."

Selznick took one look at the rushes and told Vivien, "You look too old and too ill for the scene." The ordeal of the five harsh months of working sixteen hours a day, six days a week had taken its toll. Selznick told her to take a vacation with Olivier and then come back the first week in September to shoot the scene over again. And, indeed, as she walked onto the set she looked younger and gloriously happy—which she was. Despite the war news, fears for Gertrude, Ernest, Suzanne, and Leigh that plagued her, and worry over the knowledge that Larry would eventually be called up, at the same time she was more certain than ever of his love and more optimistic that they would soon be able to marry.

Leigh was called up shortly after the outbreak of war. Gertrude took over the full-time care of Suzanne, and the house on Little Stanhope Street was rented. But England seemed far away as Vivien was swept into all the preparations for the premiere of *Gone With the Wind*, now fixed to take place in Atlanta on December 15. Howard Dietz (who with Arthur Schwartz had written the great song hits "Moanin' Low," "Dancing in the Dark," "You and the Night and the Music," and "I See Your Face Before Me") had become the publicity director of Metro-Goldwyn-Mayer, and to this gentleman, who possessed the epitome of charm and wit, went the thankless job of handling all the arrangements for the giant premiere, an affair that was meant to place the collective talents of Barnum and Bailey, Cecil B. De Mille, and perhaps Sherman's Raiders in the shade. Dietz was sent down to Atlanta to set the wheels in motion. Daily telegrams arrived from Selznick. One, a record four feet high, read in part:

> I WANT YOU TO BE VERY CAREFUL OF THE PAPER YOU SELECT
> FOR THE PROGRAM STOP SOMETIMES THEIR CRACKLING MAKES
> IT DIFFICULT TO HEAR THE DIALOGUE STOP PROMISE YOU WILL
> ATTEND TO THIS.

Dietz telegraphed back, reassuring Selznick he need not worry about the crunching of popcorn either.

> HAVE MADE TIEUP WITH GONE WITH THE WIND PEANUT BRIT-
> TLE COMPANY ASSURING EACH PATRON OF THE PICTURE A BOX
> OF PEANUT BRITTLE AS HE ENTERS THE THEATRE.

As the opening drew closer, the demand for tickets approached madness. Dietz was deluged with requests. One elderly lady practically staged a sit-in at Dietz's hotel headquarters.

"But you don't understand," she kept repeating. "I am president of the local chapter of the DAR."

At the end of his patience, Dietz replied, "But you don't understand, madam. This picture is about another war."

The day of the premiere was declared an official state holiday by the Governor; the Mayor of Atlanta arranged three days of parades and celebrations. Period costumes were to be worn by all celebrating Atlanta residents, and the facade of the Grand Theatre, where the premiere was to be held, was made over to look like Twelve Oaks. Tickets for the 2500-seat theatre were ten dollars each, but scalpers were demanding as much as two hundred dollars a ticket.

Leslie Howard had returned to England. Clark Gable was now married to Carole Lombard, but Olivier's presence in Atlanta was feared to present a problem. Vivien was asked to come alone, but she refused to do so. As it was imperative that Scarlett O'Hara attend the premiere, Selznick, aware that Vivien was not one to make idle threats, created a story for the press. He explained his plan to Kay Brown.

> I checked with Larry Olivier this morning, and it is satisfactory with him
> if we announce that he is coming to Atlanta as a trailer [a preview of a
> coming attraction] for *Rebecca*. We will arrange today to send photo-
> graphs of Olivier and stories concerning him in *Rebecca* . . .

And in another part of his memo he says:

> I would like you to consider whether it wouldn't be a smart thing to have
> the arrival in town a complete secret from the public, with a dramatic

entrance of Gable and Leigh at the ball, where they would be seen for the first time in Atlanta with all the glamour that we can surround them with. It seems to me this would be much better showmanship, especially since there will be plenty of festivities the next day . . .

In all this I haven't mentioned Miss Leigh. No mention is necessary. You know her as well as I do, and she's not going to be exactly Pollyanna about what we put her through. But in her case I feel that she owes it to herself, and to the picture. In Clark's case I feel that whatever he does for us is in the nature of a great favor, and that we should regard it as such. He doesn't need these idiotic festivities. He is the biggest star in the world, and any time he wants to show his face for three minutes, he can get a fortune for it.

True, Vivien was no Pollyanna, and she was not too pleased about just being cast in *Waterloo Bridge* opposite Robert Taylor when the role had been specifically written with Olivier in mind, and this after the disappointment of not appearing together in *Rebecca*. To compound her unhappiness, Greer Garson (newly arrived from Britain) had been given the lead opposite Olivier in *Pride and Prejudice*, and she considered the part of Elizabeth Bennet, unlike the timid second Mrs. de Winter in *Rebecca*, a natural and good role for her. Still, the publicity junket to Atlanta was to be a fine chance for her and Larry to be together before reporting for work on their next films. Therefore, she was more cooperative than Selznick anticipated.

They arrived in Atlanta on the same plane with David and Irene Selznick, Myron Selznick, and Olivia de Havilland. The Gables flew in a private chartered DC-3 passenger plane that MGM paid for, but Vivien did not seem to feel slighted by Gable's special treatment.

Selznick's initial plea for a secret arrival had been overruled. Both contingents, arriving within a few minutes of each other, were greeted by a forty-piece band splendidly uniformed, their brass shining brilliantly in the Southern winter sun. As Vivien and Olivier stepped down on the red carpet from the plane ramp, Howard Dietz met them and the band blasted out the opening bars of "Dixie."

"Oh," said Vivien, "they're playing the song from the picture."

The remark was overheard by a reporter from the Atlanta *Journal*, though he had not been sure who said it and asked Dietz whose quote it was. Dietz, thinking fast, and certain anything was better than the remark being attributed to Scarlett O'Hara, replied, "Olivia de Havilland."

"Dixie" appeared to be the only song the band knew. They played "Dixie" as the group walked across the field to their open-topped cars, "Dixie" as the parade marched into the center of town, and "Dixie" as they paused when the stars got out of their limousines and disappeared into the Georgian Terrace Hotel, where hundreds of fans crushed around them for autographs.

The Atlanta Bazaar set had been re-created for a charity ball that evening to which Gable was compelled to escort the Governor's daughter and Vivien to vote for the Atlanta belle who best fit a gown she wore as Scarlett. All the film's principals were dressed in costumes from the film, and the attending guests wore ante-bellum attire. The following day there was a grand luncheon with visiting Southern governors. Vivien met the diminutive Margaret Mitchell for the first time, and both women appeared to be mutually charmed. Later in the afternoon the Governor entertained the visiting celebrities for tea at the Governor's Mansion. Vivien was one Englishwoman who disliked tea, but she sipped it politely. Next there was a cocktail party for the press and then the procession of celebrities into the theatre through a blazing, incandescent tunnel of light. They were met in the forecourt by dozens of reporters and radio announcers behind microphones. It was Vivien's first experience of American publicity, and it startled her.

She wore a diaphanous chiffon gown, a jeweled clip held a soft veil in place on her loose center-parted hair, and a full-length white ermine coat, loaned to her by the studio, dusted the floor as she swept inside. White orchids were pinned to her evening bag. With one arm she clung quite desperately to Olivier. The audience was emotional and sentimental, and the applause and ovations were overwhelming. There were screams of "Author! Author!" and the reticent Margaret Mitchell was led by Carole Lombard to the stage, where she thanked everyone on behalf of "me and my poor Scarlett."

Vivien complained privately that the length of the film was "hard on one's ass," but seemed otherwise pleased with it. Her favorite scene was Scarlett at Aunt Pittypat's home hitting the bottle and accepting Rhett's proposal of marriage between burps.

A party followed the premiere, and then the next day a farewell luncheon was hosted by Miss Mitchell at the Riding Club for all the film people. By nightfall the plane with *Gone With the Wind* emblazoned on its side rose in a star-filled sky. Vivien clutched Olivier's hand. She was terrified and could not look down, nor did she care to look back. Four days before Selznick had cabled Kay Brown:

HAVE JUST FINISHED 'GONE WITH THE WIND' [meaning the final cut]. GOD BLESS US ONE AND ALL. DAVID

But for Vivien the time had not yet come, and perhaps never would, when she was finished with Scarlett.

Chapter Thirteen

The New York *Times* said, "Viven Leigh's Scarlett is so beautiful she hardly need be talented, and so talented she need not have been so beautiful; no actress, we are sure, was as perfectly suited for the role." For a second time in her life Viven experienced a sudden rush of fame, but it no more swept her off her feet than it had the first time. She was twenty-six and the most famous female star in English-speaking films. "I'm not a film star, I am an actress," she told reporters. "Being a film star—just a film star—is such a false life, lived for fake values and for publicity. Actresses go on for a long time and there are always marvelous parts to play."

Privately she and Olivier were hoping to star in and produce *Romeo and Juliet* (with Olivier also directing). In order for the control to remain in their hands, they decided to invest their own capital. This impelled both of them to accept immediate film work. Olivier went directly from *Rebecca* to *Pride and Prejudice*, and Vivien accepted the role of the ballet dancer who becomes a prostitute and decides to end it all by jumping from Waterloo Bridge in the film of the same name. She was loaned by Selznick to Metro-Goldwyn-Mayer for the film, obviously an attempt by Selznick to repay Mayer for his help and backing on *Gone With the Wind*. Selznick must have believed that the role of the wide-eyed innocent turned prostitute would give her a chance at a performance of star stature, but it was hardly the role to follow Scarlett.

On January 17, 1940, Vivien wrote Leigh (the letter was addressed to Leigh Holman, Esq., Bath Club, Dover, and readdressed to Sub-Lieut. Holman, R.N.V.R., Ramsgate):

I have to have ballet lessons for this film [*Waterloo Bridge*] and have asked to be between two strong girls who can prop me up! Robert Taylor is the man in the picture and as it was written for Larry, it's a typical piece of miscasting. I am afraid it will be a dreary job but I won't think about it, and just concentrate on *Romeo and Juliet*.

I am knitting Balaclava helmets which they seem to want at home. Would one be of any use to you and would you like it? I do wish you could tell me a little more exactly what it is you do, but I suppose you can't. With all my fondest love, darling—and looking forward to hearing from you again.

Vivien.

No mention was made in her letter of their divorce petition, which had been filed by Leigh in London on January 5 and in which Olivier had been named as corespondent. A curious and enigmatic pattern had been formed with Leigh before their marriage: Never discuss, uncover, or reveal any disruptive, vulnerable, or disturbing issues. She wrote Leigh that she wanted to send canned butter and bacon to Suzanne, but never asked how the child was affected by a separation from both mother and father. She commented on how adorable the little girl looked in photos that he sent, but never asked about any emotional problems that she might be having. And she continued to write Leigh loving letters without ever mentioning the rejection, the loss of pride, and the pain that she must have inflicted on him by her open love affair with Olivier. Yet she knew well that his refusal up to this time to give her a divorce and his refusal to sign the permission for her to work in the States was his own dignified way of fighting to retain the marriage.

On January 29, Jill was granted a divorce in London, naming Vivien as corespondent and winning full custody of Tarquin; and on February 19, Leigh went to court to seek his divorce. On the witness stand he said his domestic life had been happy until three years previous when Vivien had gone to Denmark to join a Shakespearean company of which Olivier was a member. On her return, Leigh testified, they had separated after she told him she and Olivier were in love. Jill had told a similar story. Larry had come to her after the Denmark engagement, confessed his love for Vivien, and left. Leigh was granted the divorce and Suzanne's custody. The path was clearing for Vivien and Larry to marry, but it would still be six months until their divorces became final.

It was no longer secret from the public that Scarlett O'Hara and the Prince of the English Theatre were lovers. Larry leased a house on San Ysidro Drive next door to Sylvia and Danny Kaye, and Vivien moved in to share it with him. Their lives were consumed with plans for *Romeo and Juliet*. Olivier would spend all his film breaks during *Pride and Prejudice* in fierce concentration on the playscript, while Vivien devoted all her lunch periods on *Waterloo Bridge* to conferences with Dame May Whitty, cast to play Juliet's nurse, and who was helping her with her voice.

She wrote Gertrude:

> I am having voice lessons four times a week and Larry has suddenly started to *compose* music and nothing will stir him from the piano. He is extremely proud of his achievements and writes them out and *signs* them! When I say "them" I mean "it"—so far, but still, *it's* very good! It's his own entrance music for Romeo. Now he's going to compose mine for Juliet—unless I can do it for myself.

It was George Cukor who first suggested the idea of their doing *Romeo and Juliet* together as a last fling in the theatre before leaving the States for Europe and war. Olivier wrote Ralph Richardson asking for his advice, and Richardson wrote back that *Romeo and Juliet* sounded "a bit too luxurious for wartime." Olivier did not heed the advice, however, and as soon as both of them had completed their film assignments they rented the old Vitagraph studio in Hollywood, investing their entire combined savings of $30,000. Construction began on an intricate revolving stage set. Olivier's intent was "to stress . . . the tight, driving tragedy that catches the characters like straws in a whirlwind and drives them on to their inevitable destinies," and he believed that a set that moved swiftly from one of the play's twenty-eight scenes to the next was part of the answer.

The press was calling them "America's most famous lovers," which was curious, since they were both English. Both were frank in their expression of love for each other. No interviewer could talk to Vivien without her mentioning "Larry." The idea of these two world-known lovers playing *Romeo and Juliet* was a publicity man's dream. And at twenty-six, Vivien was to be one of the youngest Juliets of recent times. Once it had been a tradition in the theatre that no one should play Juliet until she was old enough to play Juliet's nurse. Vivien was going to break that tradition.

They rehearsed every spare minute away from the studio. The

tour, booked for twenty weeks, would open in San Francisco, then move to Chicago, New York, and Washington. But before they were to leave they attended the Academy Award presentations. Vivien had been nominated for best actress of 1939. She looked beautiful and glowing, her chiffon gown billowing behind, her head tossed back, hair loose, as she rushed up onto the stage to accept her Oscar from Spencer Tracy. She smiled a benign Scarlett smile over the top of the microphone, but it was Vivien, her English diction perfect, who thanked "Mr. Selznick, all my co-workers and most of all Miss Margaret Mitchell."

The film won eight Oscars and several special awards. It was voted best picture; Fleming was named best director; Hattie McDaniel, beaming, accepted the award as best supporting actress (the first black performer to have won an Oscar); Sidney Howard was singled out for the best screenplay (the Guild having decided he was the major contributor); Ernest Haller and Ray Rennahan won for best photography and Lyle Wheeler for art direction, Hal Kern and James Newcom for editing. A special award went to William Cameron Menzies for his use of color. The Irving Thalberg Memorial Award, "for the most consistent high level of production achievement by an individual producer," went to David Selznick. Gable had been outvoted as best actor in favor of Robert Donat in *Goodbye, Mr. Chips*. There had been strained feelings between Selznick and Gable, and Gable somehow felt the studio publicity department had not worked well enough on his behalf and was responsible for his losing the award.

Shortly after the awards, Vivien and Larry flew to San Francisco to open in *Romeo and Juliet* and were aware almost immediately of the two problems that were to plague them for the entire tour—the revolving stage, which made it difficult for them to be heard, and the autograph seekers, who gave them almost no privacy. The notices in San Francisco were mixed. The production came in for a good deal of adverse criticism, and Olivier's performance was not liked by all the reviewers. But one and all agreed Vivien was splendid. At the end of their short run in San Francisco, Vivien and Olivier threw a rather elegant party for the cast and then they all moved on to Chicago, where the reviews filled all of them with high expectations for their New York opening.

> The much heralded production of *Romeo and Juliet* [wrote a staff correspondent for a Chicago daily], with Miss Leigh and Laurence Olivier as the star-crossed lovers, becomes a personal triumph for Miss

Leigh of a kind to make even Scarlett O'Hara seem meager. Our stages have held many excellent Romeos and perhaps that is why Olivier's performance seemed less remarkable than Miss Leigh's. She has the great benefit of immediate contrast with a generation of Juliets less than ideal; Juliets who were stiff or oratorical or middle-aged or even fat. Here the audience beheld a breathless girl, an adolescent in every detail of behavior, love-lorn and gay and terrified as the drama marched along . . . certainly this English girl is the find of many seasons.

The engagement in Chicago was eighteen days and then they were to move to New York. She wrote Leigh from Chicago:

I find Juliet an extremely taxing and difficult part. Not that I didn't know that before. However, by dint of strenuous rehearsals it is getting better and better, and by the time we open in N.Y. it should be all right. It is a perfectly delightful company, all very enthusiastic and young and eager.

I have been in bed two days with a cold everywhere, and shockingly enough we had to call off the performance tonight, but the doctor said it was useless to try to play. On Saturday night I was so hoarse and uncontrolled that I sounded like a eunuch with croup! Chicago has one good art gallery with some fine Van Goghs. And then it's quite nice to walk by the lake. But apart from these two diversions there's nothing, and we shall be very glad to leave. It is still freezing and there's no sign of spring.

We gave one benefit matinee in San Francisco, and the proceeds went half to the Finnish and half to the British. Which is what we hope to do in New York.

The theatre here holds 3,500 people—it was never meant for legitimate shows, just concerts. So you can imagine what *hell* it is to play in. I hope you are still enjoying your lodgings. My address in New York will be 51st Street Theatre at Broadway. We will actually live in the country [Katharine Cornell's house at Sneden's Landing] but I'm not sure of that address yet, and anyway the theatre will always reach me . . . Viv.

San Francisco is *simply beautiful*. I thought how much you would have liked it.

One of the young members of the company was Jack Merivale, the son of English actor Philip Merivale and the stepson of the great beauty and English stage and film star Gladys Cooper. Jack (whose real name was John Merivale) had been born in Toronto on December 1, 1917, and was only four years younger than Vivien. *Romeo and Juliet* had not been their first meeting. Educated at Rugby and at New College, Oxford, Merivale had become a student of the Old Vic

School in 1937 and played Menteith and understudied Malcolm in Olivier's *Macbeth* at the New Theatre. Vivien had, of course, been at the theatre almost every evening.

Macbeth had been a difficult production. Lilian Baylis, who had guided the Old Vic for thirty years, had died on opening night. On its second night Olivier, who always was a realistic and rather wild fighter on stage, cut open the hand of the actor playing Macduff in a terrifying stage battle. The following day just before the matinee the actor playing Malcolm took ill. Merivale had to go on without any rehearsal to do some of Shakespeare's longest scenes with an actor with whom he had never rehearsed. He was only twenty and truly frightened. As he started down the stairs for his entrance, Vivien (whom he had not yet met) was ahead of him. She turned around ("That gorgeous little face—I shall never forget it") and said, "Good luck," and let him pass.

In *Romeo and Juliet*, Merivale played the small role of Balthasar and understudied Olivier's Romeo. He was thrilled to work once again with Olivier and Alexander Knox (Friar Laurence). His dream was to get to go on as Romeo to Vivien's Juliet, but Olivier never missed a performance. For Merivale it was the happiest theatre company of his experience. Everyone in the company seemed to adore Vivien or Larry or both. One cast member considered them "the most enchanting producers."

Certainly, as heads of a company, there seemed to be little they would not do to make their co-workers happy. In San Francisco they threw the company a beautiful gay party, and once they were ensconced in New York they invited them up for weekends at Sneden's Landing. Portraying lovers on stage and being lovers off stage had even intensified their own passion. They were wildly in love and could not take their eyes off each other. This "sexual greediness" for each other could not but be observed by all the company (which also included Dame May Whitty, Cornel Wilde, and Edmond O'Brien), but for those who had worked with Olivier in the days when he had been married to Jill it was even more apparent and perhaps more shocking.

Jill was an attractive, talented lady, extremely organized, but there had been nothing of the passionate personality about her. With her, Olivier had seemed reserved, cool, and somewhat self-conscious. When together, he had treated her as he did the rest of the Old Vic players, as one of the gang. On the other hand, Vivien brought out his tremendous sense of humor. He would behave outlandishly at times. He was no longer afraid of displaying his emotions in public, and it seemed that Vivien and he were living, consuming, and enveloping each other's world. They were simply overwhelmed by each other and the sexual feelings they had for each other. If Vivien's world in their early days had been Larry, his was now totally—and even above the theatre—her.

Jack Merivale was fascinated by the two of them, but it was Vivien and Vivien alone who he felt "glittered." She would walk into a room with a tremendous presence that awed him, a marvelous glitter shining from her, conscious of herself as being known as one of England's most beautiful women (second only to his own stepmother, Gladys Cooper) but simply accepting it. She knew and admired Gladys, and this acquaintanceship brought them closer together. He was riveted by her ambition because it never destroyed but instead added to her femininity.

Their reception in Chicago had given the company a false sense of assurance. They all felt certain New York would cheer their production. They were wrong, and the reviews the morning after the opening sent them all into a near state of shock. Brooks Atkinson of the New York *Times* began his review, "Much scenery; no play." And about the leads, he stated, "Although Miss Leigh and Mr. Olivier are handsome young people, they hardly act the parts at all, and Mr. Olivier in particular keeps throwing his part away."

Atkinson's colleague, Richard Watts, Jr., of the New York *Herald Tribune* agreed. "*Romeo and Juliet* is a most undistinguished production," he said, adding, "Miss Leigh and Laurence Olivier must expect to have their local sojourn in *Romeo and Juliet* taken as a spectacular personal appearance of Heathcliff and Scarlett O'Hara, rather than as an earnest impersonation of the star-crossed lovers in the Shakespearean tragedy." Then he softens Vivien's blow somewhat by continuing: "Miss Leigh, who must certainly be one of the most attractive women in the world, is considerably more successful than Mr. Olivier, despite the fact that he is a more experienced Shakespearean player. She is assuredly one of the brighter spots in the production."

There was good reason for the failure of the play in New York. The circular stage, set far back from the footlights so it could work mechanically in the 51st Street Theatre, destroyed any possible intimacy between players and audience. It also made the dialogue frequently inaudible. But the real problem was Olivier's overlapping roles as producer, director, and star. He was determined to show the world that Vivien could be a great stage actress, and that they could be a great theatrical team. In the scenes where Vivien was on stage alone or with Dame May Whitty he succeeded. But he could not direct his own Romeo with the same objectivity.

With such reviews it was evident that, even had they changed *Romeo and Juliet* to *Laurence and Vivien*, in so large a theatre and with so great an overhead they were going to lose much of their initial investment. How much they were not yet sure. Vivien, who adored good wine and had ordered cases of the finest vintage before the reviews, got on the telephone immediately: "About that wine—don't send it!" she said succinctly. Then they moved out of the hotel and commuted daily to Sneden's Landing, which was about ten miles outside of the city. Both were concerned about their immediate financial futures, but they tried hard to keep up the spirits of their company. Weekends at Sneden's Landing there were always members of the cast.

"What are you going to do when we close?" Vivien asked Jack Merivale a few days before they were scheduled to do so.

"Well, I'm signed for a revival of *Journey's End* in Ridgefield, Connecticut."

"How long will that last?" she inquired.

"It's a week's rehearsal and a week's playing," he replied.

"Then what are you going to do?"

"Then I don't know."

"Oh, well, darling, do ring us up when you are finished and come and spend a weekend."

It was the first indication anyone had that Vivien and Olivier did not intend to return straightaway to California.

When his play closed at Ridgefield, Merivale rang up. "I've done it. I've finished. It's closed," he announced.

"Oh, how lovely," Vivien commented. "When can you come and see us?"

"Tomorrow?" he asked awkwardly.

"How marvelous."

The house at Sneden's Landing was a converted barn, but to describe it as such would be highly misleading. Set high and regally over the Hudson River, it was probably the most elegant converted barn extant. The original exterior of weathered shingles had been retained. But inside, the soaring walls and expansive ceilings had been wallpapered with gold flocking between the old and massive rough-hewn beams, and the rooms furnished with magnificent Georgian antiques. One side of the immense living room was formed of glass sliding doors that led out to a terrace with a sweeping view of the countryside and the Hudson. The main bedroom suite shared this view but was dominated by two magnificent antique four-foot-high carved wood Chinese figures set in pale gray shell-domed niches in the wall.

Larry and Vivien liked to entertain in the library-study, a Renaissance room lined with books and filled with crimson accents— damask drapes and couches and chairs, deep red Persian rugs, and Chinese porcelain *objets d'art* in the same vivid colors. There were also photographs of all Miss Cornell's friends wherever space permitted—Noël, the Lunts, Vivien, and Larry. The famous faces smiled, the artful torsos posed from polished deep mahogany wood tops framed in shiny silver. It was an imposing room, but Vivien and Larry commanded it with ease and made their guests feel instantly comfortable.

The evening that Merivale arrived for the weekend the Oliviers were alone. They dined and the three of them had "done very well" on martinis and wine and then moved to the library, where Larry sank rather heavily into a chair to study aerial navigation. (He was working to get a pilot's license in order to be fairly qualified when he returned to England.)

"Oh, well, if Ba [her nickname for Olivier] is going to do that, you and I will play Chicker Checks [Chinese Checkers]," Vivien told Merivale. They sat down at a game table, but Vivien, who had always been unbeatable, seemed distracted.

"Look, if you let me get another one there, I shall win," Merivale warned at a point in the game where she looked to be losing. "You had better get them all out."

"What absolute nonsense. Don't be silly," she snapped. "You have to let me out sometime."

"Look, I promise you I don't," Merivale insisted. "I'll put it there and that one will stay there until I am all across the board and there will be no ladder for you and I shall win by yards."

"Absolute nonsense," she repeated. "Play your own game. Don't tell me how to play." Her voice was edgy and her hands tapped the table nervously. She did not seem like the gay, glittery Vivien he adored. Something about her appeared "off," "different," and Merivale now felt uncomfortable and had second thoughts about his presence for the weekend. He was aware, of course, that they had lost a good deal of money in *Romeo and Juliet* and that that could account for what was beginning to seem a contentious atmosphere. Perhaps, he speculated, she was piqued that he, as a non-investor in the production, was not affected by the play's losses. Yet, such an attitude did not fit the generous Vivien he knew. He glanced over to Olivier, who was still totally involved in his book and unaware of any personality change taking place in Vivien. Yet Merivale was certain some change had occurred. He continued with the game exactly as he said he would and he won.

"How dare you invite yourself down here and then cheat at Chicker Checks!" Vivien shouted, turning on him.

"What do you mean—*cheat?*" he asked, pride injured and yet trying to deal with the situation in a straightforward manner. "I'm not cheating and I told you what was going to happen." She glared across the table and mumbled some obscenities. He turned to Olivier for help. "Larry, do calm her down," he begged.

Olivier appeared aware of the crossfire between the two for the first time. He put down his book. "What in hell is going on?" he asked.

A look of terror crossed Vivien's face and for a moment she was near tears. "Don't try to come between us," she accused Jack hysterically. "We've been together for four years now and nobody's going to come between us."

"I'll leave," Merivale said, rising to go.

"There isn't a train until nine in the morning," Vivien informed him.

"That's a bit early, isn't it, darling?" Olivier interrupted.

"Well, there's one at nine-thirty," she relented.

"Right. I'll be on it," Jack said.

"Good!" she agreed.

He excused himself and went directly to his room, but he was unable to sleep. Something troubled him. The sound of Vivien's voice, the curious look in her eyes, the sudden waspishness of her personality. It was as if the woman he had just played Chinese Checkers with was not the same woman he knew—the glittering, charming, always polite and beautifully mannered Vivien.

The next morning he was awake before either of them. He now decided that they had all been drunk the previous night and the chances were that his host and hostess would not even remember the quarrel. Still, on the chance that they might, he sneaked out of the house as quietly as possible to avoid any further confrontation.

Chapter Fourteen

More than anything, Vivien wanted to be like Larry, to absorb into herself all the qualities that made him who and what he was. She was so caught up, so dazzled, so constantly astonished by him that she was certain that he was unique, a genius. All the early years of her life had been filled with friends who were followers. With Olivier she was the follower. Never once did she doubt his superiority. Trying to live up to it threw her at times into complete panic. She could not understand what was happening to her. She would find she could not tolerate her friends, that she would turn savagely against those she loved, but she never turned against Larry.

Olivier attributed her short bursts of irrationality to an intolerance to alcohol and to nervous exhaustion. They did not alarm him, if only because he was too busy. Nothing seemed too much for her to do to please him. She continued to be the charming hostess, the most considerate guest, and such disasters as the evening with Jack Merivale were bizarre exceptions. The failure of *Romeo and Juliet* was a great disappointment to both of them. They had lost their entire savings, but more serious to Olivier was the disservice they may have performed to Shakespeare, whom he considered "the nearest thing in incarnation to the eye of God."

Neither of them wanted to return to Hollywood. It was the theatre that Olivier felt had true depth, actual *physical* depth, and where it was possible to portray a group of human beings as they really were. There was something about theatre—something that involved an audience and something that could almost devour an actor. It was a dangerous and exciting game, and there was nothing else quite like it. He loved more than anything else in the theatre the challenge of the great roles like Henry V, Macbeth, Coriolanus, and Hamlet. Great roles were "like cannibals," and to survive them was a thrill almost unequaled by any other experience in life—a thrill he wanted Vivien to share.

They remained at Sneden's Landing while he cast about for a proper stage vehicle that could involve them both. *Caesar and Cleopatra* was one such idea, but after the failure of *Romeo and Juliet* it would not be easy to find backers for it. Then Vivien received an offer for the lead in a proposed Theatre Guild production of *Marie Adelaide*. The part was a tour de force for any actress who played it, and it had been submitted to Ingrid Bergman the previous season. Like Vivien, Bergman was under contract to Selznick, and the Guild had not been able to get him to allow her to play the role. They now approached Vivien, who, after gaining Olivier's approval of the play, wrote Selznick, who replied:

> Forgive me, Vivien, if I call to your attention that we fought out the matter of your theatrical appearances at the time we made our contract, and that you secured certain important concessions in consideration of giving up the theater. Yet, in spite of this, I permitted you to do *Romeo and Juliet* solely because of my desire to do something important toward your personal happiness. . . . Even now, I do not regret it, because I know that despite the heartache that you undoubtedly went through as a result of it, it made you happier at the same time to do it. Frankly, though, Vivien, I didn't expect to get another request so soon.

His answer was no to both the Theatre Guild and to Vivien's personal request and he told her, "You must get three or four more films under your belt."

They seriously considered returning to England, since the war news had been disheartening and Larry felt he should be more than a tool for British propaganda in America. In the short span of three months the Germans had invaded Denmark, Norway, Belgium, Holland, Luxembourg, and France. Holland had capitulated, Belgium had surrendered, France had signed an armistice at Compiègne with the Germans, and Italy had entered the war on Germany's side.

Then Olivier received news that three-and-a-half-year-old Tarquin was seriously ill with spinal meningitis and was totally paralyzed from the chest downward. For ten days the child fought the mysterious disease until the paralysis finally left him, but then the doctors feared the danger of mental complications because of pressure of fluid on the brain. Jill had been advised to evacuate with him to America to avoid possible air raids and the associated fear, which could cause permanent damage.

Having decided that Gertrude should bring Suzanne to America as well, they needed money badly, and Larry and Vivien would have to support them all once they had arrived. Providence appeared in the guise of that charming Hungarian, Alexander Korda. He had arrived back in New York after filming a successful propaganda film— *The Lion Has Wings*. Vivien and Olivier confessed their woes to him, and not long after he rang them at Sneden's Landing from California.

"You know Nelson and Lady Hamilton, eh?" he asked excitedly.

Olivier thought he was talking about some friends of Korda's or some social figures and said no, he did not.

"Yes, Larry, you *know them!*" Korda insisted and then explained he meant Lord Horatio Nelson and Lady Emma Hamilton. "The Battle of Trafalgar, for God's sake!"

It was the answer to all their immediate problems. It was not the middle of July, and the film would go into production in Hollywood in October. Korda gave them half their salaries in advance so that they could bring Tarquin and Suzanne over. The film was to be made in six weeks, which would mean that by the end of the year they could be on their way back to England for Larry to join the forces; and with the remaining monies to be paid them, Vivien could live at home without too much financial pressure for a time anyway. As a bonus, Korda deposited money in Canada for the children's welfare.

Within a week they had returned to Hollywood and on August 9 Vivien wrote Leigh:

> My darling Leigh . . . Larry and I are to do a picture about Nelson and Lady Hamilton. I am extremely dubious about it. But now one does not plan a career much as it seems futile, and we are certainly only doing this for financial purposes which are useful in these days.

There was no mention of Tarquin's illness, of their plans to evacuate the children, or of the fact that that very day Leigh's divorce from her had become final. She was now free to wed and by August 28 so would Olivier be.

Both of them steeped themselves in biographies of the famous Nelson and Lady Hamilton while R. C. Sherriff (*Journey's End*) and

Walter Reisch (*Men Are Not Gods*) worked on the screenplay. Korda gave his writers instructions that the film was to be a form of propaganda meant to arouse pro-British sentiments in America. There were obvious parallels between the war against Hitler and the Napoleonic wars. "Propaganda needs sugar coating," Korda told them. The love affair of Lord Nelson and Lady Hamilton was to be that coating.

As expected, on August 28, 1940, Olivier's divorce became final. Following the advice of Ronald Colman and his wife, Benita Hume, he and Vivien decided to drive to Santa Barbara, a distance of about eighty miles, register with the County Clerk, who was a man who had no interest in informing the press, and then return three days later, after the legal waiting time, to be married by a judge. Benita Colman also offered to purchase the wedding ring for them as an added ruse to guard their privacy.

The Colmans planned to meet them after the ceremony in San Pedro, where Colman's schooner, *Dragoon*, was anchored and would be waiting to take them on a short honeymoon. First they had a pre-wedding party for their friends, and then with close friends Katharine Hepburn and Garson Kanin, they drove to Santa Barbara. They were married on August 31, at one minute past midnight (the earliest time they could do so legally), by Municipal Judge Fred Harsh in the living room of Mr. and Mrs. Alvin Weingand, who were Olivier's friends from earlier days.

It was an exceptionally short service, no more than three minutes from the beginning to "I now pronounce you man and wife." The couple kissed and the judge cried out, "Bingo!"

Vivien was now Mrs. Laurence Olivier.

The newlyweds arrived at the side of the *Dragoon* about four A.M. Colman's captain lifted anchor almost immediately. Standing at the prow of the ship, with dawn glowing in a summer sky, they headed out for Catalina Island.

Passage had been arranged (quite by coincidence) for Jill and Tarquin and Gertrude and Suzanne to sail to Canada on the same ship—the *Cythia*. Jill was anything but happy about the arrangement. She had been having terrible nightmares before boarding in which Vivien was about to be run over and killed by a steamroller and she had had to jump on top of her to save her. The dream had kept recurring and she had not been able to interpret it, but it left her with a strong hostility against Vivien. She avoided a meeting with Gertrude and kept the children apart to the best of her ability. But the children were enjoined to shake sticky hands once during a lifeboat drill. Jill's plans were to travel with Tarquin by train from Toronto to New York, while Gertrude intended traveling with Suzanne to Vancouver, where she was planning to leave the child at a convent school before returning to Ernest in London.

Vivien and Larry decided to fly to Canada and meet the ship. However difficult the meeting between Jill and Vivien might have been, the emotion upon sight of the children overshadowed any personal embarrassment. Tarquin's coordination was poor, and he was pale and thin and undersized for his age. Jill had to tell Olivier that the little boy's legs did not seem to be growing and that he would require special treatment and exercises that she understood were available in New York. And Suzanne was not much older than Vivien had been when she had been left alone at the convent school in Roehampton.

They returned to Hollywood heavy-hearted, Vivien not feeling sure that Suzanne should be enrolled but not knowing what else to do, and Olivier concerned for Tarquin's health. Work on the film began and became a happy release from their personal problems.

That Hamilton Woman (*Lady Hamilton* in Britain) was shot in black and white and on a spartan budget. It tended to shift the emphasis of the film from the obvious production values the film might have had to the personal conflicts of the characters. Because of this the film was the closest Korda had come to his grand success of *The Private Life of Henry VIII*. Vincent Korda built all the sets—the Hamilton's lavish Neapolitan villa and the model shots of the Battle of Trafalgar—at the General Service Studio. The script was not completed when shooting began. R. C. Sherriff later wrote:

> . . . only the first sequences were down in dialogue when they began to shoot the picture.
>
> From then on it was a desperate race to keep up with them. It was like writing a serial story with only a week between your pen and the next installment to be published. We would slog along all day on scenes that would be wanted before the week was over, and I would take them back to my hotel and work most of the night smoothing out the dialogue . . . There wasn't time for the leisurely script conferences I'd been used to. We'd sit around in the lunch-break eating sandwiches and drinking coffee, and talk about the scenes that Reisch and I had just brought in . . . Sometimes the stuff we wrote didn't measure up to what Alex Korda and the others wanted. Then Reisch and I would have to go away and spend the afternoon rewriting it.

Selznick could not have found a better follow-up for Scarlett O'Hara than Korda had in Emma, Lady Hamilton. The Lucky Hungarian had cashed in on Selznick's hard work, as he had predicted. But Selznick felt no resentment. Instead, he began frantically to look for another story that would reinforce Vivien's moneymaking potential. He was aware that Olivier planned to return to England but had a curious lack of insight into Vivien. Therefore, he was not prepared for her departure and her total rejection of her contractual commitment to him.

On October 22 she wrote to Leigh:

Oh Leigh I don't think you can possibly realize what it feels like to be away now. The longing to be back is overwhelming.

And on November 4 she wrote:

I am so very thrilled because we may be home for Christmas. If I do not come quite yet, I have got permission to come as soon as my next engagement is finished . . . the Nelson film is nearly over. We have *rushed* thro' it because apparently after Thursday there is no more money!— Alex's usual predicament.

Is Little Stanhope Street still rented? . . . I have not told Daddy about coming back yet, as it is not certain. . . . There is a stray cat here that I shall mind leaving (Old Tom).

The house on Little Stanhope Street was hit with bombs shortly after she wrote the letter and totally demolished.

Knowing she would never return to America without Olivier, she flew to see Suzanne before their planned departure, now fixed for December 27. Not wanting any publicity on the visit with Suzanne, she booked passage as Mrs. Holman, but the press found out and she was greeted in Vancouver by hordes of reporters, mystified and intrigued by her attempt at secrecy. The Mother Superior at the convent school now refused to keep Suzanne, claiming that she feared kidnapping threats. Vivien thought it might have more to do with her divorce and subsequent remarriage, but there was nothing she could do to reverse the Mother Superior's decision. This meant Suzanne was forced to go to a day school, at least for the rest of the term, and that Gertrude would now have to be separated for a long period of time from Ernest, which she agreed to but not without inflicting some measure of guilt upon her daughter.

The Oliviers, after closing up the small house on Cedarbrook Drive where they had lived since August, and leaving behind Old

Tom and a shaggy sheep dog who had come with the house, flew to New York. On December 27, as planned, they boarded the American ship *Excambion*, which had just brought four hundred passengers from Europe and was returning with twenty-three (including the Oliviers). The ship was technically neutral, but the voyage through difficult waters to Lisbon was fraught with tension and quite real fears.

In Lisbon they managed to secure a flight to Bristol and found the city cloaked in darkness. It had just been raided and all the windows of their hotel were blown out. It was bitter cold and they climbed exhausted into bed fully clothed, Vivien even wearing gloves.

The bombs began to fall. There was the sound of sirens and antiaircraft guns and falling rubble. Hollywood and Broadway now seemed a million years away.

Chapter Fifteen

Vivien was in love with excitement, but an England at war did not manage to kindle in her the spirit of battle. She found herself more often than not unutterably depressed. It was not easy for her to accustom herself to rubble and destruction. She would flinch as though seeing a life struck out when she passed a remembered house or church or archway in ruins. It was impossible for her to accept the fact that the house on Little Stanhope Street had been demolished, even when she stood at the corner of Pitt's Head Mews and stared down the street at the gaping hole where it had once been. It was somehow easier for her to accept death than destruction. The demolition of landmarks, life markings (*Here* I dreamed my first dreams of stardom, *there* I saw my first play, under *that* arch Larry held me in his arms and we waited for the storm to pass and I felt safe, *safe*), was the unkindest reminder of the temporariness of life.

She had always slept badly, now she slept less than ever. It seemed easier to lie in bed awake and listen to the sound of the planes overhead than to awake to it. In the beginning she tried to make the sound merge with fantasy. It was only the last bursts of applause after the final fall of the curtain. But the sound continued. The clapping never ceased. And there was the cold. She was constantly numb with it, unable to ever warm her hands and feet. Whatever she thought she might find on returning from Hollywood, whatever she expected war to be, it was not chalk dust and cramping cold and the smell of rancid bacon frying.

Blast had done some damage to Durham Cottage while they had

been absent, and her first task was repairing and putting things back in order. Olivier had applied immediately upon arrival for admission to the Fleet Air Arm and to his shock had been rejected because of faulty hearing in one ear. He knew he had a damaged nerve in his inner ear, but he had never given it serious consideration as a disqualification. For a month he went from one ear specialist to another and finally reversed the Admiralty's decision. He was accepted for non-operational flying.

For three months he was based in London. He took a role in a film, *49th Parallel* (*The Invaders* in the U.S.A.), about a French-Canadian trapper, and appeared with Leslie Howard and Raymond Massey under the direction of Michael Powell. It was only a few weeks' work, and he was idle too soon, as the Royal Navy Volunteer Reserve did not seem to be in much of a hurry for his services. His concern was mainly for Vivien. Her curious bouts of "nerves" came and went a bit too frequently now. She took in a stray black and white cat, which she named Tissy, and lavished too much attention on it. He decided she needed activity and convinced her to go see Tyrone Guthrie with the hope that he might accept her for the coming Old Vic season. Even though he knew she was a reliable and fine actress and that her name might serve the box office well, Guthrie had to turn her down because the Old Vic was a repertory company and Guthrie was fearful that her star status would off-balance the productions.

Before she had time to dwell on the disappointment, Olivier came up with a plan to put them both back on the stage. With Constance Cummings, John Clements, Ben Levy, and Jack Melford they visited airdromes and put on a show for the R.A.F. Benevolent Fund. They played the wooing scene from *Henry* V together, and Olivier did some comedic sketches.

In mid-April he received his first orders. He was to go to Lee-on-the-Solent to undergo a three-week conversion course to adapt his American private flying experience to British planes. Vivien refused to consider remaining in London.

They bought an old open car with a faulty radiator, and with a tow rope attached to Vivien's old car (which was inoperative after being garaged all during their American stay, and which they had packed full of luggage), they started out. Olivier, now an Acting Sub Lieutenant (A) with the R.N.V.R., drove their old car while Vivien, with Tissy sitting beside her in the front seat, steered her towed car with great dignity.

In Warsash, just a short distance from Lee-on-the-Solent, Vivien found a Victorian house with a garden and the improbable name of "Forakers," which she would spell out when giving directions. The house was sparsely furnished and Vivien was happy she had brought some of their personal treasures. The small Boudin was hung in their bedroom, the Sickert over the fireplace, the narrow Aubusson carpet graced the living-room floor, and books and pictures were placed neatly on the scarred top of the kneehole desk.

The three weeks were soon up, and Olivier was transferred to Worthy Down, near Winchester, but was still able to return home in the evenings to Warsash in less than an hour's drive. Vivien was alone a good deal of the time. The raids on London the previous summer had virtually closed down the West End. Most London theatres were dark, with companies staying alive by touring the provinces. But gardening and caring for the old house in Warsash were not enough to occupy Vivien. She felt she should be performing, and an offer from the Theatre Guild in New York to play in *Caesar and Cleopatra* with Cedric Hardwicke only stimulated this desire.

Olivier recognized how important it was for her to keep active and began busily casting about for a proper vehicle for her, one that would be within her range. Finally, he suggested the role of Jennifer Dubedat in Shaw's *The Doctor's Dilemma*. Vivien was not immediately drawn to the part or the play. To make Jennifer Dubedat an interesting character would not be easy, and she did not approve of the essential theme of the play or its resolution (the medical murder of an artist of power who was also a social bore). Though supposedly a comedy, she found it instead a rather snide and cold-blooded dissection of the theme of the artist's value to society.

She would rather, she argued, play Cleopatra, and she had heard that Gabriel Pascal was planning a film production. Perhaps he could be convinced to put it on stage first. Olivier made inquiries, but Pascal was not interested in such a proposal. He wanted to bring *Caesar and Cleopatra* to the screen, and though he agreed that Vivien would make a fine Cleopatra, his arrangements with Shaw gave the author casting approval.

Vivien then decided to play the role of Jennifer Dubedat, feeling if she proved to Shaw she could bring life to the part, he would agree to cast her as Cleopatra, which—in spite of its being a film project—she wanted more and more to do. Olivier spoke to Hugh Beaumont, who was the managing director of H. M. Tennent Ltd., and he undertook the production. The West End was still badly affected by the raids, so the decision was to tour the show until it was feasible to bring it into London. *The Doctor's Dilemma* went into rehearsal (under the direction of Irene Hentschel and with Vivien playing opposite Cyril Cusack) in August and opened in Manchester in September 1941. It was the beginning of an excessively long and successful tour. On October 14 they were in Leicester and Vivien wrote Leigh:

> Leigh Darling . . . thank you for the cheque last week. Surely you have sent quite enough now! [She was being reimbursed by Leigh for her outlay on Suzanne's care.] . . . I went riding for the first time in four years the other day at Blackpool with the result that I can still only move about with great difficulty! And my performance is not quite such a graceful one! Thank you for the criticisms of the play—they are all quite right—and of course the sympathy must be with Dubedat—that is where Cyril fails a bit, but he is such a good actor he will probably improve all the time. I speak slowly in the first act because I think it gives the weight and maturity Jennifer requires.
>
> We broke the record at Blackpool—which was satisfactory—and this is a beautiful theatre to play in—rather like the St. James.
>
> I'm dying to see Citizen Kane.
>
> Lots of love darling, Viv.

Traveling in a caravan once again, the Oliviers moved from the creaky Victorian house in Warsash to a small, cozy bungalow at Worthy Down. Vivien had developed a cough, and they thought it might come from the drafty rooms of the larger and older house. She was pale and painfully thin, but she joked away Olivier's concern and continued to commute each night after the play opened in London on ill-heated, blacked-out trains, creeping exhausted into bed, unable to sleep, reading her way through the nights with Dickens' novels, which she had just rediscovered. At dawn Olivier would try not to disturb her as he rose, made his breakfast, and then journeyed by motorcycle to the airdrome.

One night in Stratford, when the show had been touring, there was a mix-up after the performance and they missed the last train home. Vivien, along with George and Mercia Relph, who were also in the company, finally managed to get a lift from a farmer who was going their way. It turned out he had been to the play and he began, on being asked how he had enjoyed himself, to tell his passengers what a miserable time he had had, giving them several solid minutes on how lousy it was in every possible way, vehemently adding, "And as for that knock-kneed bugger in the second act—" At which George Relph swiftly inserted "That was me," and the man without any hesitation said, "Marvelous!" This became one of Vivien's favorite stories, and she would tell it in front of George imitating his grimace at the farmer's duplicity.

It was fortunate that they found things to laugh about, because each day brought depressing news: war reports, the death of friends, the destruction of familiar and loved places. The entire world seemed under the pall of death, destruction, and anxiety. Whitehall emphasized the importance of keeping up morale, but even Olivier was feeling the weight of frustration. "So many millions of people trying to feel something they don't feel or trying not to feel something they do," he wrote.

Vivien was on tour for six bone-chilling months, finally coming into the West End and opening at the Haymarket with excellent reviews on March 4, 1942. Two weeks later, Cyril Cusack took ill. For a week Vivien played opposite his understudy, and then Peter Glenville replaced him, shortly thereafter being felled himself by jaundice. John Gielgud then stepped in for a week.

Shaw was frequently at his London flat in Whitehall Court during the thirteen-month run of the play, but he did not attend a performance of *The Doctor's Dilemma*, as it was his invariable rule never to see his own plays past rehearsals. But Hugh Beaumont managed an invitation for Vivien to meet Shaw at his flat. By now both she and Pascal had agreed that if Shaw consented she would play Cleopatra in Pascal's film.

Vivien had never handled an interview better. Not once did she mention the role of Cleopatra, but from the moment she stepped through Shaw's sitting-room door she acted the Persian kitten. Just before the interview came to a close Shaw mischievously "suggested" she should play Cleopatra, and waited for her reaction with a bemused expression. She lowered her head demurely and then looked up at him with a humble expression to ask him if he really thought she was ready for such a great role. Shaw pulled back and stroked his beard, finally declaring that it hardly mattered because Cleopatra was a role that played itself.

Pascal had many production problems, so Vivien had several months free after *The Doctor's Dilemma* closed. Once again the Oliviers moved, this time to the small village of Fulmer in Buckinghamshire, to a house called "Hawksgrove," which Noël Coward had previously occupied. To Olivier's great disappointment the Fleet Air Arm was doing exceptionally little with his services. Yet his conscience would not permit him to ask for his release unless it was to do something worthwhile. After considerable thought and many meetings with film people, he decided he would go forward with a film version of Henry V if he could produce and star in the production and retain control. From the start of these negotiations he had taken it for granted that Vivien would play Katharine. Olivier cabled Selznick for permission, and he cabled back that he would not consider such a thing.

Actually Selznick had been cabling her with various suggestions for roles for over a year, all of which Vivien refused, including a production of Jane Eyre that Selznick thought Vivien would like because he had suggested in the cable that little Suzanne might appear as young Jane.

Olivier cast Renée Asherson in the role of Katharine; and early in 1943 Vivien accepted Hugh Beaumont's offer for her to join a theatrical company that included Beatrice Lillie, Dorothy Dickson, and Leslie Henson to entertain the Eighth Army in North Africa. Vivien had not wanted to leave Olivier, but he was completely occupied with work on his film and was to be on location in Ireland for a long spell. She had not been well, and both of them attributed it to the dampness in England, which was bound to be even worse in Ireland. Six weeks in the sun seemed a grand opportunity for her to regain her health and still to be doing something that she could consider worthwhile.

The revue was called Spring Party. She recited Clemence Dane's heroic poem "Plymouth Hoe," Lewis Carroll's "You Are Old, Father William," and sang a satirical song about Scarlett O'Hara. The men loved her, and she sweltered with the company under the North African sun from Gibraltar to Cairo, giving sometimes as many as three performances a day and appearing before General Eisenhower in Algiers, General Montgomery in Tripoli, Generals Spaatz and Doolittle in Constantine, and before His Majesty King George VI in Tunis on the terrace of Admiral Cunningham's villa overlooking the Mediterranean.

She adored the bazaars and would dash off between performances to search for bargains. The Miramare Theatre in Tripoli was not more than a hundred yards from the Arab quarter. Before one performance, she came rushing back to the theatre carrying several yards of a deep crimson material and swept it out before the other members of the company with pride. No one was impressed. "Oh, well," she said, shrugging her shoulders, "I can always sell it to Pascal for *Cleopatra!*"

But the sun had not benefited her as she had hoped it would. By the end of the tour she was thinner by fifteen pounds, but at least her cough seemed to have disappeared. Olivier cabled her that Pascal had gone to Hollywood to find a leading man for the *Caesar and Cleopatra* film, and she flew home feeling in higher spirits than she had been in for a long while.

Their reunion was a joyous one. Olivier was extremely pleased with the work on *Henry V*, and at last she had time to devote to simply being Mrs. Laurence Olivier. It was nearly summer in Britain. She worked in the garden and was surrounded by the kittens Tissy had given birth to in her absence. It seemed sure that Larry would not have to face serious danger, Leigh was safe, her father fine, Gertrude (though complaining) quite comfortable, Suzanne doing well, and Tarquin responding beautifully to medical treatment in Los Angeles, where he and his mother were now living. To add to her joy, she became pregnant. The doctor felt she should not be attempting a film role at this time, but she argued that she never felt stronger or happier or more confident in her life.

On June 12, 1944, just six days after the Allies' invasion of Normandy, the cameras began to roll at Denham Studios, with Claude Rains as Caesar. Shaw came to watch them shoot one day at Denham. "I pity poor Rank [Arthur Rank, the producer]. The film will cost a million," he said rather prophetically, for the film eventually cost over £1,300,000 ($5,200,000 in 1944 dollars). He allowed no alterations in the script unless he wrote them. After he saw Claude Rains, he himself decided that the actor could not be described by Cleopatra as being thin and stringy. He wrote Vivien a card from his house in Ayot St. Lawrence:

> Your Claudius Caesar is not rather thin and stringy (I have just seen him); so will you say instead: "You are hundreds of years old; but you have a nice voice, & C." I think this is the only personal remark that needs altering; but if there is anything let me know. G.B.S.

Vivien answered that she was certain she could make the original lines believable by the way she spoke them. Shaw answered immediately and with annoyance:

No. Rains is not stringy, and would strongly resent any deliberate attempt to make him appear so.

Besides "you are hundreds of years old" is a much better line, as it belongs to the childishness of Cleopatra in the first half of the play.

I never change a line except for the better.

Don't be an idiot.

G.B.S.

Why don't you put your address in your letters?

The film became increasingly difficult. The weather had turned unseasonably cold, and she had to go from the warmth of a small electric fire she kept in her dressing room to a frigid open field in Cleopatra's filmy gowns and attempt to create the feeling of the stifling heat of an Egyptian summer. Six weeks after the film began she became violently ill. She was rushed to the nearest clinic, but it did no good. Her baby was lost. After a few days of recuperation she went back to complete the film. She played the banqueting scene where Cleopatra orders the murder of Pothinus with a new maturity, and in the close-ups Pascal was taken aback by the unexpected passion in her face.

Chapter Sixteen

Larry and Vivien were the golden couple. A youthful beauty clung to them. They were the hope of the war years. England was bleak, gray, and forbidding in its wartime desolation. Faces wore grim expressions. Women dressed like men. Gone was the splendor, the panoply of the crown, the lavish balls one could read about if not attend, the resplendent military parades. A great number of Londoners ate canned Spam for Christmas. But then, just when the golden days before the war seemed lost forever, Larry and Vivien exploded in the public eye, seeming to be the two most beautiful people in the world. They gleamed with incandescent vitality, radiating charm. Everyone wanted to read about them, to see their pictures in the papers, to meet them, and to be a member of their large group of friends and even wider circle of acquaintances. In public, Vivien kept up an air of gaiety. To the unobservant she remained a dream, an apparition from the past. But Pascal had seen the truth reveal itself on the screen, and it has severely shocked him. There was something frightening in her eyes, something that made one fear for her more than for oneself.

Vivien became acutely depressed at the end of filming on *Caesar and Cleopatra*. Larry did not understand it but could easily attribute it to the strain of the work she had just completed, the loss of the baby, and world conditions in general. He was empathetic but did not take Vivien's depression too seriously. Then one night they were dining alone at home, chatting quite pleasantly, when her mood suddenly and terrifyingly shifted. She began to pace like a caged lioness who had just had her cub taken from her. Her voice changed, becoming strident and harsh; and when he tried to calm her she turned on him, first verbally and then physically. He was at a loss for what to do. She was for the first time a complete stranger to him and he could not think whom to call to help her. After a time that felt like an eternity but was actually no more than an hour, she crumpled into a heap and sobbed hysterically on the floor, not letting him come near her. When her attack of hysteria was over she could not recall what she had done or said. It terrified them both; and immediately after, she was childlike in her need to compensate. They were still totally in love, and the effect on Olivier of such an attack was overwhelming. In her hysteria she was accusatory, shrewish, saying mindless, hurting things—almost totally paranoid.

Vivien insisted she was not having a nervous collapse and refused to see a doctor to discuss the events of that evening. To the unsuspecting she remained enchanting, and as a pair they still seemed sprinkled with gold dust, even though it was the bleakest, coldest, grimmest winter since the war began. Travel was uncomfortable at best, at worst almost impossible. Taxes mounted astronomically. There were few luxuries and everyone suffered. Tensions, stress, coupons, queues, the petty tyrannies endured, and the lack of freedom were not easy to bear, even when people were united. The war with Germany was nearing its end and it looked as though life would soon return to normal. But Vivien was unsure of what returning to normal might mean on a strictly personal basis.

Selznick kept up his barrage of cables demanding that she return to Hollywood and honor her contract, but no film could help her overcome the tremendous inferiority she now felt toward Olivier. He was a genius, perhaps the greatest actor alive, and he had little respect for commercial film. *Henry V* was quite another art form. He worshiped greatness—Shakespeare, Chekhov, Sheridan, and men like Wellington and Churchill. Always men, always leaders, creators, sufferers. She was convinced she needed to achieve a stature of greatness for Larry to worship her. Nothing he said or did appeared to convince her that he loved and adored her simply for herself. She became convinced, indeed obsessed, that if she could rise to greatness on the stage—if she could compete in his arena and share his crown—then she would be worthy of his devotion, then she would have his veneration. She ignored Selznick's cables when she could, and when she could not, she sent him polite clipped refusals. Pascal and Rank had paid him a handsome sum for her to appear in *Cleopatra*, and Scarlett had made everyone rich but herself. She felt no guilt or further obligation.

Someone sent her a copy of Thornton Wilder's new play, *The Skin of Our Teeth*, in which Tallulah Bankhead had appeared in New York. She adored the play and was mad to play Sabina in London, certain that if Olivier would direct her it might be the role that would finally prove her stageworthiness to the world. Olivier had completed work on *Henry V* and liked *The Skin of Our Teeth* almost as much as Vivien did, but primarily he saw the project and their mutual involvement as a way to please Vivien. She was ecstatic in her discussions of Sabina, a woman who—whether she was in the kitchen, out winning a beauty contest, or following an army as a vivandière—was the eternal Cleopatra and the supreme survivor of the ice age, the deluge, and "bloody war, north, east, and west." Plans were begun to bring the play and Vivien to the West End.

On February 19, 1945, David Selznick sent this memo to Daniel T. O'Shea, Executive Vice President and General Manager of David O. Selznick Productions, Inc.:

To: Mr. O'Shea   February 19, 1945
                                   IMMEDIATE

There should be entire review of our dealings with Vivien Leigh. . . .

We consented to her stage appearance in *Romeo and Juliet* because of her and Olivier's urgings, although this meant passing up having Scarlett O'Hara in other films. This endeavor seriously damaged her career and reviews were terrible. This is one reason why we are so fearful of another theatrical engagement prompted and participated in by Olivier, with possibility of further serious damage to our property.

We heeded Leigh's urgings and pleas for a twelve-week leave of absence to go to England because we felt an Englishwoman should return to England during wartime and also because of her principal argument, which was that she might never see Olivier again, since he was planning on going into service. We made this gesture in good faith and at a loss to ourselves, as we did subsequent gestures leading to extensions and further leaves of absence. . . .

Olivier is no longer in service, and there is no reason why she should not return to America or at least make an attempt to do so; and it might be stressed that she has consistently refused to even consider any such attempt, although we have stood ready and still stand ready to make pictures with her that could have enormously beneficial effect on British-

American relations, with a potential audience between fifty and one hundred million people throughout the world by comparison with the small number any play could reach.

Action was certainly "immediate." Within three days, Selznick, through his British counsel, Sir Walter Monckton, petitioned for an injunction to prevent her from appearing in the play, likening her to an "exotic plant which must be exposed widely," and claiming Selznick's "right under contract" that they had signed in 1939 to decide what roles Vivien should be allowed to accept. In reply (though she did not appear in court), Vivien claimed that as a British citizen she faced possible drafting into a war factory if she did not act on the British stage. Selznick lost his bid to restrain her from doing *The Skin of Our Teeth*, and the play went into rehearsal.

Spring came suddenly and prematurely in the beginning of March. For a fortnight, summer heat force-bloomed the few flowers growing wildly amid potato patches, the trees became alive with budding green. It was almost too good to believe, but with the sun and the blossoms and the green came good news. On March 5, U.S. troops entered Cologne, and they crossed the Rhine at Remagen on March 8. British troops crossed the Rhine at Wesel on March 23. On April 14 the Russians captured Vienna. Seven days later they reached Berlin. On April 28 Benito Mussolini was assassinated, and on April 30 Adolf Hitler and Eva Braun committed suicide.

On V-E Day, May 8, Vivien was in Blackpool trying out *The Skin of Our Teeth* before bringing it into the West End. Jack Merivale was stationed at a nearby R.A.F. station at the time. Their last meeting many years before at Sneden's Landing had been most unpleasant. The play had been ill-received in the North Country, but Jack attended the V-E Day matinee and adored it. The theatre was packed. People had burned up a month's ration of petrol to see Scarlett O'Hara in the flesh. During the interval they vented their fury at what they had just seen, had not understood, and hated.

Merivale overheard one man say in a North Country voice, " 'Ere, I wish I hadn't paid my money for this muck!'"

After the performance Merivale decided to chance another confrontation with Vivien and ventured somewhat nervously backstage to her dressing room. She could not have been more openly pleased to see him. No mention was made of their last meeting. She asked him about his own plans now that the war was over and he would soon be out of uniform. "Oh, I'll return to the theatre if it will have me," he said. She offered to help any way she could. They exchanged a few personal remarks (he told her he had been married to and divorced from actress Jan Sterling since their last meeting, that his step-mother, Gladys Cooper, was fine, and that his stepsister had married actor Robert Morley). He was as charmed and dazzled by her as he had always been, and they parted at the stage door of the theatre. The next day the company moved on to London.

Flags hung from balconies, but V-E Day had not brought any spontaneous joy of deliverance. In fact there seemed to be a numbness of relief, as though everyone was simply too exhausted to express strong emotion. The night before, there had been very few wild celebrations. Instead there were sighs of gratitude that there would be no more fear of air raids and that the children could at last come home.

But for Tarquin Olivier, not quite nine years old, returning from the States was more like coming to a strange land. He had left England at three and a half, and his memories of it were vague, merely impressionistic; and he had almost no recall of his father, whom he had seen, after all, only a few times in his life. His mother had made a point of having him know and respect the fact that his father was a great actor. She had even introduced him to the profession at seven, when he took a small role in a film for Universal—*Eagle Squadron*—in which she also appeared. And he had been told that his new step-mother was "the most beautiful woman in the world" (perhaps this, by Jill, to explain Olivier's desertion). But the boy was not happy to return. He had been living in Los Angeles, where he had attended the Brentwood Town and Country School in an upper-middle-class section of the city with well-manicured lawns and wild and beautiful flora and sun shining most of the time. London appeared drab and pokey, and the people were not really as cheerful as they made out to be. The food was dreadful, their rooms cold, and worse, he did not seem to look like anyone else. He was brown and healthy, and they were pale and worn. His legs were much improved, although his co-ordination was not yet perfect. But he was used to back yards and sunny parks to run about in, and postwar London was a difficult adjustment and somewhat of a shock to a sensitive child like Tarquin.

Arrangements were made to bring him to the Phoenix Theatre to meet his father. Arriving somewhat early, he found that rehearsals were in progress. The theatre was dark except for the stage. The go-between said, "There he is," and pushed the child forward.

A man was sitting in the back row of the stalls, hardly visible in the gloom. The boy slowly, awkwardly made his way to him, coming to a halt a few steps away.

"Tarquin?" Olivier asked in a hushed voice. The child nervously nodded his head, and Olivier reached out, drew him close, and kissed him. Tarquin was conscious of the soft mouth, the murky surroundings, but the man was a stranger to him.

"Sit down and watch," Olivier whispered. "That's Bibs [a pet name for Vivien] acting."

Tarquin sat self-consciously and stared at the woman on the stage. She wore grotesque makeup and a short dress and she was moving furniture about the stage as she spoke loudly in an ugly, rasping American voice. She was terribly thin and had big eyes, and the man who was his father was totally absorbed in what she was doing. Tarquin sat nervously, afraid he might make the seat creak. When the actress had finished she looked out into the audience, straining to see, and then stepped nimbly off the stage and hurried up the aisle to where they sat.

"This is Bibs. You remember her," Olivier said, prompting him, nudging him to stand.

Vivien did not wait for the child to reply. She leaned down and put her arms around him and hugged and kissed him fondly. "It doesn't matter, darling Tarquin," she said, her voice now soft and gentle. "I remember you."

Vivien then took him by the hand and led him to her dressing room, where she chattered happily to him. As she removed her makeup she spoke about what they could all do together, asked him about all his interests, turned and listened to him attentively; and she made Tarquin feel that he was the most precious creature to her. And as he stared at Vivien, who he was now absolutely sure *was* the most beautiful woman in the world, his only desire was to be loved by her. Tarquin was awed and terrified by his father, but he immediately adored his stepmother.

The play opened on May 16. "Lovely performance by Vivien Leigh as Sabina, the hired girl, half dabchick and half dragon fly," wrote James Agate. On opening night Agate had arrived ten minutes late, and Olivier had been so furious (the first scene was important for a thorough comprehension of the play) that he actually punched Agate in the jaw directly following the curtain. Therefore they did not expect the fair review they received, which lauded not only Vivien's performance but Olivier's direction and the supporting cast. Not once did Agate in his column mention his fistfight with Olivier.

Vivien considered the play a major step toward creating the image of herself that she wanted the world and Olivier to see. What she could not and would not question were the curious spells that she seemed to be having more frequently, and the alternating bouts of exhaustion and exhilaration that had overtaken her since rehearsals had begun. She had also developed a terrible cough in Liverpool before they had come into London, and since then she had lost an alarming amount of weight. She refused to see a doctor and made light of it to Olivier.

Believing that Vivien only had another of the frequent colds she had always had a tendency toward, and with his work complete on *The Skin of Our Teeth*, Olivier went off with the Old Vic Company to entertain the troops on the Continent.

Chapter Seventeen

Shortly after the completion of *Henry V* and just before rehearsals began on *The Skin of Our Teeth*, Olivier fell in love with a thirteenth-century house that had been endowed by Henry V, and he decided they should buy it. But when Vivien saw it for the first time she was adamant in her opposition to such a move. They drove the forty-eight miles from London to Long Grendon, Buckinghamshire, where the house, Notley Abbey, was situated, on a grim February day, using a month's petrol ration stamps to do so. Notley Abbey stood gray and forbidding in the chill winter cold; and as they approached the front entrance along the wide avenue drive through pasture fields, they could see over the gently sloping high grass to the bank of the dark and murky winter waters of the River Thame. Nothing eased Vivien's depression at the sight of the massive, sprawling old stone abbey with its tangled overgrown rose gardens and its great drafty rooms.

To say that the towered twenty-two-room stone house was overwhelming would be an understatement. The grounds consisted of sixty-nine acres, with a bailiff's bungalow, a refectory barn, a six-car garage, and farm buildings (including a cowhouse for five, a chicken house for four hundred, a pig unit with twenty-four concrete sties, and four greenhouses). Vivien could admire the mullioned windows, the red tiled roofs, the ancient brick chimneys, and the central tower that had been added in the sixteenth century; but the prospect of making it habitable and home seemed quite unthinkable to her. Olivier had different emotions.

Notley Abbey's history endeared it to him to the point of obsession. Not only had Henry V endowed it, but it had been founded during the reign of Henry II for the Augustinian canons, and Henry VIII and Cardinal Wolsey had stayed there on several occasions.

Vivien could not deflect his enthusiasm even by pointing out the burst pipes, the lack of heat, the sheer immensity and number of rooms to be decorated, the total absence of modern kitchen and bathroom facilities, and the difficulties it would involve to obtain licenses, not to mention the expense of all the decoration and restoration. He insisted they could do it slowly, one room at a time, and that it did not matter how many years it took, for Notley Abbey would be their home, their refuge, for the remainder of their days.

It was senseless to argue. Larry was possessed with the idea of being Lord of the Abbey. Vivien reluctantly agreed and within a few weeks Notley was theirs at the cost of most of their savings. With the aid of Lady Colefax, who loved historic restoration, she set about the task of making the ancient house a home, while at the same time she plunged into rehearsals on *The Skin of Our Teeth*. After the show opened and Olivier went to the Continent, the burden of her situation began to overcome her. Her weight loss had continued, she was painfully overtired, and the cough that she had developed in Liverpool had grown worse. The members of the cast were alarmed by her feverish appearance. There were times she looked frighteningly peculiar to them. One night her voice, her expression, her gestures seemed strange. The woman who was her dresser prevailed upon her to see a doctor.

The doctor recognized the symptoms straightaway, and the X rays that he immediately ordered showed that she had a serious tubercular patch on her lung. He wanted to hospitalize her for the moment and then decide whether she should go to a sanitarium in Scotland or one in Switzerland. In any event he strongly believed Olivier should be summoned back and that she had better reconcile herself to the fact that her career would have to be shelved for a long time. He also assured Vivien that her "delirious behavior" (which she herself knew came upon her but seemed unable to stop or recall much about afterwards) was not unique in such cases. But Vivien refused to go to the hospital or to tell Olivier about her illness or the doctor's diagnosis. She returned to the theatre that night and managed to get through the performance, and she consulted a second specialist the next morning, who confirmed his colleague's diagnosis but felt she was in no immediate danger. She persuaded him to allow her to finish out the month of July with the play (a matter of a little more than a fortnight) before going to a hospital. Reluctantly he agreed, giving her strict orders for her personal care—absolutely no alcohol, no smoking, and rest almost the entire time she was not performing.

Still she did not write to Olivier of her condition. He was in Hamburg and about to leave for Paris when he ran into Anthony Bartley, a young pilot who was a friend to both of them. Bartley had just seen Vivien and was enigmatic and a bit disturbing in answering Olivier's question on how Vivien had looked. On his arrival in Paris Olivier contacted Lynn Fontanne and Alfred Lunt, who had just come from London and were appearing in *Love in Idleness* for the American troops. They had indeed seen Vivien only a day or so before, and she had told them she had tuberculosis (it was the first the shocked Olivier had heard of the diagnosis), but, they continued, there was no serious reason for alarm obviously, as the specialist was allowing her to complete the month before checking into University College Hospital for observation. Olivier reasoned that no doctor (and the Lunts assured him this specialist had an impeccable reputation) would allow her to perform if her condition was alarming. He wrote Vivien he would be back before the play closed and by her side when she entered the hospital.

True to his word, he took her directly from the closing night at the theatre to the hospital, where after six weeks of treatment the patch on her lung seemed to arrest itself. The doctor then insisted that she be transferred to a sanitarium for six months to a year to see if a complete cure could be effected. Vivien adamantly refused, and there was nothing even Olivier could do with her. Finally she agreed to take a year's absence from the theatre and to go to Notley with a nurse and staff. There she would occupy only the few habitable rooms, remaining quiet and in bed, with few guests. The doctor was not happy about her decision, but he was forced to agree.

The idea of a lengthy stay in a sanitarium terrified Vivien. First and foremost she wanted to be where Olivier would be able to see her frequently, and she was aware that at Notley Abbey he would be occupied and their time together would have a sense of normalcy even if she was bed-ridden. But for a long time she had been more alarmed about her nervous condition than her physical health and had delayed seeing a doctor and entering a hospital out of fear that it might be discovered that she had some kind of dreaded mental illness. She equated a sanitarium with a mental institution, and the thought of having to spend time there threw her into a panic. Neither Olivier nor the doctor guessed her true motives in refusing the facilities of a sanitarium geared especially to her illness, but they were fully conscious of the strength of her refusal to accept what would seem to be a natural course; and feeling that her condition could deteriorate under the emotional pressure, they allowed her to have her way.

Olivier helped settle Vivien at Notley and then, leaving her in the care of the nurse and a qualified staff, began the intense rehearsals required for the October 1945 Old Vic season in alternating roles at the New Theatre in *Oedipus* (Sophocles, translated by W. B. Yeats) and as Mr. Puff in *The Critic* (Sheridan).

The Oliviers' bills were mounting with staggering velocity. Vivien would not be working for at least a year, and her care was oppressively expensive. Then there was Notley, its restoration and upkeep, his own living expenses, and, of course, his responsibility to Tarquin and Jill. His salary with the Old Vic was a hundred pounds a week, hardly enough to cover. He was not only working hard but was under constant tension with Vivien's condition, and he motored back and forth from London to Buckinghamshire almost daily. Then he barely escaped a serious accident in his role as Mr. Puff.

At the end of *The Critic*, Mr. Puff exits in a startling acrobatic climax as he straddles a painted cloud and is hauled off stage out of view of the audience by a rope, to reappear moments later clutching the curtain as it swings down to end the play. At one performance Larry missed the rope. As he began to fall, he desperately grasped some wires that were attached to the cloud, and after clinging to them over a drop of thirty feet, he was finally rescued by stagehands. He began having nightmares that he would have a fatal accident, that he would fall from the flies or crash in a plane.

It was a harsh and difficult winter. For four months Vivien was unable to rise from her bed. Her life revolved around the one room she had selected for her bedroom. It was an L-shaped room on the first floor with an attractive fireplace and windows looking south and across the gardens. By the spring of 1946 she was able to see the chestnut trees bloom with white flowers and watch the gardeners from her windows as they pruned and replanted trees and vines and flowers. She read constantly, worked on plans for the house, and refused to let the gardeners plant a single seed without her approval. By the time the flowers bloomed, Notley Abbey had become her home and she loved it perhaps more than Olivier did now.

She was permitted to get up for short periods in the day and to have a few visitors, Tarquin among them. He, too, was swept into a great feeling of emotion for the Abbey. He saw it for the first time that spring.

Memory of it [Notley Abbey] moves me deeply. In a great valley it lay—the heart of leafy Buckinghamshire, the River Thame meandering in weedy shallows through the elm woods, the willowed fields. This place where Henry V once stayed, breathed heraldry. In the attic were priceless frescoes of the emblem of Notley embracing the hazel nut and the lovers' knot. There was an exhausted sexuality about the place, regretful black rooks high out of reach, umbrella poplar trees silvering against the sky in unlaboring cascades, a cruelty unearthed in the corpses of monks once buried under The High Alban before the dissolution of monasteries by Henry VIII.

It was a great house for the imagination and sensitivity of a child like Tarquin. It seemed in fact to answer all its occupants' needs. Olivier fed his sense of history, Vivien her great love of beauty. The house began to take shape as she furnished it with valuable pieces—an admirable mixture of brocade and comfort. There were antique and scholarly manuscripts and a modest wealth of fine paintings; tinseled illuminations of plays and players decorated the library walls.

Tarquin recalls:

One could lie in a bath on Sunday mornings, look through the casement windows under the original stone masonry arches, see the ancient pear trees in their white orgasm of spring when the daffodils had died, and hear the church bells of Chearsley, Haddenham and Thame in their medieval peal.

It was a house that possessed its occupants, a demanding place, which seemed to insist that one don a gown before descending the staircase for dinner. Vivien did not leave its refuge for nine months from the date she had arrived there from the hospital. She had regained fifteen pounds and did not tire as easily.

The Old Vic was scheduled to take its current program to New York in May 1946, and, of course, that meant Olivier with it. Vivien could not bear the thought of leaving Notley, nor could she imagine herself separated from Larry by an ocean for the length of a summer. Also she had become concerned about him. He looked exhausted, thin, and seemed too nervous. She worried endlessly that he might have infected himself with her disease. The doctor assured her that was not true, but he did feel that Olivier was approaching a nervous collapse if he did not slow down his pace.

That convinced Vivien. She would go and care for him in New York.

Chapter Eighteen

Vivien's spells of hysteria, though infrequent, had occurred even during the nine peaceful months at Notley. At those times Olivier experienced helplessness and terror. He was beginning to note a pattern. For a few days prior to an attack Vivien would be exceptionally nervous, all of her reactions—speech, laughter, gestures—accelerated. Then would come the insane outburst, lasting several hours, followed by a severe depression, and finally a humble, embarrassed contrition. He had thought it had some relation to alcohol intake. Exceptionally small amounts could set her off. But as far as he knew, she had followed the doctor's dictum and not touched alcohol or cigarettes during her rest cure. Yet the bonds that inextricably linked them were as strong as ever. He deeply loved Vivien, and Vivien continued to regard him as the center of her universe. By the side of her bed there was a picture of him as well as several boxes containing gifts he had given her and notes he had written to her, and they remained there even when he himself was by her side.

It was difficult for him not to feel some share of responsibility for her condition. The physical illness was something he could cope with, but the descents into hysteria were out of his reach and grasp, and left him feeling stranded. Under the circumstances it was no wonder that he feared the act of falling through space.

Vivien's decision to accompany him to New York presented something of a dilemma. On the one hand, he was relieved that he could keep his eye on her; on the other, he was not sure how he was going to cope with both his performance and his concern for her.

They flew to New York, each with mixed and deep emotions.

Neither had been back since the war, since the time as Romeo and Juliet, as Scarlett and Heathcliff, when they had been the most famous lovers of the day. Much had happened in America in the six years they had been away. President Roosevelt had died. Harry Truman was President. There had been long years of casualty lists, then the bombing of Hiroshima, the long-awaited victory, and peace. It did not seem that with all the recent national upheaval they would be remembered in America with any degree of their past attention; but there was a mob of fans to greet them at the airport, and crowds were standing outside their hotel and the theatre.

Vivien was glowing and happy, and more beautiful than ever. As always, wherever she went she carried some of their lovely possessions to insure a sense of home even in a hotel suite. She dressed in exquisite taste, impeccably, the white gloves spotless, shoes never permitted a scuff, stockings the sheerest made, her hair shining, a cloud of perfumed air wherever she was. There were masses of flowers in their rooms, many from well-wishers, but as many were bouquets that Vivien ordered and personally and fastidiously arranged. From the moment she awoke (always early, even if they had been out until dawn) she seemed to be charged with vitality. She was on the telephone by nine making plans for the day. Her breakfast tray had to be perfect, with fresh cut flowers on it. Her clothes had to be as carefully attended as the roses at Notley. No soiled clothes were permitted to remain or accumulate, and she still covered the garments she had worn the night before with a satin and lace square, as she had done when a child in the convent.

All day she would exude energy and shop endlessly like an excited child on a round of Christmas buying. She adored beautiful things and could not resist them and wanted to bring presents to everyone at home. She accompanied Olivier every night to the theatre, arranged special dinners afterward; and even if he was exhausted and excused himself to retire, she would talk animatedly with friends until three of four in the morning. By eight she was up, making sure that room service got the breakfast tray *exactly* right; and at nine, bathed and dressed and bubbling with enthusiasm, she made plans for the new day.

Olivier was in a constant state of anxiety that the tension would suddenly break, that Vivien, like some exquisite, fragile piece of porcelain, would crack and disintegrate. His neurosis and the recurring nightmare of falling to his death were intensified. He was worried more than ever about money and took on a weekly radio show to help pay for their enormous hotel bill. The last night he played Mr. Puff he somersaulted from the side of the curtain and fell to the floor. Experiencing severe pain, he nonetheless rose to his feet for his curtain call and then hobbled back to his dressing room. A doctor who was called diagnosed a torn Achilles tendon in his heel.

He could barely walk, but somehow the accident took a great weight off his mind. He was certain, having now fallen from a height, that nothing further would occur. Therefore he insisted they fly to Boston the next day, where he was to accept an honorary degree by Tufts College as "the real interpreter of Shakespeare of our age." The ceremony extended longer than anticipated; and Olivier, fearful they would miss their return flight, sent Vivien ahead to the airport to make arrangements for him to bypass the check-in counter if he arrived late, while he went through the remaining formalities.

At Logan Field Vivien managed to detain the plane and arrange to facilitate his immediate boarding. But she herself boarded to wait for him. Finally the pilot could wait no longer, the motors were revved, the stairs withdrawn, the doors sealed. Olivier arrived at that moment, his academic hood with its brown and light blue lining over his arm. An ill-defined panic overcame him at the thought of Vivien alone on the plane. He limped painfully onto the field, shouting at the plane as it moved down the runway for take-off; and then, losing control of himself for the first time, he broke down and stood there sobbing. A girl reporter helped him back inside the terminal and to a private office to wait for the next plane to follow Vivien to New York.

He rested in the hotel for two days after his return; but though neither his foot nor his nerves were healed, he decided they should fly home, where they could spend a month at Notley, ostensibly for him to relax. But also, if Vivien's behavior indicated, as he thought it might, an attack of hysteria to come, he wanted to control her and keep the matter private. But Olivier claimed later that they could not have remained anyway as they had less than twenty dollars between them.

Late in the afternoon of June 19, 1946, they boarded a giant Pan American Clipper with forty-one other passengers and a crew of ten. They were only in the air a short time when Vivien let out a terrified scream and rose from her window seat. Olivier attempted to calm her, and then noticed for the first time that the wing of the plane was on fire. The passengers were informed by the staff that an engine had dropped off and the wing ignited but that they were close to a field and would attempt a landing.

The huge plane crash-landed on tiny Windham Field near Willimantic, Connecticut, at six-ten P.M., a little more than an hour from its New York take-off. The wing was still on fire when the ship pancaked onto the field. Miraculously, no one was injured; the passengers were driven to Hartford, and by nine that evening were put aboard a relief Constellation Clipper for England.

It was their first summer at Notley and the fates were kind. The sun shone, the roses bloomed and Vivien never did have the awesome attack Olivier feared she would. A life style developed on the beautiful estate reminiscent of the golden days at Pickfair when Mary Pickford and Douglas Fairbanks had still been married. During the week, Vivien would weed the flower beds and Olivier would supervise the management of the new cattle and the planting and tilling of the land in his role as gentleman farmer. But on the weekends, Notley's hallowed halls glittered with the presence of the aristocracy of the English theatre and film worlds. Cecil Beaton, Noël Coward, John Gielgud, the Redgraves and the Millses, the Kordas and the Fairbanks Juniors, David Niven, Tyrone Guthrie, Alec Guinness, and Margaret Leighton—the Notley guest book was a theatre *Who's Here*. There were bucolic pleasures during the day, walks by the Thame, picnics on the bank, croquet and tennis, bicycling into the neighboring villages (not, however, by Vivien, who could not coordinate well on the vehicle), breakfast and lunch on the terrace, tea in the small garden room, cocktails in the drawing room, and lavish dinners in the dining room. Then there would be games until the wee hours. Vivien still adored games—card games and checkers and charades—and was masterful at all of them. It was all a bit like life in a Noël Coward song.

> Everyone's here and frightf'lly gay
> Nobody cares what people say . . .
> I've been to a marvelous party,
> I must say the fun was intense,
> We all had to do what the people we knew
> Would be doing a hundred years hence.

Noël was always inventing new games, and Vivien was the happiest when playing hostess, seeing after her guests, supervising the meals, selecting the linens, the silver, the china, and arranging the flowers she would pick herself. She had curbed her smoking and drank only small quantities of red wine. The doctor said her lung was healing nicely. There seemed no reason why, in this state of calmed nerves and growing good health, she could not return to the stage in the fall.

Olivier was busy with his own ambitious plans to produce and appear with the Old Vic Company in September as Lear. That meant he could not spend much time at Notley in the fall, and certainly the weekend guest list would dwindle. It seemed more provident for Vivien to move back to Durham Cottage for the months to come so that they would be close. And it did make sense that she would be better off if occupied. His decision was to revive *The Skin of Our Teeth* to open in September. It was a wise compromise because Vivien already knew the role, most of the original cast were available, and the play, unlike a new production, would not have to be taken first on the road.

The play reopened at the Piccadilly Theatre on September 11. *King Lear* premiered at the New Theatre with Alec Guinness, Margaret Leighton, Pamela Brown, Joyce Redman, and George Relph in fine support of Olivier, whose reviews the next morning were brilliant. He had infused Lear with "tender humor."

"If there is a better, a more impressive Lear in human recollection, it is certainly not in my experience," wrote Alan Dent in the *News Chronicle. The Times* review began "Mr. Laurence Olivier, lately come to the plenitude of his powers, plays the part with the magnificent ease which testifies that it is for him a completely solved problem." He was hailed not only as a great Lear, but as England's greatest contemporary actor.

It was exactly what Vivien had always believed. Olivier had been the Prince of Players. Now he was the King. But this would make it even more difficult then for her to become Queen.

Gertrude had returned to London with Suzanne the previous summer. At thirteen the girl attended a boarding school and was back in Leigh's custody during holidays. Vivien felt a curious remoteness toward her daughter. She was a warm, fair-haired young girl, a bit awkward, but she was cheerful, good natured, and not the least bit spoiled. It is hard to know what was responsible for Vivien's aloofness to Suzanne during that time. There could have been many reasons—a sense of guilt and of inadequacy as a mother, the long separation that had caused a lack of shared experience, the natural competitiveness often existing between mother and daughter, the confrontation of her being faced with a thirteen-year-old child when she thought of herself as still very young, or perhaps, simply that Suzanne as a young woman had little in common with her mother.

Leigh had come through the war unscathed, and Vivien had remained in touch with him. They were, in fact, quite good friends, and his approval of what she was doing was extremely important to her. Never once did Leigh chastise her for the past. He was devoted to her and concerned about her health, her career, and her security. The fall of 1946 was a particularly difficult time for her, as after forty-eight performances Olivier took *King Lear* to Paris, and Leigh's presence was a steadying influence.

The success of the revival of *The Skin of Our Teeth* did not seem in her mind to match Olivier's achievements. This was an ongoing and recurring pattern between them now. She would do *Cleopatra*, even though it was a film role, because it was Shaw, and then he would do *Henry V*. She would meet with good critical notices as Sabina, and then he would be readying *Hamlet* for the cameras. Hollywood offered them *Cyrano de Bergerac*; and though they could well have used the high salaries the roles of Cyrano and Roxanne would command, Olivier was obsessed with the idea of filming *Hamlet*.

Vivien had a spell of hysteria just before Christmas. After it passed, Olivier for the first time tried to get her to consult a psychiatrist, but Vivien would not hear of it. As an alternative, Olivier thought a holiday would be an escape for her. They were low on cash, and he managed to convince Filippo Del Giudice, the producer (he had also backed the highly acclaimed *Henry V*) who was arranging the financing of *Hamlet* with Rank, to include a working vacation on the Italian Riviera as part of the budget.

England was suffering through one of the coldest winters modern England had known. The gas and coal supply had not lasted, and there was so little fuel that Vivien walked around Durham Cottage in a fur coat and gloves trying to keep warm, and Olivier was fearful her frail health might regress.

Del Giudice came through, and within a month Vivien and Olivier were on their way to Santa Margherita Ligure, a small, beautiful seaside village near Portofino, with sandy beaches and magnificent views; and though February, even in the Mediterranean, was certain to bring rain and cool breezes, there would be hope that the sun might on occasion break through. Del Giudice took a five-room suite for them at the Miramare Hotel and decorated all the rooms with rented antique furniture, which he thought would please Vivien.

The journey by train was slow and the cars badly heated, and Vivien felt some minor discomfort in her chest that worried them. Fortunately, the sun was shining over the Gulf of Rapallo when they reached Santa Margherita. They were to have ten days to themselves before Alan Dent arrived to work with Olivier on the script. They would be alone for that time, able to think of nothing but each other, to walk among the olive trees, the yews, and the sea pines, to take short drives along winding scenic roads, and to go into the lovely small fishing port of Portofino, with its artists' colony and lively cafes.

What Olivier dreaded was the discussion to come on the casting of Ophelia, a point he knew was totally absorbing Vivien's thoughts when she was not gazing across the blue gulf waters. Vivien was thirty-three years old, and though still one of the great beauties of the world it was doubtful she could convey the teenage youthfulness of Ophelia on film. That was not the only reason that casting her in the role was impossible. She was a great international film star, recognized immediately and anywhere she went as Scarlett O'Hara. Olivier was concerned that she would destroy the balance of the production, just as Tyrone Guthrie had been hesitant about her appearing with the Old Vic Company.

Ninety-four girls were interviewed and thirty tested before a lovely eighteen-year-old with natural ability but not much previous training was chosen by Olivier to play Ophelia. Her name was Jean Simmons, and, as it happened, she resembled Vivien slightly.

Once Alan Dent arrived, Vivien was left much to herself, although she listened in on story conferences. Giudice also joined them, staying on a lower floor in the same hotel. Giudice, very much in awe of Olivier, listened like a hypnotized schoolboy to Olivier's production plans and to his perfect diction as he read a speech. The sun did Vivien much good physically, but being merely an appendage to Olivier—the star, the great director, the greatest Shakespearean actor in the English theatre—was difficult for her emotionally. *Hamlet* also evoked too many memories of the past—happy days for sure, but ones when she was still young enough to have played Ophelia and hopeful enough to believe that someday she would equal Olivier's stature on the stage.

Olivier and Vivien returned to London before the spring. *Hamlet* was to go into production on the first of May at Denham Studios, and it promised to involve a long shooting schedule and would consume Olivier's time almost completely for months to come. Vivien was in an extremely depressed state when Alexander Korda came to see her to discuss the possibility of her appearing in the remake of Tolstoy's *Anna Karenina*.

The idea of playing Anna appealed tremendously to her, though from the start she was worried about comparisons to Garbo's Anna, made only twelve years before. She was also pleased to be working with Korda again. The new script had been written first in the South of France by Jean Anouilh, the French playwright, and Julien Duvivier (the French director of *Pépé le Moko*, *Un Carnet de Bal*, and Korda's *Lydia*), who had transposed the story to France. Korda was passionate in his loyalty to Tolstoy and brought in a young writer, Guy Morgan, to work with Duvivier to return the story to its original Russian setting. Morgan was inexperienced, but Sir Alexander defended his selection on the basis that the young man could therefore be depended on to write as he was told. Having signed Vivien, Korda scheduled the film for immediate production.

Cecil Beaton was to do the costumes; and unable to find couturiers in London who could obtain the proper fabrics, Korda dispatched Vivien and Beaton to Paris to have her clothes for Anna made there. Vivien, Gertrude (who Olivier insisted accompany her), and Beaton were guests of British Ambassador Alfred Duff Cooper (known as Duff) and the flamboyant and beautiful Lady Diana Cooper at the ornate, heavily gilded grand British Embassy on the Rue Faubourg St. Honoré. The two women had a great deal in common. Lady Diana had for many years been renowned as England's greatest beauty. She was a perfectionist, a superb hostess who adored parties, games of wit, and shopping expeditions—an apparently extroverted woman who was fundamentally a serious person and appeared to exist mainly for her husband. The embassy was alive with the electric presence of these two women.

Olivier came over for a week's stay to talk Beaton into taking on the stage designs for a production of *The School for Scandal* which he hoped to take on tour to Australia the following spring, and to see Jean-Louis Barrault in a Parisian stage production of *Hamlet*. He also wanted to be certain Vivien was quite all right. At night they played what they called "The Game," which was an elaborate form of charades. Olivier was in great humor and very excited about his plans for what he considered his "abstract production of *Hamlet*."

Beaton recalls:

With arms flailing he emulated with a big *whoosh* a great curtain falling down here—a pillar "pffutting" down there—"a hell of a lot of smoke and emptiness all over the place." Instead of using words that could be found in a dictionary, he would illustrate his intentions by making prep-school sounds—of pops, bangs, and corks being drawn, of internal combustion explosions, farts, and all sorts of other coarse noises. The camera would "raspberry" down onto the castle at the beginning of the film ("an old-fashioned idea, but then I'm old-fashioned"), and then "raspberry" away at the end—and the castle that was shown wouldn't necessarily tally with the sets but the atmosphere would be the same. Larry is, heaven knows, serious about his career, but the project on hand is referred to only in ribald terms. No question of "would it be beautiful to have . . . ?" "Mightn't it be extraordinary to . . . ?"—just: "A great blob here (Bang! Bang-ho!)"—"A great cowpat there (Bungho!)"

It was a most gymnastic performance that we were treated to. Larry's imitations have about them something of the original clown or, at least, the essential entertainer, who can be found in some remote music hall or performing in the street outside a pub. This was the real Larry— the mummer, the ale-drinking Thespian—not the rather overwhelmed and shy cipher with wrinkled forehead that goes out into society.

With Larry in Paris, Vivien was her gay, witty old self. Then, after he left to return to London, she became quiet and withdrawn. The days were spent listening to Duff Cooper read stories by Elizabeth Bowen in a dry, slow, and rather sad voice while outside there was a forlorn, melting snowscape.

By May they were in production at Shepperton with *Anna Karenina*, bathed in a premature heat wave during which all the cast members wore furs and trudged through ersatz snow while prop men nailed icicles on the windows. Vivien became depressed and somewhat difficult as the strain of picture making began. She nagged and complained to Beaton that her gloves were too small. Finally, piqued to the point of exasperation, he turned on her. "It's not that the gloves are too small"—he glared—"but that your hands are too big."

According to Beaton, the difficulties were becoming overwhelming and absorbing. One morning he went into her dressing room confident that he would find her in a great stage of elation, for it had just been announced that Larry was to be knighted.

I open the door [Beaton writes]. "Oh, I'm so happy for you about the great news!" A face of fury is reflected in the mirror. "Really, it's too stupid! Would you believe it—the dressmaker from Paris was waiting at her hotel the entire day yesterday and the studio forgot to order a car for her. Really—I've never worked on such a film as this!" Later Vivien instructs me: "Please tell Clarissa how to behave when she brings journalists on the set. I don't want them turned off, but I want to have them announced first and presented." When the message is relayed to Clarissa, she has already received it from half a dozen other sources.

It had indeed been announced in *The London Gazette* in the King's Birthday Honors list that Olivier was to be made a Knight

Bachelor ("Laurence Olivier, actor. For services to stage and film"). His investiture was to follow in two months. Vivien, who had worshiped royalty with a passion all her life and who would now be Lady Olivier, experienced a surprising reaction. The news set off one of her manic attacks and this time it seemed of a longer duration and was followed by a painful period of depression.

She had crossed swords with the director (Duvivier), who had not proved an easy man to work with. Korda was in California on legal matters and there was no one strong enough to handle the situation. The crew could not work with either Vivien or Duvivier as matters stood, and they revolted. Fortunately, Korda returned from California in time to keep the cameras rolling. Vivien was giving a curiously remote performance, lacking passion, and Korda was puzzled by her lack of spirit. The film was beautifully mounted and magnificently produced, even within the limitations that black and white film imposed, but unfortunately it never seemed to come alive. George Moore, the Irish novelist, once wrote, "*Anna Karenina* was written to prove that if a woman lives unhappily with one husband and leaves him for the man she loves, her moral character will deteriorate." Vivien revered Tolstoy and identified with Anna. Given these two factors and her ability to totally immerse herself in a role, it is understandable that she fell into a state of depression as the film progressed.

As soon as *Anna Karenina* was completed she went to visit Leigh at his country house, while Olivier remained at Notley. With Leigh she never seemed to "misbehave." She wanted desperately to meet with his approval. After a very short time with him, her depression would disappear, only to reappear when she was away from him.

On Tuesday morning, July 8, 1947, Vivien accompanied Olivier to Buckingham Palace. In direct contrast to her own presentation at Court fourteen years before, she wore a stark and simple black suit, no jewelry, and a brimmed black hat. She looked beautiful but sad, a piquant mourner, a subdued butterfly. Olivier, wearing Ralph Richardson's black waistcoat (Richardson had been knighted in the previous list), his hair bleached blond for *Hamlet*, left her standing alone in the Grand Hall as he stepped forward and walked up the long aisleway to His Majesty, King George. Then, head bowed, he went down on one knee on a red plush stool as the King lightly touched his sword on each of Olivier's shoulders. When he rose he was Sir Laurence Olivier, Knight Bachelor, at forty the youngest actor to receive the honor.

Vivien as Cleopatra and Flora Robson as Ftatateeta in Gabriel Pascal's film version of Shaw's *Caesar and Cleopatra*, 1943.

ABOVE: Notley Abbey, 1945.
BELOW: The sitting room at Notley Abbey.

BOTH PHOTOS: MESSRS. JOHN D. WOOD & CO.

ABOVE: Vivien as Sabina in Thornton Wilder's *The Skin of Our Teeth*, 1944, when no one knew she was suffering from tuberculosis.
BELOW: Sir Laurence and Lady Olivier, 1947. Blond hair for the newly knighted Olivier, who was filming *Hamlet*.

CECIL BEATON

ABOVE: As Anna Karenina, 1947.
LEFT: On the set of *Anna Karenina*. From left, Harold Keel, Maxwell Coker, Vivien, Vincent Korda, Sir Alexander Korda, and Gemze de Lappe.

MICHAEL KORDA

ABOVE LEFT: Vivien as Blanche DuBois in Olivier's London stage production of A *Streetcar Named Desire*, 1949.
ABOVE RIGHT: Katharine Cornell and Vivien in kitchen of Miss Cornell's home.
BELOW: Vivien, in blond wig, with Marlon Brando in film of A *Streetcar Named Desire*, 1951.

The world's most
famous theater couple,
Laurence Olivier
and Vivien Leigh, in:

Caesar and Cleopatra, 1951.

Antony and Cleopatra, 1951.

The Sleeping Prince, 1953.

Macbeth, 1955.

Titus Andronicus, 1955.

ABOVE: Vivien in a blond wig, astride the horse that has just thrown her, *The Roman Spring of Mrs. Stone*, 1961.
OPPOSITE: A portrait of Vivien as the Lady of the Camellias.
RIGHT: Holding her newly christened grandson.

IVANOV

RIGHT: With John Gielgud in
Ivanov, 1966.
OPPOSITE: Dancing   the
Charleston   with   Byron
Mitchell in *Tovarich*, 1963.
BELOW: At her desk at Ticker-
age. Her right hand is poised
beside a bronze model of her
left hand.

UPI

LEFT: Tarquin Olivier, 1961.
OPPOSITE ABOVE: Sailing on the *Queen Elizabeth* with Jack Merivale, 1961.
OPPOSITE BELOW: With Noël Coward and Poo Jones, 1963.
BELOW: At Zeals, Wilshire, with Leigh Holman in 1965.

ABOVE: Taking the sun beside George Cukor's pool in Hollywood during break in filming of *Ship of Fools*, 1965.
OPPOSITE: In the rose garden at Tickerage Mill, 1966.
BELOW: Living room of Tickerage Mill.

Twilight at Tickerage, 1967.

That weekend Ivor Novello visited them at Notley and kept referring to Vivien in a teasing manner as Lady Olivier. Finally Vivien blurted, "Oh, you bloody fool, will you have some fucking tea?" and they both broke up with laughter. She appeared unimpressed with her new status, and she had even expressed surprise that Olivier had accepted the honor. Had she been made a Dame, that would have been another matter. But Olivier's knighthood only meant that he had once again outdistanced her.

Hamlet was completed by November, which was a bitterly cold month. Olivier and the doctors were concerned about Vivien's lung. Leigh Holman's brother offered them L'Oulivette, his house in Cannes. They took both children and Gertrude and planned a family holiday. Vivien was soon her old self, sparkling like champagne, her smiles sweet and winning, considerate of everyone. It was easy at such times for Olivier to put aside all his anxieties about her.

She had worked hard to bring Tarquin and his father closer together, though a chasm of emotion still existed between the two which made it difficult for them to communicate. Tarquin loved his father painfully. He thought of him as the "king of the castle" when they were at Notley. And although Olivier was tender to the boy on these visits, Tarquin sensed that his father was afraid of him. One time he came back from a visit to Notley and told Jill, "Daddy seemed less afraid of me this time." Tarquin appeared to make Olivier feel somewhat off guard, while Vivien was freer and more giving in her kindness and understanding. She encouraged him often, where Olivier criticized him. She was enthusiastic about his playing the piano for them. He could talk to her about "things." She took him for walks, and she always asked kindly after his mother, which Olivier could not do. Vivien handled her role as go-between to father and son. Bridging the awkwardness of her own relationship to Suzanne was not as easy, but the two young people, who shared a cottage a little way along a hill and a short distance from the main house, got along well together, despite the three-year difference of age.

Vivien bloomed with all this happiness about her, and Olivier felt more relaxed and at ease about her health. He was certain that *Hamlet* was a fine film, equal and perhaps superior to *Henry V*. Vivien had earned some money from the Korda film. The tour they were planning to Australia, now scheduled to begin early in 1948, was falling into place. It seemed to them both that the dark days of illness and despair had passed.

Chapter Nineteen

Some seventy intimate friends came for a bon voyage party at Durham Cottage the night before they were to sail on the *Corinthic* for Australia. By five A.M. Danny Kaye and Roger Furse, the last guests, left, still in very high spirits as they revved the motor of their car and drove away, taking some of the whitewash on the front gate wall with them. Three hours later Vivien stood amid the debris of the abused drawing room where the party had been held and bid a tearful goodbye to her Siamese cat, New (named after the theatre).

At Euston Station, where they were taking the boat train to Liverpool, they were met by the forty-odd members of the Old Vic Company traveling with them (with Olivier as their head), an alarming number of reporters, photographers, film and television cameramen and interviewers, friends, fans, the high commissioners of Australia and New Zealand, and the stationmaster in a top hat. It was Saturday, February 14, Valentine's Day, and the Oliviers looked like the perfect lovers as they boarded the train, Vivien's arm entwined with Larry's, smiling up adoringly at him. They reached Liverpool by three, to find more friends, fans, and many flashbulbs on the dock and masses of flowers and about a hundred telegrams in their stateroom. By four-fifteen, tugs were pushing them out toward the open sea. Vivien managed to wave from the ship's rail to Cecil Tennant and Dorothy Welford, who had come to see them off, but then she went down to their cabin exhausted and remained there for the rest of the night, not eating much of the food sent to the room, and in poor spirits, her public face cast aside. Olivier explored the ship and walked the decks wearing a duffle coat, hands deeply buried in his pockets, lost in his thoughts, not glancing up when one of his own company passed by. He was hoping that the four-week sea trip would complete Vivien's recovery. He knew she was enthusiastic about the tour and about her roles as Lady Teazle in *The School for Scandal*, Sabina in *The Skin of Our Teeth* (a rather daring and controversial inclusion on Olivier's part), and Lady Anne in *Richard III*. She loved ships, seeing new places, facing new experiences. That was one of the wonderful things about Vivien. She had an adventurous spirit. New things excited her.

The winter sea was the color of gun metal, and cold winds blew down even the most protected deck areas. But in a few days they would reach warmer southern waters, and Olivier hoped that with bluer waters and under a golden sun Vivien would cast aside her depression and once again become the radiant creature he adored, overflowing with activity, taking every opportunity to display her charm, wit, and intelligence. In their early days she had never seemed a complicated woman to him. He recalled the holiday in Venice in 1937 and the childish delight she had taken from its sheer physical splendor, the relaxed days on the sands of Malibu, the car trip through France before the war, and the first informal and gay parties they had given at Durham Cottage. Perhaps it was impossible to go back to the beginnings. Her fame as Scarlett O'Hara could not be swept under a carpet. She had played the most famous woman's role ever put on film and had reached the top of her profession, yet it had not been enough for her. It was of major importance to her now to compete and equal him in his arena. Her ability, professionalism, and talent could not be denied, but Vivien's extraordinary beauty and the high pitch of her voice would always get in the way of her attaining greatness as a Shakespearean actress. In order to present her to her best advantage, he had been meticulous in his choice of roles she was to play, making certain they were well within her range physically and vocally.

Lately, a new and difficult problem had to be dealt with. She seemed to want to provoke his jealousy. As he limped back to their stateroom, his foot hurt him curiously. He was suffering a "burning pain like a white-hot needle in [his] right toe." He ran a bath but was too exhausted in the end to step into it, so he crawled in bed to read Logan Pearsall Smith's *English Aphorisms*.

On the third day at sea Vivien finally began to move about the ship, and she joined him for dinner at the Captain's table. Someone had given Olivier a travel diary, and later that night (February 17) he wrote, "Tonight at dinner at the Captain's table Vivien turned to me suddenly with an alarmingly wild look and said, 'Tonight I should like to play dominoes.'"

But by February 21 she had returned to her loving, charming self. The Old Vic Company rehearsed in the dining saloon from ten-thirty A.M. until eleven forty-five, then cleared out so that it could be prepared for lunch. They returned at two forty-five until teatime, when they would move to the forward lounge. Vivien worked hard and long on her role of Lady Teazle in *The School for Scandal*. The quarrel scenes between Lady Teazle and Sir Peter (Olivier) in the play were difficult for her. She was feeling deeply apologetic about her "moods" for the past weeks. Even in performing she wanted no more cross words to pass between herself and Larry.

"Sun directly overhead," Olivier wrote on the 27th. "No shadows." They were three days from Capetown, where the boat was to dock for a two-day stopover. Vivien was bubbling and happy. Never had she looked more beautiful. Her eyes took on the color of the sea, and she dressed in greens and blues and flowing fabrics, her white-rimmed sunglasses like sea foam on her deep blue lenses. She dazzled the Captain, the crew, and fellow passengers, and treated the company as though they were all aboard a seagoing Notley. Olivier meanwhile relaxed, concentrating on his work.

They were met at Capetown by flowers, messages, the press, fans, and by Ivor Novello, Gwen ffrangcon-Davies (who had known Olivier since their Birmingham Rep days in the 1920s), and Vanessa Lee—all of whom were appearing in Novello's *Perchance to Dream* at the Alhambra Theatre. It was a marvelous reunion for Vivien, and she was in peak form.

"Vivien looking v. lovely in New Look black and white," observed Olivier. "Ivor's car took us to the Alhambra to see 'Perchance to Dream.' Wonderful having to come all the way to Capetown in order to see it. [It had been playing in London for the previous season.] Lots of rippling applause from the publique on the way in [for him and Vivien]."

Wherever she went, everyone recognized Scarlett O'Hara. Autograph collectors followed them. Fans crowded around them. It was a small indication of what would happen once they reached Australia. *Gone With the Wind* had assumed the stature of a classic with continuing appeal. It had only recently premiered in the liberated cities of

Europe—Paris, Amsterdam, Vienna. Everywhere else it had been reissued several times. Vivien enjoyed the instant recognition, the return to star status.

The flat summit of Table Mountain was shrouded in the famous white mist called the "Tablecloth" for the entire two days of their stay in Capetown, but it did not seem to keep them from having a wonderful time and seeing every tourist attraction—the Botanical Gardens, the Sea Point Aquarium, the Anglican and Roman Catholic cathedrals, the National Gallery, the seventeenth-century castle. Olivier's foot was still somewhat painful, but he was glowing and happy as he watched Vivien enjoy herself in the South African sun.

There was a big party given for them by Sir Evelyn and Lady Baring at High Commission House, and then the next morning the *Corinthic* left the Cape on its way to Perth, arriving there on schedule at eight A.M. on Monday (March 15) morning, right in the midst of an unpredicted heat wave and after a late farewell night on board, at which Olivier had consumed more whiskey "than I remember since an evening with Roger [Furse] and Dallas [Bower, Olivier's associate producer on *Henry V*] in Dublin, 1943."

Vivien was wide awake at seven, an hour before they docked. She smiled winningly at the cameras, did not blink at the flashbulbs, and welcomed reporters warmly aboard. Eventually they went ashore. The Australians fell in love with her immediately. She looked miraculously cool in spite of having to wear a tweed suit in sweltering 100-degree weather, her light dresses having been packed and already sent ashore.

The theatre in which they were to appear in Perth was a movie house. They were the first live show to appear in it, and there were no dressing rooms. The Oliviers finally screened off with wire netting a part of the stage to each side, and the men used one area, the women the other. Vivien did not complain and even helped to iron costumes. Olivier, upon seeing the immense old theatre for the first time, said, "We'd better dress up as Christians and throw ourselves to the lions!" Working in shirtsleeves in the unbearable heat, his foot intensely painful, he managed to do wonders on the narrow stage. Once again wherever they went were crowds, but they were treated not as film stars but as visiting royalty. In fact, since King George VI and Queen Mary were scheduled for a royal visit the following year, the Oliviers appeared to be giving officials and the public a chance for a grand rehearsal.

They opened with *The School for Scandal* the evening of March 20 to overwhelming applause. A week of receptions and speeches followed. "Straight from Lord Mayor to University for lecture on 'The Use of Poetry in Drama.' Dear Professor Currie introducing V. She makes the most damn awful fuss but I think she's beginning to like it," wrote Olivier. By March 27 his foot was well enough for him to execute some dance steps in the play. He was not entirely happy with his own makeup for Sir Peter, or his interpretation, though he remarked, "Show getting better. Vivien loosening up no end, but she must bubble with delicious laughter both inner and audible."

He was beginning to feel his new authority as head of the company and as Sir Laurence. His old friend Peter Cushing, who had appeared with him in *Hamlet*, was in the company, and Olivier confessed to him how lonely he felt in his position: "No one has the temerity to tell me how my performances are standing up to so much repetition. I wish they would, because we all need a sounding board and it's of no help to be told that you were splendid tonight because you can't be—always."

The last night in Perth the company as a curtain call joined together in rousing choruses of "Waltzing Matilda." The audience went wild. More crowds waited en masse outside, and a police escort on motorcycles had to clear the road to the airport, where another crowd of several hundred waved and cheered and sang "Auld Lang Syne" as they boarded the plane for Adelaide.

Olivier was playing Mr. Antrobus to Vivien's Sabina in *The Skin of Our Teeth*, and the press conducted a small private war of pros and cons on his performance. But there was no doubt Vivien had captivated Adelaide. The press named her "Miss Vitamin B" because she was so full of smiling energy. And Olivier entered into his diary, "V is wonderful—better than ever."

They were again the world famous lovers. Neither could take his eyes from the other. They took private trips. Vivien was fascinated with the Daliesque terrain and wrote Hugh Beaumont:

> We drove . . . through the most wonderful country imaginable . . . great shallow blue lakes surrounded by glistening white sand, black and white branches of trees sticking up out of the water and birds of every kind and description everywhere. Then through great forests to Mount Gambier where we spent the night in a very strange hotel. The midnight clock struck eighteen and the fire alarm was sent off every two hours just to see if the poor old thing was all right (and that we knew it).

They arrived in Melbourne on April 19, and again were met by swarms of people and cameras, as well as having to face a press conference. "V carried the wretched thing off with superlative charm," Olivier wrote. Entering the conference room at the Menzies Hotel, Vivien, not able to bear the stiff formality of a prearranged row of chairs, pushed them all out of the way so that everyone had to stand and mill about, somewhat as though they were guests at a cocktail party.

At Canberra it was more of the same, with an even more terrifying benefit appearance at the Capitol Cinema added to the schedule (Food for Britain), with "arc lights, two movie news cameras, four microphones, 2,000 people. Vivien looked wonderful in pale lime green and a blood red rose at her waist. Halfway through she hesitated, but went on finishing with Sonnet 116."

They had a two-month engagement in Melbourne alternating the three plays. Next came Sydney, then Brisbane. They had been away six months, and Vivien was beginning to feel homesick, a sentiment shared by the entire company. The crowds, the receptions, the speeches continued. They flew from Brisbane to Auckland and gave nine performances in eleven days. They closed on a Saturday night, and then flew 1500 miles on Sunday to Christchurch to open that next Monday evening. Olivier's knee (injured in Sydney during the *Richard III* duel scene) began to give him trouble. Eight days and twelve performances later they flew to Dunedin and performed that same night of their arrival. By then Olivier's knee was causing him extreme pain. After the first show in Dunedin, and as Vivien stood holding his arm, he told a reporter, "You may not know it, but you are talking to two walking corpses."

The next day his knee was operated on to remove some cartilage, and he remained in a nursing home while the company continued their engagements in New Zealand, with an understudy taking over Olivier's roles. October came, and the rains with it. The *Corinthia* stood in dock at Glasgow Wharf in Wellington waiting to carry the victorious and exhausted Old Vic Company home. Vivien stood on the quayside in her wet mackintosh as Olivier was lifted out of an ambulance on a stretcher, then hoisted in a canvas sling by a crane.

The trip home was as depressing as the trip over had been high-spirited. The ship rolled constantly and monotonously. There was almost no sun, and worst of all, Vivien received word that New, the Siamese cat, had been run over. But Olivier's knee healed, they brought home about £42,000 for the British Council, and they were planning on opening at the New Theatre in January 1949, replacing *The Skin of Our Teeth* with *Antigone*, but retaining *Richard III* and *The School for Scandal*. Vivien had wanted to play the tragic role of Antigone for a long time and had tried to persuade Olivier to include it in the Australian tour. Now he was finally agreeing to put it on, and she was deliriously happy about it.

Tragic heroines were, in fact, much on her mind. *A Streetcar Named Desire* had opened in New York on December 3, 1947, not long before the Australian tour. Cecil Beaton had rung Vivien on the telephone to tell her he had seen it and that it was an ideal role for her. She had secured a copy of the play just before the tour and had read it many times during their travels, dog-earing it as she had once done to *Gone With the Wind*.

On a gray November day they drove from the dock to Durham Cottage. Olivier, to Vivien's great delight, had arranged for a new little Siamese kitten to be waiting. Leaving the boxes and crates of boomerangs, paintings, aborigine knives, and stuffed koala bears that they had brought home with them, Vivien swept the little frightened creature into her arms and stroked it until it began purring contentedly. Then she carried it with her into the bedroom with the one new acquisition of the trip that seemed to have meaning to her—the playscript of the Tennessee Williams play.

Except for Scarlett O'Hara, she had never wanted to play a role more than she did that of Blanche DuBois.

Chapter Twenty

Their oversized beds at both Durham Cottage (where cupids were painted on the headboard) and Notley were shrines. The satin covers were not allowed a crease, nor the polished wood frames a fleck of dust. By simply studying the objects on the nightstand on Vivien's side of the bed one could tell whether she was in residence or not; for the picture of Larry, the boxes containing mementos from him that she deemed sacred, and the few notes he had written her that had special meaning were set down with the same exactness on her bedside table wherever she was. She had originally kept her Oscar for her performance in *Gone With the Wind* on the mantelpiece of the living room at Durham Cottage. Its presence had been a bone of contention between them for a number of years during which Larry was jealous of it and did not like to be reminded that he had not been awarded one. But since then he had won an Oscar for *Hamlet* and received a special award for *Henry V*, and now the three statuettes were kept on a bookcase in their Durham Cottage bedroom.

They were once again the passionate lovers. Australia had been a great healer. The overwhelming ovations paid to them, the royal receptions, and the tributes had given her a renewed faith in herself and an even greater belief that Larry had now become King of Players. In a sense she thought of herself as his queen, but in actuality she played the role of dedicated handmaiden. And Olivier treated Vivien with a new professional respect, doubtless because of her emergence as a fine tragedian in the role of Antigone.

It was Vivien who had fought to include Anouilh's version of

Sophocles' Greek classic into the Old Vic repertory season of 1949. The play had been rewritten by Anouilh as a parable of wartime France and had been a great success in its opening season in Paris. When the curtain rose, Vivien, as Antigone, sat at the back of the stage, a white-faced, wild-eyed creature, arms clasped on crossed knees, while Olivier, as the one-man chorus, stood wearing modern evening dress as he described the tragic destiny that the gods had waiting for her. Her performance was one of great power, and Olivier was startled into a new assessment of her capabilities as a stage actress. Two months after her first appearance as Antigone, he enthusiastically agreed to produce and direct the London production of A Streetcar Named Desire with Vivien as Blanche DuBois.

Vivien was always drawn to characters of queenly dimensions—Scarlett, Emma Hamilton, Cleopatra, Antigone, and now Blanche—all women whose passions gave stature to a play or film. Tennessee Williams says of Blanche, "She was a demonic creature, the size of her feeling was too great for her to contain without the escape to madness." Vivien became more and more obsessed with Blanche, seeming to understand her with even greater intensity than she had Scarlett. Blanche was different from anything she had ever done, and as far from Scarlett as another woman could be. Yet they were both true daughters of a romantic tradition that harbored nostalgic regret for the loss of the past. Like Vivien, Blanche was a creature living on frayed, snapping nerves, a woman constantly aware of madness, but who could still conjure up the white pillars and trimmed lawns of the past, while living in squalor.

"Everyone," Blanche tells her insensitive brother-in-law, Stanley, "has something he won't let others touch because of their—intimate nature."

Vivien had not seen Jessica Tandy in the New York production, so the image she had of Blanche came from her own interpretation of Williams' play. The New York production and the playscript differed strongly in one respect—Blanche's costumes. Williams had indicated rather sleazy clothes for Blanche ("a worn-out Mardi Gras outfit . . . a dark red satin kimona"), but Lucinda Ballard, the play's costume designer in New York, had seen Blanche as a delicate, uncertain woman and dressed her in mothy whites and faded flowered organdies. One of Olivier's first important decisions was to adhere to the author's costume descriptions. This of course altered the New York production's concept of Blanche and might account in a great part for the critical attacks on the play when it opened at the Aldwych on October 11.

The critics called Blanche a nymphomaniac and a prostitute and the play was snidely referred to as "low and repugnant" in the House of Commons and condemned by the Public Morality Council. *The Times* came to the conclusion that "the purpose of this play is to reveal a prostitute's past in her present." But Vivien had never once believed that Williams had written about a prostitute. To her, Blanche was a tragic woman whose past was too lonely and loveless to support her fading, aging beauty, a woman fighting for a last desperate chance of a life of gentility, one whose fantasies finally career her into madness.

There was only one allusion in the play to Blanche's possible past immorality. Brother-in-law Stanley declares, "Sister Blanche is no lily!" and then elaborates with a bit of gossip garnered from the supply-man at his plant, who supposedly traveled often to the town of Laurel, where Blanche lived. "This supply-man stops at a hotel called the Flamingo," he goads his wife, Stella, who is Blanche's younger sister. "A second-class hotel which has the advantage of not interfering in the private social life of the personalities there! The Flamingo is used to all kinds of goings on. But even the management of the Flamingo was impressed by Dame Blanche! In fact, they were so impressed by Dame Blanche that they requested her to turn in her room key—for permanently!" Then he adds that she got "mixed up with" a seventeen-year-old boy and "they kicked her out of that high school [where she had been teaching] before the spring term ended."

Olivier found the undertaking one of the most painful he had experienced. Irene Selznick, now divorced from David and a successful theatre producer on her own (she produced the New York production of *Streetcar*), arrived in London and crossed swords with Olivier almost immediately as she fought to prevent cuts he was making in the original script to create a faster moving play. Olivier had problems with the Board of Censors, which refused to allow them to have Blanche describe her young dead husband as a homosexual, a point that all concerned felt was basic to the understanding of the character. In the end, Vivien could only indicate that there was a problem, and then break down sobbing so that the problem could only be guessed at. Further conflicts arose with the presence of the play's original director, Elia Kazan, in London to rehearse *Death of a Salesman*. Olivier had been sent Kazan's prompt script with all his notations. He tried to ignore it but was constantly drawn back to refer to it and to incorporate some of Kazan's bits of stage business in his own production. This weighed heavily on Olivier's conscience, and finally he had a credit line inserted in the program following his own which read, "After the New York production."

"Miss Vivien Leigh drifts to ruin on a tide of words many thousands strong," wrote the reviewer for *The Times*. "Her performance, considered merely as a feat of memory, is impressive. It is impressive also for its delicately insistent suggestion of a mind with a slowly loosening hold on reason. She is ridiculous, she is indomitable; she is lost. But the impressiveness of the performance grows as the violence of the action deepens."

But although the critics praised the production highly, many of the audience considered the action on the stage obscene and were quite vocal in their disappointment that Vivien should appear in such a "sooty" play. Vivien refused to be disturbed by this and was fond of telling a story she claimed one of the tea ladies had told her. At intermission when this lady passed among the audience to sell tea, a woman rose from her seat. " 'Ere," she said at the top of her voice, "don't give this place another penny!"

The play had now been bought by Warner Brothers. Kazan and Irene Selznick both felt Vivien should portray Blanche on the screen. But if Olivier had not accepted the lead opposite Jennifer Jones (now Mrs. David O. Selznick) in William Wyler's film version of Theodore Dreiser's *Carrie*, it is doubtful that Vivien would have agreed to play Blanche in the film. This way they would be in Hollywood together.

Shortly after Vivien signed for *Streetcar*, Lucinda Ballard flew to London to meet with and discuss her film costumes for the role. Kazan, who was to direct, felt this was a rather touchy matter (Olivier had, after all, adamantly rejected Lucinda's costumes for the London stage production) and one that had to be settled before Vivien arrived in Hollywood.

Lucinda and Vivien met for the first time at a party given by Ivor Novello. When Lucinda first saw Vivien, she was sharing a large crimson chair with Danny Kaye. They were laughing and whispering to each other, but the moment Ivor said, "This is my sweet Lucinda," Vivien looked up and rose at once, "like a good little girl," and Miss Ballard, who hails from the South and is a descendant of the Confederate President Jefferson Davis, was struck immediately by her impeccable manners and with her most unusual beauty. Vivien smiled in greeting, the corners of her mouth turned up naturally, and yet Lucinda had never seen this lovely curve of the lips on anyone else. It gave her a look of eagerness and a sweet sort of innocence which, combined with her startling beauty, made her absolutely unique.

But it was more than Vivien's beauty that attracted Lucinda. It was her joyous and ebullient nature, the spellbinding way in which she could tell a story. That night Robert Helpmann was also at the party, and Vivien had everyone in hysterics as she related and re-enacted a story about the time the two of them had appeared in *A Midsummer Night's Dream* with the Old Vic Company and the royal family with the two little princesses had been in the audience and Vivien and Helpmann had turned to bow to them. To their immense horror their elaborate headpieces locked and they could not draw apart. Vivien smiled inanely at the royal family and nestled in closer to Helpmann and the two of them backed off the stage with Vivien in a position that made her crowned head seem to grow out of her backside. Novello's guests roared with laughter.

Lucinda, who, with her copper curls and freckled fair complexion, possessed a childlike openness and enthusiasm, won Vivien over; and it was not long before the two women became good friends. Lucinda took her costume sketches to Notley Abbey. England was still crushed by rationing, but the food, the service, and the atmosphere at Notley were so exquisite that she felt she was removed in time to Edwardian England, for Vivien, with ingenuity and infinite pains, and without ever using black market foods, had been able to make her table and her house gracious and welcoming. Before Lucinda returned to the States, Vivien had agreed to all the costume sketches, and a special understanding had grown between them.

Lucinda was struck by the distinctiveness of the Oliviers' marriage, the sense that they were still young lovers and all their friends were conspirators to an illicit affair. Vivien's subjugation of her own status to Larry's, the complete and genuine idolatry she had of him, and the fears that she would not please him, troubled and confused Lucinda. It seemed incredible to her that a woman who seemed even more beautiful at night, with her face creamed and without makeup, should be distraught because "Larry thinks my legs are too fat," but such was the case.

Money had been the major factor in Olivier's agreement to do *Carrie* and Vivien's to film *Streetcar*. He had recently formed Laurence Olivier Productions, realizing his lifelong ambition to head his own company as actor-manager. Vivien was made a director of the company along with Alexander Korda, Anthony Bushell, and the scenic designer Roger Furse. After much searching it was decided that they would take over the St. James's Theatre, which was once a gem among London theatres but had lost its prestige over the years. Olivier had hopes of restoring the theatre to its former glory. To this end he spared no expense in refurbishing it. His first production, *Venus Observed*, Christopher Fry's complex verse play, ran successfully (and concurrently with *Streetcar*) for seven months in 1950, with Olivier starring as the Duke of Altair. But production costs had been so high that it made no money. Disastrously, Laurence Olivier Productions' second entry at the St. James's—*Fading Mansion*, an Anouilh play which starred Siobhan McKenna—closed after a fortnight. There had seemed to be only one recourse if the company was going to continue. Hollywood would have to foot the bill, and as Larry confided to Vivien, "It will be a pleasure to snoot old monsters!"

It had been nearly nine years since either of them had been there. Many dramatic changes had taken place. Vivien no longer considered herself a film star, nor did she believe she needed Hollywood to advance her career. And they were now Sir Laurence and Lady Olivier, which in a society based on fairy tales very much changed their social status. It was difficult not to reflect on the last time she had left England for Hollywood, a runaway lover determined to remain at Larry's side in spite of all censure.

She was still on close and fond terms with Leigh. It was a relationship that she had not yet come to fully understand, and she struggled inwardly with many emotionally disturbing thoughts. During the periods of depression that still plagued her she had sexual fantasies that distressed her, believing that if she were left alone at these times she might be moved to pick up a stranger on the street, bring him home, and seduce him. Occasionally she would feel a compulsion to ask a taxi driver in whose cab she had ridden to come back to the house with her. This same kind of desire would at times overwhelm her when she was alone with a deliveryman. Certain comparisons could be made to Blanche DuBois' sexual behavior in *Streetcar*. But Vivien's needs were considerably different from Williams' character's. Loneliness was not the motivation. Nor did she ever "misbehave" during periods when she was not ill. But within Vivien was a childhood guilt so deep-rooted that none of the psychiatrists who had treated her were able to dislodge it. The thought of having relations with a man who was "working class" appeared to lighten the guilt for short periods. Unfortunately, such fantasies left their mark upon her, so that one guilt seemed only to be traded for another.

There was no way she could bring herself to discuss these schisms of behavior with Larry. She was certain that madness waited around the corner for her. The thought terrified and consumed her. Leigh calmed her fears considerably. Not that she could reveal her private thoughts or sexual aberrations with him either. It was simply that they seemed to disappear in his presence. He made her feel free and clean, young, beautiful, untouched—still innocent. It would never occur to her to use indecent language before him or to dispute any arguments he might have. She hated variations of her name and yet she never complained when he called her Vivvy. At the same time she never felt sexually drawn to him either, and this was a great relief to her. It meant she could relate to Leigh as though he were a fond and loving parent.

Suzanne was now sixteen, and Vivien wanted very much to form a closer communion with her. The girl appeared to be leaning toward a career in the theatre and hoped to attend the Royal Academy of Dramatic Art. In the beginning Vivien tended to dissuade her, reminding her that there were about 12,000 actors out of work in England at the time. It was a curious attitude for Vivien to take in view of her own experience, but she did not believe that Suzanne had the natural ability to make a success of it without a terrible and hard struggle. When she saw that Suzanne was serious, she backed her up. There was no apparent bitterness on the girl's part for past indifference, and Vivien felt Leigh was responsible in the main for that. But try as she did, she could not relate to her daughter in a true maternal fashion.

With Tarquin it was another matter. Tarquin was more openly demonstrative and of a more sensitive and artistic nature. She encouraged his aspirations to play the piano and tried hard to make Larry take a keener interest. Strangely, she was not as close as she should have been to Suzanne, and yet she desperately wanted father and son to bridge their chasm.

Tarquin had entered Eton shortly before the production of *Streetcar*. Before that he had been at Cottesnore School, which was a boarding preparatory school in the wilds of Wales near Snowdon, where the boys were housed in a crazy historical mansion alleged to have secret passages, priest holes, and ghosts—a marvelous place for vigorous little boys—and he had been very happy. Eton was entirely another matter. As Olivier's son and heir, a great deal was expected of him that he did not feel capable of delivering. Most painful, perhaps, was the fact that he was small for his age, which was a handicap in sports. He majored in Spanish and French, but was not doing at all well.

He had a good relationship with Jill, never hesitating to bring friends home when he had time from school, and he was pleased that she easily fit in as "one of the boys." But it was his father's approval that he needed most desperately, and no matter what he did he seemed unable to get it. He took up rowing with enthusiasm, and despite his size was a welcome addition to the Eton junior rowing team. He gave small concerts at school for friends and won the junior piano competitions, but Olivier did not attend.

Vivien's relationship with her parents very much occupied her thoughts. She had a far greater understanding of Gertrude than she had had in her younger years. She was aware of her father's infidelity, and her allegiance had turned to Gertrude. But now Ernest was ill and she found their meetings were charged with emotion that she could not disperse.

It was not an easy decision for Olivier to remain in London to complete his current engagement while Vivien left for a conference with Elia Kazan at his home in Newtown, Connecticut. He was well aware that her dependency on him was great and that their separation often threw her into one of her attacks of depression. She had "taken ill" during the last weeks of Streetcar, and it had closed without her. But she had rallied quite well, and lately there had been none of those little signs that indicated that she might turn on him—and ultimately upon herself. Feeling that her "spells" might be behind them, he saw her off on a flight to New York.

Vivien had "terrific admiration" for "Gadge" Kazan, who was going to direct the film version of A Streetcar Named Desire. She had first seen him as an actor in the role of Eddie Fusili in a London production of Golden Boy in 1938, and had gone back several times to watch him perform. And she and Olivier had staged the London productions of The Skin of Our Teeth and A Streetcar Named Desire, which he had directed first in New York. Kazan planned to film virtually the entire playscript—including the speeches Olivier had cut from the London production—and he and Vivien went over it line by line. There had been ticklish problems raised by Hollywood's censorship office (known then as the Breen office). Once again, as in England, the reference to homosexuality had to be removed, and Williams was working on that passage to get it past the censors while retaining what he could of the original concept.

Kazan and Vivien differed on the interpretation of Blanche's motivations, and it looked as if there might be trouble ahead between them. After two days as a guest in his home (he found her "full of grace, and intelligence, and clever enough not to say all she thought"), she boarded a train for California, stopping in Wisconsin en route to visit with Alfred Lunt and Lynn Fontanne. Vivien had always felt able to confide in Lynn, to confess many of her anxieties. At this time she seemed most obsessed with the idea of Larry's possible infidelity. Both women agreed that they would much prefer their husbands to have homosexual rather than heterosexual affairs, neither feeling able to cope with the threat to her ego that another woman would pose.

Tennessee Williams met her in Hollywood, where he was still working on the script. One troubling sequence was Scene Nine in the play, in which Blanche after having had her past exposed by Stanley, brings down the curtain by yelling, "Fire! Fire! Fire!" The Breen office banned this on the basis that it might send patrons out of the theatre in panic. Williams also had the problem of the scenes dealing with the homosexuality of Blanche's dead husband, her supposed promiscuity with soldiers and sailors, and the accusations that she had been involved with a seventeen-year-old boy.

But by the second week in August 1950 the film was ready to go before the cameras, and Vivien, as Blanche, was unveiled to the press in Jack L. Warner's private dining room at the studio that bore his and his brother's name. She entered on Kazan's arm wearing one of Lucinda's costumes for the film—a dotted net negligee—a yellow straw-blond wig on her head. She was introduced to her co-star Marlon Brando for the first time. Brando was clad in brown slacks and a T-shirt, his naturally blond hair died dark for the film—as it had been for the play at Lucinda's insistence. (His first Broadway appearance had been as a blond young Scandinavian boy in a production of I Remember Mama.)

Vivien talked to him about his performance with Katharine Cornell in *Antigone* (he had played the Messenger). She replied to the reporters' queries in a straightforward manner and rejected their calling her Lady Olivier. "Her Ladyship is fucking bored with such formality," she told one reporter, "and prefers to be known as Miss Vivien Leigh!" The film's producer, Charles K. Feldman, laughed nervously beside her.

She was asked questions like "What do you suppose happened to Scarlett O'Hara after Rhett Butler walked out?"

"I think she probably became a better woman, but I don't think she ever got Rhett Butler back."

Did she read her lines to Sir Laurence?

"No, I always know my lines."

Did Sir Laurence read his lines to her?

"Yes, it's perfectly wonderful because he puts me to sleep."

Did they go out often?

"On Saturday nights and maybe one night during the week."

Did she think the American public might resent her playing a Southerner again?

"A great many Americans saw me when I played the same role in London on the stage and I didn't get any rude letters, so I must have sounded all right."

In answer to other questions: "*Streetcar* is a most wonderful, wonderful play. . . . The role of Blanche is very exhausting—in the theatre anyway. . . . I am extremely flattered Mr. Kazan chose me."

"Lord, I'm famished," Vivien finally announced after more than a half hour of being questioned. Brando nudged her from behind. "Go ahead and fuckin' eat your meal," he advised her and then slouched off to order his own.

Before *A Streetcar Named Desire* went before the cameras, Olivier had arrived from London accompanied by a wide-eyed, sixteen-year-old Suzanne, just finished with her secondary school studies and looking forward to a summer holiday and her entrance in the fall in the Royal Academy. Olivier began work on *Carrie* immediately, and they moved into a manorial house with a huge pool that no one except Suzanne ever had the time to use. The young woman would join her mother and Vivien's secretary, Sunny Lash, in Vivien's dressing room for lunch, but the role of motherhood seemed an added and most difficult pressure and the relationship was not good.

Kazan had seen Blanche in an unsympathetic manner, and Vivien did not share his view. They had come no closer to an agreement once in production. For two weeks they were at an impasse. Then their differences suddenly dissolved. Kazan claimed that Vivien came over to his side; Vivien said in interviews that he had come over to hers. What seemed to have eased the tensions between them was Vivien's final agreement not to go home each evening and work out her next day's scenes with Larry. Kazan blamed her stagy performance in those first weeks on Olivier's "subversive" direction.

What Vivien found important in the character of Blanche was her beauty of spirit, imagination, and mind. She was trying through her interpretation to let people see what Blanche was like when she was seventeen and in love with her young husband. The key to her was Blanche's sister Stella's line "Nobody, nobody, was tender and trusting as she [Blanche] was." The reading by Stella of that line created a tremendous schism between Vivien and Kazan. Vivien felt the words "tender" and "trusting" should be elongated because they evoked the young Blanche when she was tender and trusting, as opposed to what she had become—cynical, hard, mad.

During the three months it took to shoot the film, Vivien could hardly wait to get to the studio each day; and once again, as with *Gone With the Wind*, she was the last to leave in the evening. Williams' final script was frozen, no further changes could be made, and cast and crew felt dedicated to bringing it to life to the last detail. The prop man would question Vivien: "What sort of things do you think Blanche would have on her table next to her bed?" She decided it would be a picture of Blanche when she was young, and objects that came from her past—a dance program, a gift from an admirer, a picture of her family home.

She adored Kim Hunter, who played Stella; but in the beginning there was tension between Brando and herself. She found him affected, and he thought she was stuffy and prim. "Why are you so fuckin' polite? Why do you have to say a fuckin' good morning to everyone?" he asked. It was difficult for him to understand how important good manners were to her, but after a while they became friends. Brando would sing folk songs in a pleasant voice to the cast and do imitations of Olivier as Henry V. Larry was difficult to mimic, but Brando was able to imitate him perfectly.

Olivier was concerned because she was sleeping very little. Blanche seemed constantly on her mind. There were moments when those close to her were startled by the thought that she had times when she fully believed she *was* Blanche. Olivier was under terrific pressure on *Carrie*, for though he admired Wyler he was beginning to feel that the film had been a mistake and his role too downbeat and not dramatic enough. There were also the coming theatre productions for the Festival of Britain in less than six months for which he was partially responsible. Every night the two of them would read Pirandello, Sheridan, and Shaw until they were red-eyed, searching for plays.

When Sylvia Fine and Danny Kaye decided to throw them a glamorous party at the Beverly Hills Hotel, Olivier was extremely pleased, since he thought it would relax Vivien's increasing nervousness. The Kayes had decided that no producers would be invited and that the guest list would have to be limited to 150. Invitations to "a party in honor of Sir Laurence and Lady Olivier" immediately became the key to social status in Hollywood. Everyone surreptitiously inquired of everyone else if they had been invited, and those who had not, and knew Vivien, besieged her with requests to secure invitations for them. It soon became more than she could bear, and she would lock herself in her dressing room with Sunny and weep. She begged Larry to speak to the Kayes about canceling the affair, but he thought that would be a terrible breach of etiquette and she was forced to agree with him.

The party was held in the hotel's grand ballroom, which glittered with crystal and gold. An orchestra augmented with additional strings played at the far end of the room, and there seemed to be as many uniformed waiters as guests. A tuxedoed Danny Kaye, his hair dyed a brilliant red for an appearance in a Technicolor film, strode exuberantly through the crowds of his guests to greet each newcomer. To Vivien it recalled her Court presentation, and though no one loved parties more than she, the pretentiousness of this one struck a wrong chord with her. Certainly it was the most elegant of parties. Men as well as women who considered themselves Hollywood royalty were strutting like peacocks, and each seemed to be wearing more jewels than belonged to the British crown. Vivien looked exquisite in a green gown that made her eyes look like two dark emeralds. She smiled, she laughed, she flirted, but she was not happy. It disturbed her that Larry was enjoying the party so much, that Danny Kaye seemed to completely ignore his wife, Sylvia, indeed that she and Larry were being used as an excuse for a party.

No guest who was unattached was allowed to come alone or with anyone who had not been invited, so Lucinda Ballard, who had recently fallen in love with Howard Dietz, was escorted by a rather dandified Otto Preminger. At the end of the party Lucinda announced to the Oliviers that she and Howard were going to marry. Vivien was genuinely happy for the first time that night. "Oh, how marvelous, Cindy darling." She beamed and hugged Lucinda to her.

But Larry commented, "What? Not that publicity man?" (He remembered him from the Atlanta premiere of *Gone With the Wind*.)

"Howard Dietz is one of America's finest lyricists!" Vivien retorted sharply, then turned and walked angrily out of the room. It was one of the few times the Oliviers were ever seen to argue in public.

At the conclusion of the principal photography on *Streetcar*, Vivien took a train trip to New Orleans with Kazan. Even so, they never became intimate. Their relationship revolved around their work. Kazan was aware that she experienced extreme ups and downs, but as she was happy when she worked, indeed thrived on it, he ignored them. Yet his first impression of her as a great beauty being devoured by something that she was trying unsuccessfully to control remained unchanged from the first day of the film until the last.

As soon as Larry had completed *Carrie*, the Oliviers made plans to leave, but Vivien was unable to cope with the idea of a long air flight. There were no ocean liners scheduled for departure out of San Francisco, so they booked passage on a French Line freighter, the *Wyoming;* and with five other passengers, 40,000 crates of apples, 10,000 cases of sardines, and 2000 bales of cotton they sailed a rough winter sea looking forward to Christmas at home.

Chapter Twenty-one

Rehearsals for the 1951 Festival of Britain productions had to begin immediately if they were to open as scheduled, but Larry and Vivien had not yet found a play that would give them roles of equal stature. Finally, all the board members of Laurence Olivier Productions Ltd. (Cecil Tennant, Anthony Bushell, Roger Furse, Alexander Korda, Olivier, and Vivien) met at their office in the St. James's Theatre to reach a decision. The majority were in favor of Shaw's *Caesar and Cleopatra*, but Vivien did not think the sixteen-year-old Cleopatra, which she had already portrayed on the screen, ambitious enough.

"Let's do the two Cleopatras"—Roger Furse laughed nervously— "the Shaw and the Shakespeare, then Vivien could age over twenty years in one evening." He meant it as a humorous remark and was immediately sorry he had said it, thinking Vivien might have been offended, but she leaned forward, eyes shining.

"It couldn't be done in one night, of course," she said excitedly, "but it could on successive nights." She looked up at Larry, who was pacing the room.

"Too expensive and too massive a cast," he muttered.

The others agreed, but Korda was the only one frank enough to question Vivien's ability to tackle the arduous and difficult role of the aging Cleopatra. The meeting disbanded with the idea having been rejected and with no other substitute in mind. The Oliviers flew to Paris for the New Year's weekend and Vivien tucked a copy of the two plays in their luggage. No sooner had they settled into their hotel suite than Olivier felt a chill. By evening he was bedded with flu. He was unable to leave his room, so Vivien insisted he read *Antony and*

Cleopatra and *Caesar and Cleopatra* with a view toward the intense challenge of his appearing on successive evenings in two such dramatic roles as Antony and Caesar.

By morning he was convinced that Roger Furse's crazy idea was a true stroke of genius. Never before had the two plays been presented together. Combining a comedy and a tragedy about the same bewitching woman could make stage history, and Vivien was indeed right—Antony and Caesar were powerful, uniquely different characters. He rang Furse in London and asked him to set up another board meeting that same week.

His enthusiasm for the project grew each day, and yet he was deeply concerned about how Vivien would cope with the pressures of shifting one day to the next from the naive young Cleopatra being taught the manners of a monarch by a fifty-year-old emperor to the mature and calculating Serpent of the Nile who brings about the ruin of her lover, Mark Antony.

From the first day of rehearsal, Vivien felt the strain, worrying constantly that she might let Larry down. More and more she was convinced that he was a genius, and day after day her fears would increase that she could not keep pace with him. He sensed her growing apprehensions and was pleased that he had decided he would not direct the dual productions (Michael Benthall took on the task), so that he could give Vivien whatever time he could spare. But certainly his brilliance was behind the entire conception.

Sets were designed for the revolving stage that would tie both plays together. Costumes were created with the same duality of use. The militia wore the same uniforms, Cleopatra's female attendants appeared in both plays dressed in flowing boudoir silks, and Cleopatra wore the same splendid coronation robes for her crowning at sixteen as she did for her suicide at thirty-nine. The most singularly memorable link between the two plays, however, was the use of a sphinx to open the Shaw play and to close Shakespeare's. But Benthall, working hard to give each play a character of its own, made the Shaw play rather realistic and the Shakespeare as poetic as possible. This involved a "Shavian dry delivery" for the first and "a rich Renaissance treatment" for the second.

Vivien's greatest problem was handling the twenty-three-year age difference of the two Cleopatras. Special makeup was created for her alternate roles, applied in a slightly different way to alter the shape of her face. For the young Cleopatra, rouge was painted high on her cheeks to make her face appear plumper. Lipstick was applied heavily to give an unsophisticated look. The older Cleopatra wore her rouge lower down, making her face leaner and more interesting, and used less lipstick.

"My neck's too long, my hands too big, and my voice too small," Vivien complained and then set forth to torturously correct each "fault." She stood six hours one evening while Audrey Cruddas, the costume designer, worked to drape material to disguise the length of her neck. She wore massive rings and bracelets to distract from "my big paws," but it was the constant coaching to help her deepen her voice that gave her countless extra hours of exhausting work that no other member of the cast had to endure.

Rehearsals were beset with illness in the cast. Maxine Audley, who was Charmian in both plays, contracted measles and feared she would lose the roles, as she had to be absent for three weeks. Vivien sent her a magnificent bouquet of spring flowers and a note that read, "You poor little measly one, hurry up and get well and come back quickly." Peter Cushing, who was cast as Britannus in the Shaw play, suffered a nervous breakdown. The Oliviers advanced him money (of which the company had little enough) to see him through his hospitalization and held the role open for him (he gave an excellent performance when he recovered). Elspeth March, who played Ftatateeta in the Shaw play, broke her ankle. As she had done for Maxine Audley, Vivien sent massive bouquets and notes of encouragement.

The cast adored Vivien. She made them laugh a lot and was concerned about each member and remarkably never forgot a birthday or anniversary. Jill Bennett (who played Iras) and Maxine Audley were especially devoted to her, and as they were in almost all of her scenes, they supported her in every sense of the word. It was no secret by now that Vivien was having "emotional problems," and the cast rallied to her magnificently.

But Olivier was viewed quite differently by the cast and crew. Those who had worked with him before found he had become "more austere and a little remote." There were those who firmly believed knighthood had gone to his head. He was, of course, in a difficult spot as actor-manager, unable to show favoritism; and perhaps he thought it improvident to be too informal with members of the company. One old co-worker, however, said forthrightly, "Any acquaintance who slaps Olivier on the back expecting to find *Larry* risks a rather disconcerting experience. The danger is that his present Olympian perch may isolate him from the contacts every artist must maintain if he is to keep in touch."

It was generally agreed that "Larry is not the great fun he used to be," but there were times when the old Larry reappeared. One example took place during the rehearsals, after Peter Cushing had returned to the cast. He had just acquired false teeth, along with all his other troubles, and found that they caused him to spit considerably. To avoid splashing fellow actors he lowered his voice. Olivier shouted out to him, "Go on, Peter. It doesn't matter if you spit! Spit for all you're worth! Drown us all! It will be a glorious death!" The cast cheered and Cushing raised his speech level.

Olivier still maintained his sense of humor with Vivien and their guests at Notley, and would do comedic bits and impersonations. But the closer they got to May 10, the date of their opening, the more delicate Vivien's nerves became, and the more aloof Olivier seemed to become.

The Shaw play opened first. In one scene Vivien had to slap Elspeth March's face. Elspeth was wearing a false rubber nose as Ftatateeta, the nurse. One night Vivien slapped too close to it. The nose flew into the air and Vivien fielded brilliantly with her left hand and returned it to Elspeth who was then able to get off stage holding her hand to her face, the audience having noticed nothing!

Shakespeare's play was received more enthusiastically by *The Times* after its premiere. "Allowing that the Cleopatra of Miss Vivien Leigh," the review began, "is in the heyday of her power a somewhat cool enchantress, and that the production on an open revolving stage may sacrifice some speed to continuity, memory recalls no more satisfying performance of this play, no palimpsest so imposingly strong in line and color, so harmonious in its total impression. Cool Miss Leigh may be as she exhibits the wiles of a courtesan of genius, but she exhibits them with a beautifully exact expressiveness and she grows in momentousness to meet her doom. When Antony has died and she is left alone to bring the play to its wonderful ending she is faultless." *The Times* also found Olivier's performance "a mounting excitement."

The fact was that the plays, different as they were, fit curiously well together. The Shaw play seemed a kind of prologue to Shakespeare, although Shaw might have snorted that Shakespeare's play was a mere epilogue to his. Still, all the critics did not agree, and indeed seemed to be at great loggerheads of opinion. The battle was on. Some said Vivien was holding Sir Laurence back and that no matter how he surrounded and supported her she would never be his equal on the stage.

A young critic, Kenneth Tynan, who had only recently "floated down from Oxford," had brought out a book on theatre and had taken his place as a theatre critic to be reckoned with. His review of the two plays set off a rocket of anger from Vivien that she was never quite able to successfully discharge or abandon. Though, at a later date, Olivier was to become a very close friend of Tynan's, he too was incensed at Tynan's devastating criticism of Vivien.

Life was becoming increasingly more painful to Vivien, at times almost intolerable. She knew she could never free herself from her obsession to accomplish theatre greatness, and yet she feared failure irrationally and with true and mounting terror. Tynan's slashing diatribe cut deep and wounded her mightily. She was convinced that *they* (the critics) thought Larry's greatness was being diminished by her own ambition. *They* thought her small voice blunted his authority. *They* thought her mediocrity caused him to compromise. Rumbles of Tynan's attack—a nod in his direction—appeared here and there in other published pieces, but no other critic actually served up such dispraise, and as many, if not more, were extremely laudatory. It did not balance the ledger for Vivien. She held her suffering close to her, but it was discernible to those sensitive artists who worked with her and admired her amazing stamina and the hard work and sweat she put in. The last was a new problem for her to bear. In the short time of perhaps ten or fifteen minutes before her first appearance on stage she would become drenched from perspiration. After the second or third time this occurred she had Audrey Cruddas sew dozens of protective pads into her costumes, but the problem continued, causing her great apprehension and adding to her tension.

Olivier rose in defense of Vivien and angrily called Tynan to task. It was even whispered among the company that he had "landed a smart one on Tynan's chin, causing it to recede even more," but Vivien sensed an admiration on Olivier's part for Tynan's intelligence and attributed his defense of her to "gallantry." There that word was again! Tynan had used the word "gallantry" in his article to refer to Olivier's casting of Vivien opposite him even though she possessed what Tynan considered an inferior talent.

Small signs of disharmony between Larry and Vivien began to be noticed among the company. She turned on him in public from time to time, and he grew more aloof. One night during *Antony and Cleopatra* he splattered spots of stage blood on her gown, and she grew intensely hostile toward him immediately after they came off stage. And another night when they were taking their curtains he neglected to bow and smile at her, and she strode furiously ahead of him into her dressing room and slammed the door. These were the few times that she had ever displayed anything but admiration for him in public. Yet his picture remained on her theatre dressing table at all times and by her bedside in both houses. In truth, she adored and worshiped him and was even more miserable when she thought she had made him the slightest bit unhappy by her behavior. What most frightened her—and him—was that she often did not recall her actions and was baffled and humiliated by them.

Still, the production was a particularly happy one for the company, which included Robert Helpmann, Norman Wooland, Elspeth March, Peter Cushing, Jill Bennett, and Maxine Audley. The two Cleopatras played five months in England, closing on an unusually balmy October evening. The Oliviers threw a fabulous party for all the company on a barge on the Thames after the last performance, a particularly creative idea and certainly one of the few—if not the only—parties of its kind ever given an English theatrical company.

In December the Oliviers took the plays to New York with many members of their company. (Maxine Audley, Jill Bennett, Elspeth March, and Peter Cushing remained behind with other commitments.)

As George Jean Nathan wrote in the New York *Journal American*, "Not since John Ringling North imported Gargantua from the wilds of Bermuda, to say nothing from Austria of Unus, the man who could stand on one finger, has anything created such a stir as the importation from England of the Olivier-Leigh two-ring circus currently in operation on Billy Rose's Ziegfeld lot." Besides being called a two-ring circus, the plays were heralded in New York as "The Mixed-Doubles" and as "Two-on-the-Nile." It was the theatrical event of the season, and perhaps of the decade.

Vivien's performances dominated the reviews, as she did the stage of the Ziegfeld with her long straight flaming wig and flowing wings of sleeves which gave her an erotic, somewhat morbid look of an imperious Aubrey Beardsley drawing. New York, more than London, was overwhelmed at the sumptuous pageantry, the sense of pomp, the circusy aspect that the revolving stage created, making the play an amphitheatrical carousel, which, though adding flow and speed to the productions, occasionally gave the audience vertigo.

By itself neither of the Cleopatras would have been likely to arouse much furor, but as a duet they were a theatrical treat never before available and perhaps never to be repeated, at least by a company headed by the most distinguished couple in the British theatre. There were nearly a million dollars in advance bookings before the play opened, and after the first nights there was hardly an available ticket remaining for the sixteen-week run. Still, because of the extravagance of the spectacular productions, and the huge imported cast (thirty-eight including Alec McCowen, Niall MacGinnis, Wilfrid Hyde White, Pat Nye, Robert Helpmann, Harry Andrews, and Donald Pleasence), the play at full capacity would little more than break even.

Opening night the Ziegfeld was unbearably hot. The next night, and because of a seven-twenty curtain, there were a great many latecomers. In spite of these difficulties and some confusion in the light cues, the plays, and especially Vivien's performances, seemed to have grown more powerful than they were at the St. James's.

Walter Kerr in the *Herald Tribune* wrote, "Laurence Olivier and Vivien Leigh have performed the near miracle of pulling the sprawling canvas into a coherent and increasingly exciting whole." All the critics thought the Oliviers had brought glamour, theatricality, and a renewed vitality back to the theatre. Vivien and Larry ruled regally over the New York 1951–1952 theatre season. Crowds of autograph hunters and fans waited at the stage door of the Ziegfeld after each performance, parties in their honor were given in droves, and the press and media coverage nearly overwhelmed the McCarthy Senate hearings on un-American activities in Hollywood and the tragic death of King George VI.

One might have thought that Vivien would at last be a happy, contented woman, for she now shared the stage with Olivier with seeming equality. The truth was that she never could believe this in her heart. Then on March 20, 1952, she was awarded an Oscar for her performance in *Streetcar*, Greer Garson accepting for her in her absence. This certainly should have been a crowning glory. But the art of film acting remained secondary to Vivien. She seemed as grief-stricken by the British monarch's death in February as she had been at his father's sixteen years before.

Then, in April, she suffered another of her attacks of hysteria. Olivier was beside himself. She was like some wild creature, and when he tried to calm and comfort her she turned on him with no cause or provocation. He was now becoming convinced that Vivien was seriously mentally ill. The idea overwhelmed him, and he was not at all sure how the two of them would conduct their lives under such a burden.

Act Three

"I am not going to lose my dignity, no matter what happens I am not going to lose it," but just as continually she caught herself doing things that were not at all consistent with that resolve.

—*The Roman Spring of Mrs. Stone*
Tennessee Williams

Chapter Twenty-two

The magnifying mirror on her dressing-room table told her that though she remained an extraordinarily beautiful woman she was no longer a young one. She was nearing her fortieth birthday and the thought terrified her. Youth was constantly on her mind and she was becoming obsessively jealous of anyone who had it. She would swing between happiness and misery and she cried easily. One minute she wanted more than anything to give Larry a child, the next she considered having an affair. Her reason was blurred by panic. She had to prove to Larry and the world that she could top her New York performances of Cleopatra. She could not stop—not now. Nor could she continue—for what if she failed?

"I'm a Scorpio," she told an interviewer, "and Scorpios eat themselves out and burn themselves up like me." She was smoking incessantly, which was bad for her lungs, sleeping less than ever, and surrounding herself and Larry—when he was home—with a constant barrage of guests. She was drinking more heavily than she had ever done before, and the alcohol brought on periods of hysteria as it interacted disastrously with the drugs she took for her lung condition. For Vivien the world was filled with either splendor or sadness. There seemed no in-between. She wanted things to be as they had been before, but she did not know how to achieve this.

Coping with the acceleration of her hysteria and the manic-depressive periods was weighing Olivier down. He guessed alcohol was at least partially responsible and did what he could to convince her to abstain. He was becoming more and more aware that they were losing what they once had and that nothing would ever quite be the same. He felt—as did Vivien—that because theirs was a superior, sublime love it could survive most difficulties. Yet he was growing increasingly alarmed that her extremes of manic behavior could change that, and that the direction of their relationship was moving out of his control. Work seemed the only antidote to the sense of inadequacy her illness gave to him, and he thrust himself compulsively into it.

He presented Peter Finch in *The Happy Time* at the St. James's and planned a film of *The Beggar's Opera* that he would both co-produce and appear in as Macheath. But Vivien was not to be in the film, and her exclusion was a terrible blow to her. Her great love for Larry began eating away inside of her, severing her emotional contact with the world beyond her body.

At the time she was under the care of both a medical doctor and a psychiatrist. And during her illness she developed a trust in and a childlike dependency on Gertrude, who was nearby. At these times she thought that men, both acquaintances and strangers, were always trying to seduce her, and she would have spells of fear that she would not be able to resist them.

So in 1953 Notley once again became her safe retreat. The doctors had recommended rest. Compulsion to be active overwhelmed her and she seldom took to her bed. She would sweep Notley's stately halls, dust the nooks and crannies, spend hours pruning trees and plucking dead blossoms. The end of summer brought Olivier home to rest. Immediately she showed signs of improvement, but *The Beggar's Opera* was soon to be filmed and he would be forced to leave her alone again.

There were rumors of her "illness," but her friends were faithful and no one verified them. Olivier was in a torturous dilemma, plagued by guilt and yet driven by his own need for survival. Then Irving Asher, a Hollywood producer, appeared, as though in answer to Olivier's silent prayers. Asher was planning to go into production on a film to be called *Elephant Walk*, which was the story of an English tea grower and his wife living on a plantation in Ceylon and of the plantation foreman with whom the wife has an affair. Asher thought the Oliviers would be ideally cast as the married couple. Olivier could not consider the film even if Asher postponed his plans for an immediate production, because he had theatre commitments for the entire coming year. He therefore suggested the possibility of Vivien appearing in the film with Peter Finch, whom he had had under his management. Asher, having met with Vivien, was now fearful of "her delicate state of health." But her doctors felt a change of scene might benefit her condition, so Olivier assured the producer that though Vivien had suffered a lung flare-up she was perfectly able to make a film, and, indeed, that the work was exactly what she needed. The suggestion of Vivien having anything other than a physical illness was never hinted at, and it would seem that Asher had not heard any of the rumors.

Vivien was not terribly impressed with the script, but she knew there were other considerations, money not the least. The proceeds from *Streetcar* and *Carrie* were now depleted, and production costs for all the endeavors planned by their company were not only rising but nearing crisis proportions. Asher had agreed that Paramount would pay $150,000 for Vivien's services, $50,000 of which would be paid over on the signing of a contract. It is difficult to fathom how Olivier, the doctors, or even Vivien herself thought she was going to be able to endure a most trying role which called for a month of location work in Ceylon, where the heat would be close to intolerable and where she would be called upon to ride horseback, escape a herd of stampeding elephants, and play one scene with a snake wrapped around her neck. But they were all quite confident, and Olivier put her on a plane with Peter Finch and his wife and then went off to Italy for some location work of his own.

Ceylon, situated southeast of India, was a part of the world that she had not been in since childhood, and it evoked many memories—blurred and only dimly recalled. She had not really known what to expect, and it was far more beautiful than she imagined. Everywhere there was an abundance of nature. It was the most scenic of islands. The big sea stretched blue to the horizon, the tropical jungles were emerald green, and the seashore was palm-fringed. There were the ruins at Anuradhapura, the mountains and glaciers that rose above the jungles, the sense of witchery and legend. Ceylon (called Serendib in Arabic) was where Sinbad the Sailor played out his adventures, and it seemed a part of the *Arabian Nights*, with nothing real or tangible; and the unreality loosened Vivien's hold on whatever security she had left.

The film was directed by William Dieterle. Dana Andrews played the foreman. She did not identify well with either man. The heat was worse than she had anticipated and the loneliness was terrifying. For the first time in her life she had difficulty memorizing her lines. She found it impossible to sleep and walked around all night, haunting the beaches and the coves and alarming the rest of the cast and crew.

The rushes were not good. She looked tired, old, and somewhat wooden. Dieterle took her aside and told her so. "I'm not young," she retorted. "What's wrong with that?"

In the last week of location she began to hallucinate. She followed Finch around the set with hungry eyes and called him "Larry." He had a great fondness for Vivien and tried to do what he could to protect her and to conceal what he feared was the truth—that she might be building to a complete nervous collapse unless she got out of Ceylon.

It took an entire day and two huge but harmless snakes to film the sequence where the reptile was wound around Vivien's neck. By nightfall it was fairly obvious to everyone that the day's work had unnerved her, but Finch was aware that it had done a great deal more than that. She had begun to recite Blanche's dialogue from *Streetcar* and sobbed uncontrollably throughout the night.

The remainder of the film was to be shot on the Paramount lot in Hollywood. The plane trip took seventy-two hours and only moments after take-off Vivien suffered an attack of hysteria. She was sedated, and Finch remained staunchly by her side. Flying had always sent her into a panic, and seventy-two hours was a terrifying ordeal. She tried to tear off her clothes and to jump out of the plane. By the time the plane was ready to put down at Burbank Airport her hysteria had been subdued, and Finch and his wife were able to take her to their rented home. No one knew exactly what to do next. An astronomical amount of money was at stake. If Vivien was replaced, all her location scenes would have to be reshot. If she continued, there was always the possibility that she would break down at a stage when nothing could be salvaged and the film would have to be scrapped. Nonetheless, forty-eight hours later, the decision was to continue. Vivien, though looking spent and seeming unusually edgy, appeared considerably improved.

Olivier was vacationing on the island of Ischia near Naples, having completed work on *The Beggar's Opera*. It was to be a short respite before he plunged into a mass of responsibility and ambitious plans. He had been put in charge of film and theatrical activities for the Queen's coronation that summer. (A production of Terence Rattigan's *The Sleeping Prince*, to star Vivien and himself was a part of those plans.) A decision was made by those close to Vivien not to notify him of her attack.

In Hollywood that Monday, Vivien appeared at the studio not

quite her old self but very much composed. The columnists had got wind of the situation and were bombarding the film's publicist with requests for interviews. The studio, feeling it would augur better for all concerned if Vivien saw at least one member of the press, insisted she agree to this. Vivien sent word to Louella Parsons that she would like to see her. The meeting was arranged for Tuesday, the following day. The two women chatted, Vivien quite gaily, if somewhat drawn and nervous. "I think this will be my last picture," she told Parsons. "Life is too short to work so hard." She was charming and pleasant to the writer as they walked in the Paramount gardens.

Vivien tired quickly and Parsons had the grace to cut the interview short. They had spoken about generalities—Ceylon, the coronation, the danger that wearing high heels posed for your voice, since it threw your body out of line. Parsons departed and Vivien retired to her dressing room. She was scheduled to appear on the set in half an hour's time to shoot a scene. When called she could not remember her lines. She took a drink to calm her nerves and began to sob hysterically. Finch came to her dressing room to see if he could help, but she turned on him, calling him "Larry." She screamed at Sunny Lash and would not let the studio doctor near her. Dieterle stood helpless in the doorway.

"Get out of here quick before I start screaming fire!" she shouted, her voice taking on Blanche's Southern lilt as she repeated *Streetcar*'s famous Scene Nine curtain speech. "Get out of here quick before I start screaming fire!" she repeated, bolting for the door. "Fire! Fire! Fire!" she gasped desperately, and then collapsed into a sobbing heap on the floor, refusing to rise. Someone thought of calling David Niven because he was an old and close friend of both of the Oliviers. Niven immediately came over to the set. He saw her alone and remained with her for quite a time. Eventually they both came out, Vivien resting against his lean body for support. Her co-workers tried to avoid looking at them, but they stopped what they were doing and fell silent. She was in a dazed, uncomprehending condition as Niven led her across the cavernous and hushed soundstage to a waiting car.

Olivier set out for Hollywood as soon as he was notified. The trip took nearly three days. The only way out of Ischia was by boat to the mainland. Olivier was then driven to Rome, flown to London, where he met his agent and good friend, Cecil Tennant, and the two of them continued on to New York, finally to board a connecting flight to Burbank.

Vivien, confined to bed, remained there until Olivier's arrival. Announcements had been made that Elizabeth Taylor, then twenty-one, would replace her in the film. All the doctors concurred that, despite the possibility of further trauma induced by an extended flight, Vivien should be returned to England. Calls were made to her English doctors, who suggested a hospital they claimed had treated similar cases with dramatic success.

Vivien, heavily sedated, traveled by ambulance on a stretcher to the airport with Olivier, Tennant, and two nurses. Olivier hovered by her side as photographers flashed their cameras. "Be careful with the flashbulbs," Olivier pleaded. "She's a very sick woman." As Vivien's stretcher was carried aboard the TWA Constellation, Olivier began to shake with sobs. Niven put his arms around his shoulders. The two men stood clasping each other in emotion for several moments. Finally, Olivier pulled away and followed Vivien's stretcher into the aircraft's lounge. He sat down beside her and took her hand, but she was not aware of his presence.

Danny Kaye met them at New York's LaGuardia Airport with his chauffeured limousine. Then conscious, Vivien smiled at reporters as she leaned heavily on Olivier. The two nurses and Tennant closed ranks behind her as they walked from the plane across the field to Kaye's car. An uneasy moment followed as Kaye came to greet her and to help Olivier. The two men had been extremely close friends for many years, but since the time of the making of *Streetcar*, Vivien had grown intensely jealous of the relationship. She got into the car, however, and was driven to the Long Island home of a friend of Kaye's, where she was once again sedated in preparation for the long overseas flight to London.

Plans had been made for her stretcher to be used to carry her aboard the BOAC plane that was to fly them home. Wrapped in a blanket, her sleeping figure was placed across Olivier's and Kaye's laps for the ride to Idlewild International Airport. The two nurses sat on the jump seats, Tennant in front with the driver. The sedation did not last, and at the airport Vivien belligerently refused to be moved from the car to the plane on the stretcher. Both Olivier and Kaye tried to quiet her, but in the end Kaye got out of the limousine, which then drove onto the field and directly to the ramp of the waiting plane. Finally, after Larry's pleading and Tennant's cajoling did no good, she was pulled from the car screaming. Flashbulbs exploded on all sides, and Viven sobbed and wildly shook her fists at the photographers. The nurses pushed her forward and into the plane, with "Uncle Cecil" and Larry close at her heels.

It was unreal, surreal actually, and Olivier followed her flailing figure into the cabin with pain etched heavily on his famous brow. Where had the young beautiful years gone? Were they to end with Vivien declining into madness? He stood by and watched as the nurses sedated her and got her settled into a seat. He could not bring himself to look at her until she had slipped into a heavily drugged sleep. Even in that state and after all she had put herself through, she was unbelievably lovely. At that moment—her head back, her eyelids sealed in sleep, her profile to him, her neck bare and the color of pale veined marble—she looked like a carved Rodin head. The rest of her was covered by a blanket, but even so, he could see how heavily she was breathing. He did not know what he would do if her illness caused her to be institutionalized. She slept throughout most of the journey and he sat across the aisle, unable to close his eyes.

When the BOAC plane set down at the London airport, Vivien was calm but extremely weak, and Larry was exhausted but relieved that they had made it home. Three doctors and another nurse came on board as the rest of the passengers left the aircraft. Vivien seemed dazed and not quite sure of where she was. Larry helped her apply some makeup and comb her hair, and a representative of BOAC sent a bouquet of red roses aboard. A half hour later Vivien, grasping the flowers to her, her hands trembling, smiled as she walked haltingly down the ramp on Olivier's supportive arm, with the entourage of medical staff following closely behind.

By nightfall she slept under heavy sedation in a private room in a wing of Netherine Hospital, which stood in tree-fringed park land near Coulsdon, in Surrey. Administered by the South-West Regional Hospital Board, Netherine was famous for its work in the treatment of nervous conditions. Vivien was placed in the care of a top psychiatrist, who immediately barred any visitors, including Olivier; and all messages, gifts, and flowers were forbidden. Olivier, having been told she would be isolated for several weeks, drove back to Notley exhausted and disheartened. He was terrified that Vivien might never regain her sanity and he felt quite helpless. There was no peace, even at Notley. The telephone rang incessantly, reporters brazenly trespassed, photographers stood ready at the gates, their flash cameras poised. Unable to see or speak to Vivien, he returned by plane to Italy the next day so that he might at least have some privacy to think things out.

For three days and three nights Vivien was kept sedated with round-the-clock nurses in attendance. Then a course of psychiatric treatment was begun. She was packed in ice to lower her body temperature as far as it could safely be lowered. From time to time the ice packs would be removed and she would be fed raw eggs for nourishment. After several days of this her confusion and apathy began to pass. She would scream out whenever the eggs were to be fed to her, the smell helping her associate "feeding times" as her only conscious chance to rebel. "I thought I was in an insane asylum," she told intimates later. "I thought I had to scream so that someone would help me get out."

After three weeks Vivien left Netherine and went home to Notley, but she had suffered a trauma that had left her permanently scarred.

Chapter Twenty-three

Vivien refused to accept the fact that she was a manic-depressive. She and Larry had been trying for a number of years to have children and she desperately longed to give him a child. Her youth was gone, and her talent did not seem enough to prevent her from feeling sterile. Always energetic, able to go on little sleep, with each waking hour programmed and accounted for, she was losing her ability to concentrate or relax. The horror of her illness was that it caused her to turn on Olivier. The memory of this was often blurred, and when the attacks had passed she was once again his adoring handmaiden.

Olivier faced each day not knowing what to expect, grateful when she was "my Vivien," and treating the other—the manic Vivien—as an untouchable. Work and his career were the only constants he knew, and he concentrated wholly on them. But there never was any question of his deep love for Vivien, and when she was her loving, giving self he was as bewitched by her as he had always been. He thought of her in much that way—a witch, a sorceress: the air, the wind, the sky. She was the most beautiful woman in the world, an enchantress, not like any other mortal being.

Olivier was not the only one to be mesmerized by Vivien. In childhood it had been the Mother General and her peers at Roehampton. Hadn't she received special privileges without arousing the jealousy of the other girls? Leigh had worshiped her and gone on loving and caring for her long after she had left him for Larry. Jill had never been able to be unkind to her. Old friends of Jill's and Larry's, who at first thought her behavior reprehensible, were immediately won over by her. Men adored her and pandered to her, but women seldom felt envy or competitiveness. "Can one envy a goddess?" a close woman friend inquired. "Or hate the sea because it storms or the sky because it darkens? No. One waits, grateful to be alive, until the storm calms and the sea is breathless and glittering blue again and the sun rises in a matchless pastel dawn. That's how it was with Vivien."

When Larry returned to be with her at Notley, she was slimmer, paler, more beautiful than ever. There was a new aura about her, not a sadness, but a pervading sensitivity, as though she had somehow ascended to a higher level of perceptiveness and understanding. She was humbly appreciative to be home, to be with Larry. She had received a warm and moving letter from Noël Coward that she read and reread constantly and kept in her pocket or in her purse at all times. "Dear Lord, I'm so grateful I'm still loved," she would say and pat Coward's note.

Plans remained for Olivier to stage Terence Rattigan's *The Sleeping Prince* that August of 1953 for the coronation festivities, and he was quickly becoming convinced that no medication, treatment, or rest would be as beneficial to Vivien as her active participation in the project. He consulted the doctors, who warned him it was chancy but nonetheless worth the chance. Only six weeks after she had been released from Netherine Hospital, it was announced at one of Vivien's first outings—a party in honor of Rattigan—that she and Larry would star as the Prince and the showgirl in his new play to be directed by Olivier at the Phoenix Theatre.

"Am I finished with Hollywood? Good heavens, no!" Vivien told a reporter at the party. "I shall certainly go back there if there is a film to make and fly there, too. I did some hard thinking while I was ill. I just felt all washed up and never wanted to see a camera or a stage again. But I stared myself in the face and mapped out a new way of living. I shall work just as hard, but rest harder, too. It's early to bed from now on. And as for *Elephant Walk*—well, you mustn't blame the elephants." She grinned wickedly.

She flew to the Riviera, where she relaxed on Alexander Korda's yacht, *Elsewhere*. Korda's influence on her was always steadying, and much like Leigh's. She admired him intensely and greatly respected his sense of family loyalty. And wherever Sir Alex was, other Korda family members were sure to be. The yacht was at once a place of luxury and a floating family home, as Alex restlessly alternated between the desire to anchor in the harbors of idyllic fishing villages and his equal passion to play chemin de fer at Monte Carlo or Cannes.

Rattigan's fairy tale about a rather unpleasant Balkan prince who is lured by an American showgirl into a romantic affair on the eve of his coronation was rescheduled for a November 1953 opening, which meant that it would not be on the boards at the same time as the coronation. This somewhat eased the pressures on Olivier. Back in London in time for the gala event, they watched the majestic procession from the large windows in Olivier's private office. It rained throughout. The spectators huddled under umbrellas in the street stands, but guards and statesmen rode unprotected on horseback and in open carriages. Winston Churchill, without the usual stout cigar, waved, and the people shouted and cheered him.

On a small table in the office sat a television set, the sound turned up high so that they could hear the running commentary. When the procession was over they gathered about the set. The young Queen Elizabeth looked glowing in her splendid costumes and magnificent royal jewels. There was about her a sense of humility as she sat with her hands crossed and resting on her robes. Vivien watched with tears in her eyes. "How sad it must be for the Duke and Duchess of Windsor not to have been invited," she commented. She cried when the crown was placed on the new Queen's head.

Later thousands stood outside Buckingham Palace. A thunderous roar came from the crowd as the new royal couple (looking like tiny waving specks on the small TV set) stepped onto the balcony. Vivien sighed so deeply that one of the secretaries took a step forward, thinking she might be feeling ill.

They previewed *The Sleeping Prince* in Manchester, and Vivien's dressing room was filled with huge baskets of flowers. They were warmly received and she was given a standing ovation. She appeared to withstand the rigors of the performance and took several curtains smiling radiantly. The same empathy and enthusiasm marked the London opening at the Phoenix Theatre, on Thursday, November 5, 1953, Vivien's fortieth birthday. She never looked more beautiful than she did in the costumes for her role as Mary Morgan, the showgirl, but it was Martita Hunt who was the great success of the evening, making a gorgeous thing of the comic Grand Duchess. Vivien, though she made a gallant try, was truly miscast as a Brooklyn chorus girl. Rattigan had feared this was the case all during rehearsals, but Olivier had felt confident he was wrong.

There was one moment when the audience always broke up with laughter. Olivier, as the aging Prince, and with little time to lose in which to seduce the chorus girl, glances impatiently at the clock and delivers the line "Ah yes, my child, here I am, having reached the age of forty . . ." There was a split second freeze of alarm, the most imperceptible of pauses, and then the continuation of the speech: "I have never found true love," spoken on a slightly hysterical note and telegraphing to the audience the truth that the Prince was about to reveal his true age—forty-five—and then stopped. The line appeared to disturb Vivien in each performance. She was forty and there was little she could do to forget it.

The Oliviers still brought magic to the theatre, but the play did not seem to have the effervescence it should have, and though Larry—made up with a pasty complexion, a thin, rather humorless mouth, his hair parted grotesquely in the middle and brought unattractively downward over his ears, and wearing a pompous monocle on his right eye—had caught Rattigan's Prince Uncharming perfectly, he had also taken his role too seriously, imparting a certain weightiness to an evening that should have been served up much lighter. The coronation had brought flocks of Americans to England, and tourists were everywhere. The theatre was packed at each performance with audiences eager to see the glamorous Oliviers on stage together. One American visitor was heard to describe the play as "a breath of old caviar." By the time it closed, however, the pressures it had placed on Vivien had taken their toll. She was exhausted, and the spells of depression came and went alarmingly close together.

In 1954, Olivier was preparing to film *Richard III*, and he cast the young Claire Bloom in the role Vivien had played on the Australian tour six years earlier.

During those days there was little they dared talk about. A silence was growing between them that terrified Vivien. She tried to reach him with the right word, but Larry no longer seemed to hear her. She began to guess that behind his dark, intense stare, his silence, his constant preoccupation with his own needs, something she had no part in was developing. Her Larry had embarked upon a private and locked-away life of his own. They both now invited their own friends to Notley, and many of their good companions were drawn into separate camps. Vivien became flirtatious with other men, especially with Peter Finch. No other marriage could have sustained what theirs did, but the fact was they were held together by the same strong passion and need for each other that they had had from the very beginning. Neither was willing to give up the past, which they clung to as reality, for the present, which they refused to see as anything other than a bad dream from which both would one day soon awaken.

Tarquin had graduated from Eton and was in national service in the Coldstream Guards. He was commissioned in early 1955, carried the colors, changed guard at Buckingham Palace, and marched through the streets of the City to guard the Bank of England. Father and son seemed to be losing ground in their struggle for a working relationship. Olivier by then had suffered several years of Vivien's illness. There was no doubting his pride in Tarquin and his growing fondness and admiration for the young man. Expressing it seemed too difficult, however. At Eton, for his last piano concert, Tarquin had hammered away at Chopin's "Revolutionary Study," hoping that his father would come to hear it at the school concert. Olivier did not attend and it had been a crushing blow to his son. Tarquin therefore steeled himself upon receiving his commission, certain his father would take no note of the occasion.

That night the sergeant on guard burst into the barracks room chuckling, a buff-colored envelope between his five thumbs. He knew Tarquin was the son of Sir Laurence and he was a great fan of the theatre. " 'Ere, sir"—he grinned—"some ruddy message for *you!*"

In the envelope was a poem dictated via telephone from Notley by Olivier to the sergeant. Tarquin took out the Army message forms from inside the envelope and read the following written in the sergeant's somewhat clumsy hand:

Hail resplendent Ensign, you young blade.
But why dost tempt to put thy father in the shade
With plume, mirrored leather and gold braid?
Coulds't not remain a private economical?
Must Dad now find thee wardrobes astronomical?

Must Dad now curb his splendid voyage into wrong
To keep his son in wine, in women, and in song
While St. James from the theatre to the Palace throng
Fashion insists true feelings be denied
And this poem must try father's doting pride.

For most of 1954 and 1955 Vivien remained at Notley under the care of doctors, fighting desperately against what she feared might become the permanent loss of sanity. There were few friends who were not aware of her battle or of the enormous courage she employed to overcome her illness. She was beginning to recognize the signs of an approaching attack and would send for Gertrude when they occurred. During her well periods she was the same grand and gracious hostess, the same thoughtful friend, the same sensitive and caring companion. For Larry and Gertrude it was like living with two different women.

To all those close it seemed that even though work exerted pressures on her it created a discipline in her life that stabilized her condition. Except for the horror of filming *Elephant Walk*, she appeared able to control her emotions when performing. She would, as did happen while doing *The Sleeping Prince*, stand brooding and mumbling incoherently in the wings. But as soon as she was on stage there was no evidence of her problem. Some of this could be explained by the fact that Vivien was an exceptionally ordered, controlled performer. Her performance was always set by the end of rehearsals and she relied on an exact assured technique. Nothing, not even a hand gesture, would vary once a show had opened. What she did on the stage, therefore, was very much rote, allowing her to park her own psyche in the wings to be collected after the last curtain. Film was different, however, for one had to create a sense of immediacy for the camera, and it took a good director to "get at" a performer incisively enough to elicit the actor's best response.

Terence Rattigan's *The Deep Blue Sea* had been a fair success on the stage starring the great Peggy Ashcroft. Alexander Korda had plans to film it in 1955 and had signed Anatole Litvak to direct and Rattigan to write his own screenplay. Vivien, always secure in Korda's hands, agreed to make the film. Rattigan described his play as the story of "an affinity between a man and a woman who are mutually destructive to each other." The woman, Hester Collyer, is married but obsessed with another man who is of inferior clay.

Both film script and play suffered from a basic dishonesty. Hester's feminine gender seemed a cloak to appease theatregoers and censors, for an underlying story of a homosexual triangle came through in almost all the strong confrontation scenes. Vivien was therefore handicapped from the start because film glaringly magnified this sham. Her performance also suffered because of the lack of sexual chemistry between her and Kenneth More, who played her lover. Vivien appeared to have checked all immediate emotion the other side of the camera, just as she left it in the wings when she was on stage. Perhaps because she was able to do this she was also able to get through the film.

This ability heartened Olivier. So much so that he decided she should appear with him in a season at the Shakespeare Memorial Theatre, Stratford-upon-Avon, beginning that April of 1955 with a production of *Twelfth Night*. In June they would present *Macbeth*, in

August *Titus Andronicus*. He wanted desperately to negate her illness, to prove that it had all been a bad dream. He did not want to make a lot of money, and in truth Vivien liked being Lady Olivier more than he enjoyed being Sir Laurence. First and foremost he was obsessed with acting the great stage roles, becoming the English-speaking world's greatest classical actor. No lesser ambitions befogged that desire.

Vivien knew he remained very much in love with her but that his ambitions came first. She wanted the world to acknowledge his greatness as much as he wanted it for himself. A king ideally should have a queen, however, and Lady Olivier had always been to the royal manner born. Vivien, therefore, struggled to rise to the challenge he presented her. So, enthusiastically and gratefully, she tore into the difficult and diverse roles of Viola, Lady Macbeth, and Lavinia. She wanted to share Larry's work, to be given another chance to prove her worthiness, and she wanted to be loved.

For Vivien to want to play opposite Olivier was one thing, but for him to expect her to master and to perform the roles of Lady Macbeth and Lavinia, both seething with horror and madness, seems, considering her recent medical history, to have been a dangerous step. He could not have been unaware of the fact that these three roles would have been an almost impossible challenge to her even before her collapse.

Titus Andronicus is above all else a horror story that takes place in a nightmare world. It is filled with violations and madness. It is an anthology of atrocities. The play had never before been presented at Stratford, perhaps because it was so horrific. But also it had been a matter of debate for generations whether or not, in fact, Shakespeare had actually written this gargoyle tragedy of bloody revenge. The old Roman general, Titus Andronicus, disaster raining down thunderbolts on his wiry gray head, was a role Olivier could act on the grand scale. Titus severs heads with abandon and his own hand in a vain effort to save his two sons. He kills Queen Tamora's sons and serves their heads to her in a pie, and he finally stabs his daughter, Lavinia, to death before he himself is killed.

In Act I, Lavinia is a spirited character, but by the end of Act II she is led back on stage after having been ravished, her hands cut off, and her tongue cut out—a pathetic mute creature who after three more profoundly moving acts is murdered by her father in the last scene of the play. "Die, die Lavinia," cries Titus. "And thy shame with thee . . ."

Horror, death, and madness were also themes of *Macbeth*, which

Olivier had first played in 1937. He saw it differently now, more as a domestic tragedy really. He felt that an intriguing aspect of the play was the fact that Macbeth had imagination, Lady Macbeth none, and that Macbeth saw what was going to happen and she did not. "That's what gives her the enormous courage to plot the whole thing," Olivier explained. "She persuades him, cajoles him, bullies him and he allows himself gradually, bit by bit, to be teased into it. But he knows the result and she doesn't and it's sort of—it's the passage of two people doing that. One going up and one going down."

As they moved into rehearsal for the season at Stratford, it became obvious that in both *Titus* and *Macbeth* Olivier was reaching for a deeper psychological penetrativeness. Certainly with *Macbeth* he was the psychiatrist probing his own and his lady's diseased mind. Each of the three plays was to have a different director: John Gielgud for *Twelfth Night*, Glen Byam Shaw for *Macbeth*, and Peter Brook for *Titus Andronicus*. But Olivier came to each production with his own interpretation, and for a director to countermand this would have been like flying directly into the eye of a hurricane. Olivier had always sought the psychological motivations of his characters along with an identification that he could, with the greatest concentration, feel within himself. The summer was therefore spent with madness and its examination.

The initial play of the season was *Twelfth Night*, which opened in April, and Vivien's role, Viola, a happy, romantic one. She adored Gielgud, but as director and actress they were not on the same wavelength. Rehearsals became successively more chaotic, with Gielgud changing his mind about interpretations every other day. Olivier was playing his role, Malvolio, in an unusual and realistic manner, as if he were appearing in a psychological drama. Vivien acted her part as romantic comedy. The play seemed shapeless.

Olivier's lust for acting greatness had finally taken precedence over his love for Vivien. Perhaps this was not a conscious move on his part—the actor had usurped the man. He could rationalize this by noting that Vivien was also being given the chance at three marvelous roles. But somewhere there had to be an awareness that her finest performances were those that allowed her to be charming and beautiful or a fading beauty, as with Scarlett, Emma Hamilton, Juliet, Cleopatra, and Blanche. Viola could have been a successful role for her, but it was impossible to be charming and romantic as Viola when Olivier played Malvolio as a plain, unlikable man, turning away from any familiar interpretation. Much of the laughter that usually sprang from Malvolio's dialogue was gone, and so her own frivolous reactions as Viola seemed painfully shallow. It was like combining a Wagner opera with a Strauss waltz. Yet Olivier hushed the entire audience in the moment when Malvolio cries out, "I'll be avenged on the whole pack of you," with a poignantly accusing and exquisitely studied cry.

The critics spent most of their words lauding Olivier's performance, where only a few lines were given to Vivien. "Lovely to look at," said *The Times* critic, ". . . like some happy hunting boy," adding, "She is in her romantic way a little too 'knowing' to convey the natural and transparent honesty which is designed for those who are dupes of their own sentimentalism."

There were weekends at Notley between performances. Olivier never was happier than when he was in Notley's stately library in his smoking jacket, looking every inch the lord of the manor. He would stand at the window with a guest gazing out at the lovely grounds that were his and confide how he would like to have children to play on those lawns. He spoke quite often about children being a man's only true bid for immortality. Tarquin had received his honors degree (M.A.) in philosophy, politics and economics at Christ Church, Oxford, and he was a frequent visitor at Notley. One weekend he met Quentin Keynes, the explorer, and a tremendous interest in the underdeveloped countries was kindled in the young man, who seemed gripped at the time by a desperate need to feel morally committed to a cause that he could embrace emotionally.

Vivien was the same marvelous, generous hostess she had always been as she filled the house with friends and cast members. It never ceased to amaze new acquaintances and co-workers how knowledgeable she was on all subjects. In one weekend she would startle guests with her depth of understanding of art, architecture, antiques, music, animals, trees, and flowers. It seemed that whatever came up in discussion Vivien was well acquainted with the subject. She always rotated the groups of cast members so no one would feel slighted. Some, of course, she was closer to than others.

She was quite friendly with Maxine Audley, whom she had asked Gielgud to cast as Olivia in *Twelfth Night*. (That season Miss Audley also played Lady Macduff in *Macbeth*, and Tamora, the fiendlike Queen, in *Titus Adronicus*.) Miss Audley had recently become a mother, but children were a subject Vivien did not care to discuss. "Well, I do long to have another baby," she confided when pressed. "But I would have to stop work if I became pregnant and do precious little for nine months and I don't think that would suit my nature."

If she meant her restlessness, it was much in evidence as they began rehearsals for *Macbeth*. From the start things seemed to be going badly between Larry and Vivien, and it was noticeable to all the cast. Curiously, everyone thought it indirectly helped their individual performances. Then Peter Finch began turning up more and more frequently at Notley and at Stratford. He and Vivien could be seen hand in hand together all the time. Olivier reacted with a rather shoulder-shrugging attitude. Nonetheless, one could see he was far from happy. It was a great source of gossip among the company and a solemn concern for all, for both were very much loved, and as *Macbeth* came together on stage so did their anger and hostility. The deeper they got in the production, the more distraught Vivien became. Finch was tremendously supportive, and certainly after his experience with Vivien in Ceylon he knew what he might be faced with at any time.

Macbeth opened on a Tuesday night, June 7. Once again there were more than a thousand words by *The Times* critic containing praise for Olivier and only two lines about Vivien. "Miss Vivien Leigh appears as a small, baleful, gleaming Lady Macbeth but her looks and her voice are disconcertingly at odds."

They all spent the following Sunday at Notley, Finch included, where they gathered together all the Sunday papers to read the reviews.

Tynan had written in the *Sunday Observer*, "Last Tuesday Sir Laurence shook hands with greatness, and within a week or so the performance will have ripened into a masterpiece." He ended his review by stating, "Miss Vivien Leigh's Lady Macbeth is more niminy-piminy than thundery-blundery, more viper than anaconda, but still quite competent in its small way. Macduff and his wife, actor-proof parts, are played with exceptional power by Mr. Keith Michell and Miss Maxine Audley."

Vivien was furious at Tynan's slighting review of her performance. But Olivier did not turn his anger on the young critic this time. To the contrary, he was becoming quite interested in him and commented on the young man's obvious intelligence. It wasn't long before Tynan was a frequent guest at Notley, and Vivien was forced by her own instinctive good breeding to treat him as graciously as her other guests, a gesture made more difficult after his review of *Titus Andronicus*.

Tynan wrote, "Sir Laurence Olivier's Titus, even with one hand gone, is a five-finger exercise transformed into an unforgettable concerto of grief. This is a performance which ushers us into the presence of one who is pound for pound the greatest actor alive." He then notes that "Maxine Audley is a glittering Tamora. As Lavinia, Vivien Leigh received the news that she is about to be ravished on her husband's corpse with little more than the mild annoyance of one who would have preferred foam rubber. Otherwise, the minor parts are played up to the hilt."

It did not seem to help that *The Times* critic thought she had played Lavinia "with statuesque pathos," certainly not as long as Tynan was in Larry's camp. Her condition was becoming treacherously shaky. One night she went with Maxine Audley to see John Gielgud in *King Lear* and cried throughout the performance. The fear of madness was beginning to obsess her, and the company was concerned that she might collapse before the end of the season.

Everyone was relieved when the season ended. Vivien, Finch, and Olivier went to Notley. Vivien was feeling incredibly insecure. She had let Larry down. Somehow she should have been able to reach down inside herself for a deeper and newer understanding of Viola, a more tortured Lady Macbeth, a Lavinia who rose to greater stature. But she was forever fearful of digging deeply and perhaps unleashing some of her own private passion. If she did that, then where would it end? How could she stop the flow?

Once they were home, Larry retreated to the library and his voluminous correspondence and plans for the future. He did not appear threatened by Finch's presence. An aura of Victorian forbearance pervaded the ancient halls of the Abbey and everyone was impeccably polite. Vivien's nerves were at the very edge. If she wanted and expected Larry to create a row about Finch she was wrong. A few days later she packed a bag and without a word to Larry boarded a train with Finch, planning to run off with him. But as she sat in the first-class compartment staring out the window at the countryside she began to panic. Part of it was the extreme claustrophobia she suffered at times, but apparently she also had second thoughts about leaving Larry and feared that, in fact, he would not come after her.

A few moments later she pulled the emergency cord and left the train with Finch. They returned to Notley, where Vivien rang Gertrude and asked her to join them.

Then she collapsed into one of her terrifying attacks of hysteria.

Chapter Twenty-four

Vivien held friendship to be one of the most important elements of life, and few people could number more intimates. She corresponded regularly with thirty or more "dear friends," never forgetting their birthdays, anniversaries, weddings, opening nights, and celebrations. She adored flowers. Notley was always filled with massive bouquets in each room, as were Durham Cottage and any hotel room she ever slept in. She keenly loved sending flowers for any occasion, always in beautiful and elegant profusion.

Often in the mornings she would sit at her Queen Anne desk by the leaded glass windows of her bedroom at Notley and write eight to ten personal letters consecutively on her soft blue stationery and in her most-difficult-to-read but strong hand. She thought it a complete breach of good manners to dictate or type personal correspondence. "My Darling Sweet Cindy," her letter to Lucinda Ballard Dietz would begin, "Dear, dear Master" to Noël, "Darling Leigh"—effusive terms of endearment were sent across the Thames, the Channel, and the Atlantic. Vivien did more than keep in touch, she maintained an involvement in all her friends' lives. Depressions and happy occasions were shared, illnesses were discussed, disappointments were met with cheery support. There always seemed to be a special gift to buy, a wedding, a christening, a funeral to attend. Her flower bills were enormous, her postal charges exorbitant, as gifts, letters, and flowers were sent to Leigh, the Dietzes, Noël, Bobby Helpmann, Katharine Hepburn, George Cukor, Lynn Fontanne, Margalo Gilmore, Madeleine Sherwood, Cedric Hardwicke, Clifton Webb, Cyril Ritchard,

"Sweet darling Maggie" and Jean-Louis, Radie Harris and Percy Harris and Arnold Weissberger, the Bogarts, the Harrisons, the Redgraves, the Millses, the Nivens . . . and, of course, Victor Stiebel, Kit Cornell, John Gielgud, Suzanne, Tarquin, Larry's sister Sybille, his sister-in-law Hester, his nieces Caroline and Louise and . . . the list was endless.

Her vast correspondence helped fill the time of her intermittent periods of "convalescing," though when she was working or enjoying good health she still kept it up. Contact with close friends was essential to her well-being. She had to feel that there were many loving thoughts being held of her. And she wrote everyone whom she thought might have been hurt by one of her attacks—humble letters begging forgiveness.

The gardens of Notley took a great deal of her time and energy. She still devoured books and she had also taken up painting (though not noticeably exceptional at it). Both she and Larry greatly admired Winston Churchill, who claimed that *Lady Hamilton* was his favorite film and that he had seen it many times. He encouraged Vivien to paint and had given her a painting he had done of three roses, and she had it hanging opposite her bed so it would be the first thing she saw upon awakening.

The closeness to Finch had for a time placed a strain on the marriage, but in actual fact the nature of Vivien's illness and its ramifications were the major cause. When she had one of her attacks Larry was the worst person she could be with. For several years he had clung to the hope that some miracle would come along to change things. But that period had passed. He now carried around a deep ache of pity for her and for himself. She was a beautiful child whom he had loved, but things could never be as they once were.

In their private worlds both lived in the shadow of past memory for each other. The picture of Larry remained at all times by her bedside, and they would spend evenings in front of the open stone fireplace in the small garden room at Notley fondly recalling the laughter and tears of past experiences.

The year 1956 started off hopefully. She had not had an attack for quite some time and was in fine spirits. Then on January 22 Alexander Korda suffered a fatal heart attack. Vivien was distraught. Losing a dear friend was always a tremendous shock and threw her into instant depression. But Korda was more than a dear friend. He was her mentor, a man she looked up to with almost the same reverence and intensity as she did Larry. His death was a hard and difficult blow for her to take and set her back considerably.

About this time Olivier received a most unusual offer to direct and co-star in a film version of *The Sleeping Prince*, to be shot in England. Milton Greene, an American photographer and close friend of Marilyn Monroe's, had bought the rights from Rattigan with plans for Marilyn to play the showgirl. Immediately the title was changed to *The Prince and the Showgirl*. By the end of February Larry had made up his mind to go ahead with the film, but he did not tell Vivien of his plans. The reasons were perhaps two-fold—Vivien remained in a state of depression and he was concerned she would react badly to being replaced by the younger Monroe in a role she had created. If he played opposite, no matter what the considerations, it would certainly compound that injury. With the offer coming so soon after Korda's death and at a time of her inactivity, he was incapable of dealing her yet another blow, though it would seem he was sufficiently self-oriented not to turn aside the project on her account.

Noël, "the Master," as they called him, seemed heaven-sent when he came to spend a weekend at Notley and talked about his new comedy, *South Sea Bubble*, hinting that he would love to have Vivien take the role of Lady Alexandra Shotter. Vivien, of course, asked to read the playscript. It was not good, but, as Larry said, it was still "the Master," and there were some splendid moments of Coward's brittle humor. Her decision to do the play, though, was more attributable to Larry's great enthusiasm. Granted, with Vivien cast in a play, his own conscience about doing *The Prince and the Showgirl* was eased. But it also meant Vivien would be participating in a production that would not tax her as classic theatre did and that she would be appearing with Noël, who—like Leigh and George Cukor—was one of the people with whom she simply was never "naughty," and with whom she felt secure. The play went almost immediately into rehearsals, for it was to open at the Lyric Theatre in eight weeks' time.

With Vivien settled, Olivier flew to New York to meet Greene and Monroe. A press conference was held and it was so widely covered that full details reached Vivien in England. There were pictures of Marilyn clinging seductively to Olivier's arm and wearing a tight black velvet sheath cut so low her breasts were almost entirely revealed. A reporter asked Olivier his opinion of Marilyn as a film actress. "She has an extremely extraordinary gift of being able to suggest one moment that she is the naughtiest little thing and the next that she's perfectly innocent, and the audience therefore leaves the theatre gently titillated into a state of excitement," he pronounced.

Not to be upstaged, Marilyn's shoulder strap broke, and with a soft and seductive cry that made all eyes turn immediately to her, she saved herself from total exposure. One reporter was ungallant enough to ask if she had purposely broken the strap. She looked at him with wide innocent eyes and smiled, saying nothing.

South Sea Bubble was stale champagne to the critics when it opened on April 25, 1956. "Miss Leigh brings cool effrontery to the business," said *The Times* critic. Still, as Olivier had noted, "it was the Master," and so when Marilyn and her new husband, playwright Arthur Miller, arrived at the London airport at the beginning of July, the play was still running.

Vivien accompanied Larry to the airport to meet the newlyweds. The press stampeded them all, and one photographer was injured in the crush. The Oliviers drove with the Millers in a limousine to the country estate that they had rented for the American couple in Egham in Windsor Park, a thirty-car caravan of baggage (Marilyn had twenty-seven pieces) and press following them.

The two women could not be said to have "got on well" together. Marilyn was ill at ease. The chauffeur called Vivien "your ladyship," the press "Lady Olivier," and Vivien had an elegance along with her musical and beautifully articulated English accent that made Marilyn self-conscious.

It is difficult to imagine that Olivier did the film for any other reason than money. The script was charming, and Olivier had enjoyed playing the Prince on stage; but there seemed little advantage in terms of his own greater ambitions in doing the role over again. And he was almost immediately regretful that he had done so, for Marilyn was impossible to work with, attempting to bring to the screen her newly acquired Method approach to acting—which he abhorred—and bringing with her Paula Strasberg, her drama coach, for constant advice (none of which Olivier agreed with) on how to play a scene. She was invariably two, three, or four hours late on the set. Sometimes Miller would call in that she was ill and would not be able to work at all. It was unheard-of behavior in Olivier's eyes, the height of unprofessionalism, and he thought of her as "a troublesome bitch."

But it was Vivien not Marilyn who was in the headlines when *The Prince and the Showgirl* went before the cameras. She was pregnant after sixteen years of marriage and at forty-two years of age. She announced to the press that she would soon leave the Coward play, as the baby was due in five months. No sooner done than she was a daily visitor on *The Prince and the Showgirl* set. Maxine Audley was in the film and the two would chat on the sidelines. There were many ugly rumors floating about that Vivien was not pregnant at all, that she had announced the event to draw attention from Marilyn. "Why had she waited until she was four months along?" they buzzed. She remained her slim self and each time she came onto the set her detractors would be watching for "signs."

Sitting with her feet up on another chair one day, she confessed to Maxine Audley, "The only trouble with being pregnant is that I have to have my feet up all the time and that bores me stiff. I guess I'm just not a maternal person, after all."

Four weeks after the first press release, Olivier announced that Vivien had suffered a miscarriage and had been ordered to take a complete rest and not to see anyone.

"We are bitterly disappointed and terribly upset," he said. "The main concern now is Vivien. The important thing is that she should make a complete recovery."

She had suffered more a mental than a physical collapse. There was ahead of them the slow agony of trying to learn to live with her illness, for Larry knew she was not just a neurotic or hysterical woman. She was a manic-depressive who had been diagnosed by more than one doctor as schizophrenic. Fortunately, she had suffered no serious lung flare-up, for as the doctors had explained to Larry, her tubercular condition aggravated the manic problem. To Vivien, who had so many times suffered extreme feelings of helplessness and terror, it seemed there was no escape. She went along with every effort to help her (drugs, shock, and psychotherapy), except suggestions that she return to the hospital.

It took the entire fall of 1956 for her to fight her way back from what she was terrified might be a final descent into madness. Although no one was quite sure what brought on her attacks, a pattern was beginning to show itself. First she would enter into a depressive phase, which was of gradual onset. She would become increasingly depressed, find it difficult to think and concentrate, lose her appetite and weight, be unable to sleep without help, and hold suicidal thoughts (though suicide did not seem an actual threat at the time). The manic phase would be of sudden onset. She would feel a marked elevation of mood and begin to lose her natural restraint and normal reserve. She would always turn on Larry, say whatever came to her mind, and suddenly lose judgment, reasoning power, and insight. Then severe claustrophobia would set in. She would tear her clothes off, feel the desperate need to jump out of a car, train, or plane in which she might be riding. The attention to impeccable grooming would disappear and she would slip into slovenly habits.

Dr. Arthur Conachy, who did not believe she was schizophrenic but diagnosed her as a manic-depressive, was the one doctor she truly trusted. In a report that traveled with her, in case she should be seized with an attack beyond the range of his London offices, Dr. Conachy wrote, "She develops marked increase in libido and indiscriminate sexual activity. These illustrations of her symptoms, particularly her overt sexuality, loss of judgement and persistent overdrive, make me feel, that for a person in her position, from the social and publicity consequences that arise from this, that her manic phase is much more undesirable than the depressed phase."

He explained that during her most recent attack "I administered five electroconvulsive treatments under general anesthesia of sodium pentothal and with scoline as a muscle relaxant given by an anesthetist. I used a Shotter-Rich electronarcosis machine to avoid memory loss, but any good E.C.T. machine, providing it is certain that a convulsion has been triggered off, would be adequate.

"The one undesirable factor in this pattern," he concludes, "is her tendency to take considerable and regular amounts of alcohol particularly in moments of stress. She refuses to modify this, but is in no sense an alcoholic." It was a known medical fact now that liquor accelerated her attacks.

If Vivien was beginning to lose a foothold on her confidence, Olivier had begun to react to success with a complete confidence that he had never quite felt before. The public approved wholeheartedly of him. He had come to feel a certain hypnotic power over his audience.

At the time he felt a great need to appear in a contemporary play, and he spoke to the Royal Court's George Devine to ask if John Osborne might be writing a new play that had a role for him in it. Osborne, in fact, was working on *The Entertainer*, and was stunned by "the King's" request; but he sent him the playscript when it was complete. Vivien read it and immediately wanted to play the wife, if Olivier played Archie Rice. This was the early spring of 1957, and she had had several months to recuperate from her last collapse.

They no longer had Durham Cottage and planned to stop at the

Connaught Hotel when they were in London. Osborne came over to the hotel to discuss the possibilities of Vivien being cast in the play opposite Olivier. "The trouble is that Vivien is too beautiful to play this kind of part," Olivier kept saying. Then they sat around for hours debating the ludicrous suggestion (Olivier's) that Vivien wear a rubber mask to make her look plain and ugly.

In the end she did not appear in *The Entertainer* (Brenda de Banzie took the part) and Olivier was greatly relieved. He was meeting a new challenge, breaking away from the world of Establishment theatre and Vivien's world as well, and going it alone. It was the first time since before *Romeo and Juliet* that he had no other responsibilities than to be an actor, for once he was not playing with Vivien or directing her or himself.

Vivien did not accept the situation with grace, and she came to the theatre a great deal during rehearsals. Olivier had chosen a young actress, Joan Plowright, to portray his daughter in the play. Vivien did not think she was right and Osborne did not like her, but Olivier insisted, feeling that she represented the new school of acting. Vivien's presence at rehearsals made Olivier terribly nervous—a new effect she was having on him. She also made her influence felt, criticizing Larry, Joan Plowright, and director Tony Richardson. Finally she had a furious quarrel with George Devine, and directly after the first dress rehearsal she was asked not to come to the theatre.

Archie Rice was perhaps one of the most outstanding and impressive performances Olivier had ever given. Indeed, many critics now felt he was not only the greatest classic actor in the English theatre but the greatest comedic actor as well. For Vivien, however, that entire spring was fraught with disappointment. Olivier had tried to get a film production of *Macbeth* off the ground (she was to play Lady Macbeth) but failed. Then Hecht-Lancaster Productions in Hollywood offered them the starring roles in their film version of Terence Rattigan's *Separate Tables*, but they could not reach an agreement on the script.

By summer's approach Vivien appeared to be heading into the depressive phase of her illness. Olivier, perhaps feeling otherwise helpless, set plans for a summer tour with the original cast of *Titus Andronicus* to Paris, Venice, Belgrade, Zagreb, Vienna, Warsaw, and then back to the Stoll Theatre in London.

Olivier decided that Vivien, he, and the entire company would travel by train rather than fly, taking into consideration first Vivien's fear of flying and second the chance the company would have to relax between engagements. However, it was May when they started out, the weather had grown unseasonably hot, the trains were jammed with tourists, and the distances between cities were quite tiresome.

They opened in Paris on May 16. Ten days later, at a ceremony on the stage of the Sarah Bernhardt Theatre, Vivien was decorated with the Knight's Cross of the Légion d'Honneur. Olivier was already an officer of the Légion d'Honneur. Vivien's decoration was conferred by M. Seydoux, the Director of Cultural Relations at the Quai d'Orsay, "for services rendered to the cultural relations and friendship between France and Great Britain." *Titus Andronicus* had been a huge success in Paris, and Vivien met with better treatment by the French critics than she had by the English.

From Paris they rode by train to Venice. The weather had become boiling hot and Vivien was showing signs of strain. The company was, in fact, noticing a sharp difference in her behavior patterns, and being in such close quarters they were conscious that she was roller-coasting into a manic condition much like the one they had seen at the end of the Stratford run. By the time they reached Belgrade she was smoking and drinking excessively and was in a terribly agitated state.

For Olivier, Yugoslavia and Warsaw were a new experience. The people did not know him, but crowds would follow them wherever they went and scream, "Scarlett! Scarlett!" Scarlett O'Hara was known all over, and they packed the theatres to see her, waiting impatiently, shouting for her outside the dressing rooms, hotel rooms, and train cars, practically trampling her, and pushing him to one side in an effort to get "Scarlett's" autograph. This hysteria did much to accelerate her own.

On the twenty-two-hour train journey from Vienna to Warsaw, the heat soared to over ninety degrees. The train was full, no food was served, and the company had to carry their own lunches and bottled water. Vivien paced the corridor nervously, her voice taking on a hard edge. Everyone was alerted, but no one knew what to do. Then suddenly she turned against Olivier and began to run up and down the corridor shouting. He tried to restrain her, but she broke away, picked up someone's makeup case, and hurled it, smashing a train window. Somehow members of the cast subdued her, and Olivier went into another car.

Her wrath then turned on Maxine Audley. Maxine had the rather choice role of the fiendish Queen Tamora, and Vivien berated her, also seemingly angry that Maxine had had a better dressing room than she in one of the theatres on tour. Maxine rose from her seat and moved away. Vivien followed, verbally attacking her. In an effort to escape the tirade, Maxine locked herself in the train toilet. Vivien banged heavily on the door. "Come out! Come out!" she shouted. Finally, Maxine heaved a deep sigh and stepped out into the corridor. Vivien bombarded her with pieces of bread as she made her way back to her seat. She was totally irrational and out of control. Finally, after sixteen hours, Vivien collapsed into an exhausted sleep. Most naturally the company was relieved, but the interesting and moving thing was that they felt even more protective toward her. No one took any offense at her hysterical outbursts and insults. They all recognized the severity of her illness and knew from past experience that when the attack was over she would once again be their darling, loving, kind, giving Vivien.

Once in Warsaw, a doctor was called. His visit and treatment was followed by hours of uncontrollable sobbing, but by the time of their first curtain in Warsaw she was back to a fairly normal state.

They returned to London in July, just in time to hear the news that the House of Lords was debating the issue of tearing down the 122-year-old St. James's Theatre, where Olivier had presented his first plays as actor-manager and where Charles Dickens had his first plays produced. The news set Vivien off. On July 20 she marched down the Strand ringing a handbell in protest. Two days later she swept imperiously into the visitors' gallery of the House of Lords and listened impatiently to the debate on the floor. Baron Blackford in argument for the tearing down of the St. James's declared the theatre was "simply an obsolete, Victorian, inconvenient, uncomfortable playhouse with no architectural or historic value." Vivien leaped furiously to her feet and shouted down over the gallery rail, "My Lords! I want to protest against St. James's Theatre being demolished!"

It was a terrible breach of protocol. Their lordships sat in stunned silence and Sir Brian Harrocks, the Gentleman Usher of the Black Rod, gravely put a restraining hand on Vivien's arm. "Now you will have to go, Lady Olivier," he said. Vivien tried to shrug him off. None of the lords moved a muscle as Sir Brian had to forcibly eject Vivien. And though her protest of the demolition of the St. James's Theatre coincided with one of her manic phases, it did look by the end of the week as though Scarlett O'Hara had saved Tara almost singlehandedly from the carpetbaggers. Churchill grumbled, "As a parliamentarian I cannot approve your disorderly method, but I shall pledge five hundred pounds to save the St. James's from being replaced by an office building." And American millionaire Huntington Hartford also contributed to a fund Vivien was sponsoring to save the St. James's. Within a week the House of Lords had gallantly voted a stay of demolition to the "cramped, outmoded, bomb-battered and much loved theatre." A cartoon appeared in *The Times*. In it Maxine Audley stood in the visitors' gallery of the House of Lords. "I protest against the demolition of Miss Vivien Leigh," the caption read.

It looked as if the St. James's would be saved, but the emotion spent in the protest exhausted Vivien and sent her into another deep depression. Olivier felt helpless. It seemed to him there was little more he could do, and in effect, he gave up at about that time. He was not unlike a man faced with an oncoming tidal wave. "What's the use of running?" his attitude implied. "Let whatever is to happen happen."

But Gertrude was not ready to give up the battle. She thought it possible Leigh could help because his presence always had a calming effect on Vivien. Leigh often visited them at Notley; and Olivier agreed that perhaps, since Vivien reacted so badly to him, she should take a three-week holiday and rest cure with Leigh and Suzanne. As soon as Vivien, Leigh, and Suzanne left for the Continent the press speculated that the Oliviers were about to divorce.

"There is absolutely no question of divorce," Vivien told reporters on the telephone from the Continent. "My first husband and I are still good friends and there is no earthly reason why I should not see him. Larry and I are very much in love."

To which Olivier, who was vacationing with Tarquin in Scotland, added, "I have no comment on something that does not exist."

Pictures appeared of Vivien resting in the sun at San Virgilio on the shores of Italy's Lake Gardo. Parliament immediately rose in its own protest against Vivien.

Mrs. Jenny Mann, a fiery Labourite Scotswoman and mother of five, declared angrily, "There is a woman who took the House of Lords by storm and she has gone on holiday with her first husband. Her second husband is on holiday elsewhere. I do not know of any protest about it. It would seem you can pack your first husband up— that is what our young people will be telling us—and you can go on holiday with him now and again. You might even be able to spend weekends with the first and the middle of the week with the second. It is a terrible example for people who occupy high places in life to place before young children. Where is the flood of indignation?"

Leigh was the only one to show any indignation. He cabled *The Times*: CRITICISM ILL-CONSIDERED AND UNMANNERLY. PRESENCE OUR DAUGHTER GIVES EXPLANATION HOLIDAY TO ANY REASONABLE PERSON.

The holiday with Leigh did seem to help, and Vivien returned to London looking more relaxed and beautiful than she had in a long while. No sooner had they returned than Suzanne's engagement to Robin Farrington, a twenty-nine-year-old insurance broker, was announced. They were married on December 6. Olivier and Vivien arrived at the church together, but he quickly stepped aside to let her be with Suzanne and Leigh. There was immediate buzzing in the pews. The rumors grew when, after the wedding, Vivien left with Leigh in a car and Olivier stood on the steps of the church with the other guests waving goodbye.

Chapter Twenty-five

Being manic-depressive was not like having a cold. Vivien could not simply suffer through and get over it. She had—at least until medicine became more advanced in the area—an incurable disease, and she knew it. Desperation seized her. Larry looked at her now with cool dark eyes locking away his private anguish. As matters stood, she was secretly fearful that the wounds inflicted on him by her attacks would drive him into the arms of another woman, and there were rumors that he was having an affair with Joan Plowright. Vivien did not blame him if it was true. In fact she found Larry blameless of all the somber, frightening things that had pervaded her life these past years. A dark, impenetrable fog seemed to be closing around her, and out in it stood something black and hooded, the shape of disaster. But it wasn't Larry, nor did she think he could save her from whatever or whoever it might be.

Larry was keeping her at a distance. There was no laughter between them anymore, no comfort in their bed. She was frightened and lonely. Telling him how much she loved him didn't help. They had always been meant for each other. It had been obvious from the very beginning, as had her consuming love for him. She had to dissipate his fears. He was weaker than she, not nearly as able to cope with anguish and adversity.

She read in a column that Joan Plowright might be leaving her husband for Olivier, but she refused to believe it. There was no way she could have discussed Joan with Larry. No newspaper gossipmonger had to hint that she was losing him. His detached concern confirmed it. How to hold him was uppermost in her thoughts. Joan was not yet thirty and could easily give him a family, a novice actress with great ambitions Larry could mold, and part of a new kind of theatre that excited him. But though Vivien no longer had youth, she had beauty, glitter, and taste—all things Larry greatly revered. They had found a flat in Eaton Square, which meant she would be in London when he was, and she set about making it a home that he would admire. Suzanne was pregnant, and Vivien had mixed emotions about being a grandmother. She could hardly be blamed, she told herself, for not giving Larry the children he wanted. Before her breakdown, children had not seemed to matter to him. And since, she had tried and miscarried. It was, then, God's will.

When they returned from the tour, *The Entertainer* was first transferred to the Palace Theatre, and then in 1958 the company moved to the Royale Theatre in New York. Larry and Joan were sharing day-to-day experiences; and Vivien was alone, an outsider. It seemed at the time that if she lost Larry nothing else in life would matter. What she feared most was the pity he sometimes revealed, the benevolent, somehow dispassionate sense of kindness.

In February 1958 she was offered the role of Paola in Jean Giraudoux's play *Duel of Angels*, which was to be presented at the Apollo in an elegant translation by Christopher Fry. She loved the play and the role; and it seemed to her the best way to prove to Larry that she could take responsibility and be a healthy, whole person, so she accepted the part. "When I come into the theatre at night I get a sense of security," she once said. "I love an audience. I love people, and I act because I like trying to give pleasure to people."

The theatre offered her the loving response she was not getting at home. Every night she would go in an hour and a half before curtain time and go through the entire performance aloud by herself. As soon as the makeup was on she felt like another woman. When the wig came off she was once again herself.

Duel of Angels was filled with talk of separation and a house divided, and the play took on an intimate personal meaning. "Sometimes," Vivien said at the time, "I dread the truth of the lines I say. But the dread must never show. I love the theatre for that discipline."

The play was well received. Vivien portrayed the pagan Paola, who is as hot in temper as in sex, with authority and conviction, making Claire Bloom's Lucile appear quite pallid in contrast. The Christian Dior period costumes in vivid scarlets and jeweled brocades were spectacular, and Vivien was breathlessly beautiful in them. But by summer the strain of Olivier's absence became too difficult. Manic signs again appeared, and she took a leave from the play to join Gertrude for a rest on the Continent. Olivier returned from New York and flew down to spend some time with her before filming *The Devil's Disciple* with Burt Lancaster and Kirk Douglas.

It was what she wanted more than anything else in the world, and yet it was impossible from the moment he arrived for her to control her behavior. She was delirious with happiness and felt young and wildly in love when she first greeted him. But by nightfall she began turning on him—just in small ways, but the signs were there. He left on the fourth day.

"Puss" was one of her favorite nicknames, one that Olivier called her in moments of fond affection, and cats had always been a passion of hers. Now she became obsessive about them. While holidaying with Gertrude she had two with her constantly, fondling them, watching them with deliberate attention for extremely long periods. Gertrude noted that during her attacks Vivien became quite catlike, her fingers arching, her eyes flashing strangely, a terrifying hissing sound coming from her when she was furious, and not wanting anyone to approach.

By November 5, her forty-fifth birthday, she had returned to the cast of *Duel of Angels*. Lauren Bacall was in London and remained at the theatre with her while she played two performances. Olivier presented her with a £7,000 Rolls-Royce that she had seen and liked at the motor show. Three nights later they threw a star-studded party for Lauren and 150 guests at the Milroy nightclub in Hamilton Place. Olivier smiled graciously at her side and Vivien looked incredibly beautiful in elegant turquoise brocade. The idea was to stanch the rumors that had been flowing freely in the press. They remained the perfect hosts, always making each arriving guest feel the night would not be complete without his or her presence. As each man entered he was given a red carnation by Vivien; each woman received a miniature red rose from Olivier.

Vivien was gleaming and happy flanked by so many good old friends—Douglas Fairbanks and his wife, Beatrice Lillie, the Jack Hawkinses, Emlyn Williams, Alec Guinness, Tarquin, Gertrude, Bernard Braden and Barbara Kelly, Richard Burton and Sybil, Kenneth More and his wife, Duncan Sandys, Herbert Wilcox and Anna Neagle. It was a glittering evening and Vivien was her enchanting effervescent old self, except in those rare moments when the famous Cheshire smile would fade and she could be caught wistfully watching Larry from a few feet away.

From the time of the party, Olivier seemed to make a point of keeping the Atlantic Ocean between them. On December 5, Suzanne gave birth to a son, Neville Leigh Farrington. The following morning the newspaper headlines declared: SCARLETT O'HARA NOW GRANDMA. "It's divine," Vivien told reporters. Then she added, "I've been a godmother loads of times, but being a grandmother is better than anything." She brushed away a tear, presumed to be caused by happiness, and raised a gin toast, which she drank slowly. That day she had lunch with Leigh. The fears of growing old filled her conversation. There was talk of her doing a play about Eva Perón of Argentina. "A lucky thing she was," Vivien said. "She died at thirty-two. I'm already forty-five."

Self-pity was not her nature, however. She refused to allow her ebullient spirit to be quelled. Olivier was in America for most of 1959, and Vivien surrounded herself with close friends and dazzling newcomers in her set and threw herself with headlong pleasure into London theatre life. She glowed beneath the extravagant compliments given her by the men she met casually or already knew. There was something reckless about her behavior. She was living utterly in the present. Clothes became a passion, gift-giving an expensive pastime. Lengthy letters crossed the Atlantic. She would always love Larry. No man could mean what he did to her, and so she was able to discount any discretions she might indulge in and ignore the cruelty of his new restraint. Calls went back and forth via overseas cable. His manner would be cool and detached, hers silky and affectionate.

In May she started rehearsals for the starring role in Noël Coward's new play, *Look After Lulu*, an adaptation of a Feydeau farce. It contained the kind of dialogue that had made Coward "the Master"—the gracefully impudent retort, the glorification of the normally unspeakable obvious. The play was written with elegance and ease, and Vivien accepted without hesitation.

It opened on July 29 at the Royal Court Theatre, scene of Olivier's triumph in *The Entertainer*. "The evening is Miss Vivien Leigh's," wrote *The Times* critic. "Beautiful, delectably cool and matter of fact, she is mistress of every situation."

It was a great personal success for her and should have bolstered her flagging self-confidence, but it was a Pyrrhic victory. Larry came to see her sparkling performance, they walked arm in arm smiling from the theatre, but she went home alone and he returned to Stratford, where he was rehearsing *Coriolanus*.

One cannot live nearly twenty-five years with a man and not

know when things are wrong. He was and always would be her "beautiful, shining, brilliant darling Larry," and she loved him better than she loved herself. Yet she had lost him as surely as she had lost her youth.

There was no use looking back. It only brought pain, heartache, and desperation. What she wanted more than any other one thing in life was for Larry to love her as she now was. Her illness made her feel quite bewildered, curiously more childlike than she had ever been. It would have been all right even if he could have held her in his arms without passion but with gentleness, like a fond, loving friend. She would gladly have welcomed such an arrangement. There were things that only Larry, who had shared her memories and her youth, her love, and her ambitions, could understand.

She returned alone to Notley that weekend and waited for a call from him that never came. When they next met it was to discuss the feasibility of selling Notley. She agreed. What else could she do? A Notley without Larry would be like a house without lights. But worse was yet to come. He needed time for himself, time to think things out. He suggested they spend the Christmas holidays apart. There seemed little left for her except to hold on to her dignity. As Larry had plans to go to the States for the holidays, Vivien accepted an invitation from Noël Coward to spend Christmas with him and other close friends at his home, Les Avants, in Switzerland.

Then Ernest became gravely ill, underwent major surgery, and on December 18, died at the age of seventy-five.

Vivien felt that everything was slipping away from her. Ernest's death was like some terrifying omen. The past had slipped darkly around an unknown corner and was lost. Gertrude had gone into the beauty business and was doing quite well. She was, in fact, stronger than she had ever been during Ernest's lifetime, and Vivien leaned heavily upon her.

Look After Lulu closed shortly after Ernest's death. Everyone close to Vivien feared that inactivity could be devastating to her, and they were relieved when a decision was made to revive *Duel of Angels* in New York with Mary Ure in the Claire Bloom role. In fact, except for Peter Wyngarde, the play was entirely recast, with Robert Helpmann taking over the direction. The one role that was not too easy to cast was that of Vivien's husband in the play. The actor had to be a member of American Actors Equity and yet speak with an English inflection, and he had to be able to stand on his own and not be overwhelmed by Vivien.

Chapter Twenty-six

Since their meeting backstage during *The Skin of Our Teeth*, Jack Merivale and Vivien had seen each other only a few times, and that had been in California in 1950, when Vivien was doing *Streetcar* and Olivier *Carrie*. At that time Jack had stayed with his stepmother, Gladys Cooper, and had attended two or three of the gala afternoon parties the Oliviers gave on Sundays. Once Gladys had "the most famous couple in the English theatre" to dinner. But in the intervening ten years the paths of Jack and Vivien had somehow not crossed. It was Cecil Tennant who suggested that Jack—as he was a member of American Actors Equity—take on the difficult role of Vivien's husband in *Duel of Angels*.

Tennant had always been Larry's great good friend, guide, philosopher, benefactor—everything close. To Vivien he was "Uncle Cecil," and she trusted him utterly. "Of course have Jack Merivale cast," she agreed.

There were, though, various delays before their departure for New York, and Merivale, feeling he knew her well enough to do so, rang Vivien up to ask, "Have you any news?" When the play was once again delayed he rang to find out if she knew why. It had something to do with the availability of a proper theatre, she replied. She was in one of her lows, a deep depression, and it came through in her voice. Merivale picked it up. He continued on, joking, trying to be as cheering as he knew how. On impulse he said in closing, "You ought to see the beard I'm growing for the part," and then suggested that they meet.

Her reaction to him when they met was extraordinary. For the first time in years she felt alive and female. She adored him almost immediately for saving her. Olivier's rejection had robbed her of self-esteem. His affair with a young woman cut deeply. There was no way she knew to compete, having exhausted all possibilities open to her. But here was an attractive, talented, intelligent man who from the first moment of their reunion showed signs of being dazzled by her. She listened in deep gratitude to his strong, sure, even voice that seemed to suddenly make things all right. There was a new calm in her where anxiety and fear had been.

It appeared to Jack that their romance had been fated. There were so many things in their past association only half noticed—shadow moments so fragmentary that one scarcely thought of their meaning—the curious familiarity of flesh when they had embraced fleetingly in greeting, the surprising flame of anger his words had struck in her, the faintest awareness of each other amid a group of people. Beautiful women held his utmost respect. There was something awe-inspiring in a woman so perfect in face, so exquisitely well bred as his stepmother Gladys, his ex-wife Jan Sterling, and Vivien. He was only a young boy when his father married Gladys, who was considered one of the world's great beauties at the time. Perhaps there was some relevance to that, some envy. Perhaps it was merely a predestined pattern.

"I ask only a chance for life" is what Vivien's attitude conveyed to him. She was humble, grateful, responsive to his smallest kindness. He was heady from the reactive warmth of her touch, smile, and voice. There was little doubt in his mind after only a few meetings that he was in love with Vivien and that she felt more than friendship for him. But the Oliviers were a legend, an historic pair, so closely wedded in thought one did not think of one without the other: the Fitzgeralds, the Lunts, the Windsors, and the Oliviers. To step between would be like trying to divide Siamese twins when you did not know which organs they might share. Therefore he kept a certain distance. A polite, careful man, he was always conscious of the feelings of others, always respectful of their imperatives.

One of his principles was to never interfere with anyone's marriage, and he instinctively felt that Vivien's allegiance was still with Olivier, for she spoke constantly about him. There was more than one picture of him in her dressing room and near her bed and in her purse. It was as though she was carrying around the ghost of a dead man.

One day, directly after they arrived in New York, Jack turned up at rehearsal wearing a plaid suit. "I love that suit," she said, her eyes misting, a faint smile on her lips. "Larry has got one like it," she added softly.

She took an apartment at Hampshire House in New York, and each evening after rehearsal Jack Merivale and Bobby Helpmann would go back to her flat for a drink. By the time the company was ready to move to New Haven for its out-of-town tryout, Vivien and Jack accepted their own emotions and brought their love out into the open. In New Haven they were together all the time. Vivien seemed as astonished at her own happiness as she was deeply moved by Jack's. "This will be our town," she confessed to him, and between performances he took her all over it—to the Yale campus, the galleries, the green parks, the waterfront. He was deeply and sincerely in love, and Vivien reacted to his tenderness like a rejected child might to an overwhelming show of affection.

By the time they returned to New York he was aware of many of her characteristics. Her loyalty for one; no one could say a word against Larry in her presence. Her quite extraordinary generosity for another; he had to be careful not to admire anything or she would buy it for him. The afternoon of their opening at the Helen Hayes Theatre he insisted, "Now look, I don't want anything from Cartier or Tiffany—nothing like that. I don't want any jewelry. If you want to celebrate our opening give me a packet of soap. No nonsense."

She promised to do as he asked. But then Jack had a time thinking to himself what he might give her. Recalling that Cartier made an inexpensive little gold head of St. Genesius, the patron saint of actors and musicians, he bought one and gave it to her. The minute she saw the Cartier wrapping, she exclaimed, "I think I've been double-crossed!" Vivien simply could not stand to be outdone. Immediately she ordered a matching piece for him.

The play opened on April 19, 1960. Vivien trembled on Jack's arm as they made their entrance together. What outsiders never knew was that in her low periods almost anything and everything frightened her, and it required great courage for her to see people, attend parties, and especially to go out on stage. She stood at center stage trembling and speechless. Then the entire house rose, giving her a tremendous ovation. It went on and on, Jack stepped away and it was all hers. After the curtain the street was brimming with fans and police on horseback. Vivien stepped out from the stage door to cheering crowds. One would have thought her spirits would have raised enormously. She had been brilliant in a role and a play that she greatly respected, and had done so without Larry. To Jack's stunned surprise she ended the evening in near hysteria.

Like everyone else, he had read the headlines about her being flown out of Hollywood under sedation and back to London. He knew about *Elephant Walk*, but that was years before. There had even been rumors that got back to him before *Duel of Angels*; but they had been together nearly six solid weeks now and though he had felt a pervading sadness at times, and was surprised when only one or two drinks after theatre made her overwrought, he had not been alerted to the truth, partly because of the years of their friendship. She had always been restless, nervous, unable to sleep, uniquely exhilarated and exhilarating. It was a great portion of her tremendous personal sex appeal and her magnetism as a performer. He could remember nights in Chicago, San Francisco, and New York during *Romeo and Juliet*, the Chinese Checkers game at Sneden's Landing, the way she sparkled at parties, smoked to excess, and ran, ran, ran. None of it had been normal behavior. But then she was no ordinary person.

"Why can't I have a decent, clean illness?" she cried. She hated illness of any sort, had absolutely no sympathy with it—not hers or Ernest's or Larry's or Gertrude's or Jack's—not really anybody's. If you were ill you just got over it and you ignored it or you got it fixed quietly with dignity. Having something mentally wrong was shameful.

It was out now. Jack knew she was suffering a mental illness. "Why should you feel ashamed?" Jack asked. "What an example you are to so many people who suffer from this, and to think you can lead this successful life, battling against this. It's a most marvelous example to any and all, and you should be a figure of hope and encouragement to thousands of people."

She agreed diffidently, but it was obvious to Jack that she did not really accept his rationale. But somehow his constancy, his tenderness, and his unfailing patience quite won her heart; yet her hopes and her desires for the future still rested on Larry. His portrait remained by her bed and on her dressing table; and though she wrote him that Jack was in love with her and she deeply in love with him, she begged Olivier to give her some sign of his plans for the future and if they in any way revolved about or included her.

Helpmann was now coming to Jack to enlist his help almost daily. "You've really got to calm her down," he begged, for she had slipped into some of the same behavioral lapses that had been rampant during the *Titus Andronicus* tour. She had to rest, but she simply would not go to bed and she refused to stop drinking. The illness just drove her on and on. "Everything seems to go so fast," she cried.

Olivier was told of her condition, and he enlisted the help of Irene Selznick, who was in New York and whom Jack had never met. Suddenly, Jack received a phone call from Irene asking him to please come to see her alone at her apartment to discuss Vivien and he went. "You know you have got a life of your own," she warned him. "She's ill. Mental." Jack did not seem in the least deterred. "Well, I'm going to invite her up to my country place on Sunday. Will you come and bring her? And after lunch I can have a long talk with her. She needs treatment."

Jack did accompany Vivien to Irene Selznick's home, and Vivien agreed to go the following day for a series of shock treatments. Monday morning Irene went with them to a doctor who administered shock in his office. Vivien let out a cry from the treatment room, and Jack, waiting outside, heard it and rose to go in. Irene pulled him back. "No, don't go," she insisted.

That night Vivien played with a racking headache and burn marks on her forehead (not too uncommon when shock treatment is employed). Not once did she falter in her lines. She had "the courage of a lion, really," Jack recalls. The next day she returned for another treatment. The excruciating headaches were still plaguing her. "I never feel this way after Dr. Conachy's treatment," she kept repeating. She was agitated, jumpy, unable to sit. Jack was certain she would run out before the treatment, and the doctor had not arrived yet. "Let's walk around the block," he suggested.

By the time they had returned to the front of the building she had made up her mind she was not going to have a treatment. Jack managed to get her into the office and the doctor came out. She was hostile and incoherent. Nothing the doctor said could get her to accompany him into the treatment room. Suddenly she lurched away. "No! What I'll do is ring Dr. Conachy in London. I want to speak to Dr. Conachy!"

She credited Conachy with bringing her back to life. He was the one who had said, "You are ill. I can help you." He had been the first one who *had* helped her, and she trusted him. She was perfectly coherent when Dr. Conachy came on the line. Whatever he said seemed to calm her and she handed the telephone finally to the other doctor. This time the shock treatments were abandoned and medication was substituted, but the manic phase, therefore, took longer to pass than usual. Incredibly, she appeared every night, and no matter how distressed she would be in her dressing room, a transformation would begin in the wings and she would go out on stage and give a brilliant performance. The play was now reblocked, however, so that Jack was as close at hand as possible.

She was becoming extremely dependent on him, and her love for him was growing each day. He was tall, lean, dark, and handsome, a no-nonsense type who managed at the same time to be warm, tender, and caring. He came from her world, and Vivien admired his lineage. His father had been the first Professor Higgins in Shaw's *Pygmalion* in America, and his stepmother was one of England's greatest and most beautiful actresses. He was a few years Vivien's junior and yet easily seemed Larry's contemporary. What he did not possess was Olivier's mystique, the charismatic personality that not only dazzled but stirred and uprooted the most violent of emotions. She was overwhelmingly grateful to him. She wanted him to know how much his love meant to her, and so she showered him with gifts and letters expressing her own love.

> Saturday, May 19th, 1960
> [It was, in fact, the 14th]
>
> My Darling—why I have written May 19th on this little present I don't know—but as I love you every day of the year—it matters not— I hope very much that you will like it—use it—and not lose it—it is to thank you for your kindness and goodness to me. It is to tell you that I love you— my beloved.
>
> Vivien.

On May 19, the day she had wrongly dated her letter to Jack, she received a long and moving letter from Olivier. He and Joan Plowright were appearing opposite each other in Ionesco's *Rhinoceros* at the Royal Court. They were very much in love. Joan was asking for a divorce from her husband, and Olivier, after much and great soul-searching, was asking Vivien to release them both from an obviously untenable relationship. Cindy Dietz was with her when she opened the letter. At first Vivien could not believe the contents. Then, distressed greatly and not well to start with, she became somewhat hysterical. Finally, she quieted. "What are you going to do?" Cindy asked.

"Whatever Larry wants me to do" was Vivien's immediate reply.

By the time of her evening performance she had issued a statement to the press: "Lady Olivier wishes to say that Sir Laurence has asked for a divorce in order to marry Miss Joan Plowright. She will naturally do whatever he wishes."

At nine-thirty the next morning reporters wakened Olivier with the news of Vivien's announcement. He was appalled. His letter had, after all, been of a very private nature, and he had expected a return letter from Vivien, at which point they could have taken the next step. This way Joan had been publicly named as corespondent, which, since she was still married, created a somewhat embarrassing situation. In the same circumstances years before, Jill had acted with more discretion. Olivier had no immediate response to the press other than "I have no comment to make—literally none. I have to have time to think."

Joan, who was labeled by the British press as "the black-stockinged darling of the 'vital theatre,'" drove away from her flat in Ovington Square, Kensington, moments later and was gone the entire day, presumably at her parents' home in Scunthorpe. She and Olivier were due to appear that night at the Royal Court Theatre.

Olivier left the flat on Eaton Square at lunchtime, still refusing to answer reporters' questions. When he returned that evening and found the press corps still gathered at his door he gave them a bottle of whiskey. "Have a drink with me," he offered charmingly, adding, "I'm sorry to have been so uncooperative." He put his arm around the shoulders of one man, and the reporters followed him into the flat. When they came out they had no more information than they had previously.

In New York, Vivien fell to pieces after she had made her announcement. Jack at least was there to help her get through the days and nights. His affection never flagged, nor his ability to express his deep feelings for her, but he was a proud man who carried himself and his emotions with great dignity. It was painful for him to see Vivien in the state she was in and to be aware that her love for Larry could still torture her with such deep effect. He remembered them when their love was golden and a standard of what he most desired for the love he sought in his own life. If Vivien was feeling the scalpel's sharp edge, Jack was suffering the open wound. He tried to surmount his own pain by soothing hers. And she responded to it with gratitude.

Tuesday
May 31st, 1960
Helen Hayes Theatre

My Darling,

This is to thank you most formally for my really beautiful presents. I love them and shall treasure them and enjoy them.

It is also to put in writing that I love you I love you and I absolutely love you— So there—

Vivien.

As fate would have it, Equity called a theatre strike at that time. After many days of meetings and negotiations the strike was settled, but Roger Stevens, the play's producer, decided the play would remain closed in New York and would open a month later in Los Angeles and do a tour—Los Angeles four weeks, San Francisco four weeks, Chicago three weeks, and Washington two. It was a godsend because it enabled Vivien to go back to England for a week's treatment with Conachy. It also meant Jack could get some sleep too, for Bobby Helpmann and Peter Wyngarde were seeing her home. The truth was, Jack was now not at all sure that he didn't want out.

She left June 10. From the TWA aircraft she wrote Jack, "Oh, how I love you dearest heart!" For the return address she wrote "Lady Vivien Olivier." She had always loved being Lady Olivier and Jack did not know if it would ever be possible for her to accept being Mrs. Anybody.

Reporters swamped her as she stepped out of the customs hall. She wore a beige linen suit and a high-crowned, low-brimmed brown and white printed cotton hat that half concealed her face. Helpmann and Wyngarde stood on either side of her as she puffed nervously at a cigarette and refused to answer questions about her marriage. Larry had moved from Eaton Square and was staying with friends. The first thing she did was attempt to arrange a meeting with him. At first he agreed to see her at the Royal Court and then changed his mind. "I thought I was going to see Larry at his theatre," she told reporters. "But he phoned me and said he believed it best not to meet right now." She appeared to be choking back tears as she continued. "He said he would see me later, but there are no definite arrangements."

Olivier rang Jack in New York about the same time he had refused to see Vivien. "Jackie, I hear from Vivien that you and she are in love. Any chance of a union?" he inquired. "Oh, no. Absolutely not," Merivale replied. To which Olivier—with a large degree of disappointment—simply said, "Ooooh."

It was not that Jack loved her less but that he could not envision how he was going to cope with their future, or indeed that she truly wanted him to do so. His former experience with this sort of illness was sketchy. She took so many pills for ups and downs that there was no way for him to be sure when she was behaving in a normal way. While manic she was abusive, difficult, cruel, and impossible to manage. In depression she was the clinging, dependent, frightened child. At other times she was sweet and adorable, the charming, witty, generous lady the world and her dear friends knew and loved.

Gertrude and costume designer Bumble Dawson (an old friend) stayed with her in the flat at 54 Eaton Square the night Olivier refused to see her. She was in a terrible state and Gertrude called Dr. Conachy at two in the morning much concerned. He came right over and administered a tranquilizer, but at five A.M. she was still awake. She sat down and wrote Jack:

> 54 Eaton Square
> 5 A.M. June 11, 1960

My Darling Love—

I cannot sleep without writing to tell you a) that I love you and b) that I miss you. I have been wondering all evening where and how you have been. I gave you most of my news on the telephone and there is little else to say. I have been sorting out things from Notley—placing them and hanging pictures and oddities like that. Gertrude came over looking a good 16—sends you her fond love— Armando Child came to dinner and Bumble Dawson—the latter kindly spending the night here for the telephone and the door bell ring ad infinitum and the angelic Rubyesc has enough on her hands with the cooking and cleaning and shopping without dealing with the dear reporters all of the time. They have been pleasant enough, to tell the truth, but ever present which *is* fatiguing. I feel better already. Shall have treatment tomorrow. Otherwise stay in bed or anyway knock about here—then to Notley to meet with the gardener and his wife— Lunch at Little Hasdey with Baba Metcalf. Back to London the 15th to see "Rhinoceros" [the play that starred Olivier and Plowright]—then, I don't know what. There has been no communication from his Lordship. Oh, my dear, dear dearest love—I do adore you and send great waves of love—good-good night and God bless you.

> Your Vivien.

Notley was being shown to prospective buyers, and Olivier had brought some of Vivien's personal things to Eaton Square for her before her arrival. When she got to Notley she was upset with the gardens, which had not been tended to as she thought they ought to be, and it was a painful wrench when she left, feeling in her heart it must be for the last time. She saw *Rhinoceros* in London—falling asleep in the middle—and complained that the acting was not too good, but that perhaps she wasn't quite in the mood. A few days later she was on a plane back to New York. En route, on a Pan Am Jet Clipper, she wrote Jack:

June 20th, 1960

My Darling Love— I am on my way to you with a beating heart and the only point of this little scribble is that it makes me feel nearer. I wonder every minute if you are awake (I was at 5 this morning) when you will be starting out for the Airport—if you will drive right by it?

Dear lad I long to see you—and read and reread every little thing you have ever written me to make the time pass quickly. I am feeling so very very well—it seems like a miracle— Indeed, I believe it is— This has been a very extraordinary week. I think the most extraordinary of my life— Alone—and darling infinitely close to you— Friends have been most remarkable. I have every reason being grateful— I seem to have seen everyone I meant to and there have even been some hilarious moments. To think 5 hours time I shall be able to *tell* you of them. My darling dearest dear. We have just passed over the Coast of Ireland— We have head winds so will be a little late. Sweet dear love I ache and long to see you.

With great apprehension Jack met the plane at Idlewild. But when Vivien stepped off the aircraft looking like a divine angel, sweet, loving, and full of life, he was flooded with relief. The manic phase was over. Yet deep inside he wondered how long it would be before depression would overtake her again and the whole cycle start over.

But those three weeks before they were to reopen *Duel of Angels* in Los Angeles erased all his doubts.

They took a train to the Coast, thinking they would have the time alone, but reporter David Lewin came along with them to do a profile for his English paper. Lewin was constantly at Vivien for the first day, remaining in her drawing room, following her into the dining car for meals, the questions never stopping. The second day out Jack got quite cross. "We were hoping this would be a holiday," he told Lewin. "Well, I've got to get this work done," Lewin replied. "I realize that, but couldn't we arrange say two hours in the morning and one in the afternoon?" Jack suggested. Lewin agreed and from that point in the trip Vivien and Jack had their holiday.

An amusing thing happened the first evening they boarded the train. Vivien and Jack ordered a drink before dinner in the drawing room. The porter served them and they began to talk. "Are you going to be with us all the way?" Vivien inquired.

"Yes, ma'am." The porter beamed.

"Oh, good! I'm delighted. What's your name?"

"Larry," he replied.

Vivien and Jack could hardly contain their laughter until he had gone. Then they hooted, unable to stop. After that it became their one great joke. Whenever they needed anything, Vivien would smile mischievously and say, "Oh, just ring for Larry."

For the first time Vivien did not seem upset by the restriction of the train. Jack seldom left her side. She had her new cat, Poo Jones, complete with basket and litter box and a Renoir she had brought back from Notley because, as she insisted to Jack, "I need something truly beautiful to look at in hotel rooms."

They had managed to keep the time in New York rather private and free from the press, as New York agent Gloria Safier had lent them her little house out at Old Quogue. But they would now be traveling together. It would not have mattered so much, but Olivier had not issued a public statement as to his intentions—or, for that matter, even acknowledged that a divorce might be imminent. To all intents and purposes Vivien was still a married woman.

Jack sat down and wrote Larry a letter apprising him of his new feeling of commitment and his deep love for Vivien. Olivier sent him an immediate reply on August 16, 1960, in which he confided that moments after he had read Jack's letter he had broken down and sobbed in relief with the purest kind of gratitude he had ever known and thanked him for giving him that, adding how happy he was for all of them. He obviously felt released now to proceed with his own life, but at the same time he warned Jack to watch for those little signs that at first were not easily recognizable but which grew to formidable symptoms of her illness.

Olivier was in effect now resigning all responsibility toward Vivien and turning it over to Jack. A strong sense of relief came through in the tone of the letter, an unspeakable joy. Perhaps the irony was fitting, for the same indescribable feeling had overwhelmed him when he and Vivien had decided to run off together to become the golden lovers of the 1940s.

Chapter Twenty-seven

She called him Angel, he called her Angelica. For Jack it was hard to remember when he had felt so young. She was so beautiful and softly shining as she responded to his affection. They stayed at the Chateau Marmont high in the Hollywood Hills in an apartment with a terrace that overlooked the city, and Vivien was surrounded by old and dear friends. George Cukor opened his house to the lovers. They had the use of his garden and pool any time, and he hosted a splendid gala party for them. The title role in the projected film of Tennessee Williams' *The Roman Spring of Mrs. Stone* had just been offered to her; and she was glad to have George there to discuss the part and help her decide if she should do it when it went before the cameras in January 1961.

Duel of Angels was a sophisticated play, and Hollywood did not seem able to pick up on its humor. The laughs did not come where they were expected, which put a slight tension on their four-week engagement at the Hollywood Playhouse. It did fair business and there were always crowds of fans waiting at the stage door for "Scarlett O'Hara."

Cars had always been one of her great passions and she bought a Thunderbird. She was deliriously happy as she showed it to Jack. "That was really rather naughty," he scolded. "You shouldn't have done it." He did not honestly think she could afford such an extravagant whim when she had a Rolls-Royce in London.

The fact was that Olivier had always given the impression he hadn't any money, what with taxes and theatre costs; and the theatrical set of London often conjectured how terrible it was for such a great actor—who could have been a millionaire if he had remained in

Hollywood—to be limited in any way financially. But Vivien, from her own earnings and because those close to her in London had invested well for her, actually could afford such a whim, even though she was never aware of how much money she had. When Vivien was on a "high" she went on great spending sprees—mostly gift-giving. It was part of the illness.

"We'll drive to San Francisco," she announced when they closed in Hollywood.

"What? All our gear in a sports car convertible? It will be impossible!" Jack protested.

"Don't be ridiculous, darling," Vivien replied. "We'll be traveling light."

"Traveling light" to Vivien meant twenty-eight suitcases, Poo Jones, a cat bed, a litter box, and the Renoir. Somehow they managed to pile it all in the car, though it was not possible to see in the rearview mirror over the enormous mountain of luggage. It was August and hot, and both Poo Jones and the Renoir shared the front seat with them as they drove up the Pacific Coast Highway. One hundred miles from San Francisco the car broke down. It had to be left in a garage and another car rented. With so many suitcases, only a convertible would do. Finally, after much difficulty, a fire-truck-red Chevrolet was located (a color that Vivien abhorred), and everything was transferred so that they could continue their journey.

They were now two very happy people. The weather was beautiful in San Francisco and the audiences cosmopolitan. They flew to Chicago four weeks later, where they were met by a good friend of both of theirs, Sir Cedric Hardwicke. They had a suite with a kitchen at the Ambassador East, and after the show "dear Cedric" would come by and Jack would cook a steak for the three of them. Vivien adored Chicago with its beautiful museum of art, and they were invited out by many people with private collections.

By the time they reached Washington, fall had approached and the leaves were just beginning to color. They took drives out into the country during the day and had small picnics. It was a lighthearted and loving time for both of them. Vivien had not had an attack for the entire tour, and they had pushed all the former pressures and problems out of their minds.

"How are we going home?" Jack asked when they closed in Washington.

"We'll fly," she said.

"No, we'll go by boat."

"What a lovely idea!" she agreed.

They booked passage on the *Queen Elizabeth* and Peter Wyngarde came too, though that was not exactly Jack's idea. However, Wyngarde respected affairs of the heart, and he came by their suite (they had connecting staterooms) for a drink only occasionally and joined them for dinner just twice.

At Cherbourg Jack got his first taste of the press. All the time they had been together on the tour not a word had been printed in the papers or columns. But as soon as they stepped off the gangplank they were instantly surrounded by reporters peppering them with extremely personal questions. Vivien seemed to be enjoying it and stood by smiling with Poo Jones clasped in her arms as Jack told them all, "We're just good friends."

While she had been away Cecil Tennant had ordered her old Rolls-Royce to be exchanged for a new one. En route she had received a cable from him: HAVE MANAGED TO GET YOU A SABLE ROLLS. She cabled back: DARLING UNCLE CECIL 'TIS THE ONE COLOUR I REALLY CAN'T ABIDE. SPRAY IT!

So there on the dock at Cherbourg a lovely new gray Rolls awaited them. They drove to Paris, where Vivien had costume fittings at Balmain for *The Roman Spring of Mrs. Stone*.

They had a marvelous time in Paris. Vivien seemed to be glowing with happiness. From Paris they drove to Switzerland to visit with Noël Coward. Adrianne Allen and her husband Bill Whitney were also there, as was Cole Lesley, and in the evenings after dinner they played hilarious word games at which "the Master" always won. In one you had a minute to say as many *unreal* words as you could starting with the same letter of the alphabet. No one could top Noël's ability to create the most improbable words, and they all roared with laughter until late into the night.

"Dear, dear Noël." Vivien embraced him when she and Jack were leaving. "You are the most marvelous companion."

On December 2, 1960, thirty-year-old actor Roger Gage was given a decree nisi in the divorce court in London on the grounds of the adultery of his actress wife, Joan Plowright, and Sir Laurence Olivier. Moments later, in her own divorce petition, Vivien, pale and nervous, followed Gage into the witness box, wearing a neat red and black checked suit and a wide-brimmed black hat. She held her head very erect but folded and unfolded her white-gloved hands almost as though she were wringing them. When she was asked about her own conduct, in accordance with British divorce procedure, her lawyer interrupted, admitting into evidence a written declaration of two instances of her adultery, in London and Ceylon. Vivien bowed her head. The man involved was not named, but her lawyer contended that since reconciliations with Olivier took place after her adulteries were committed this constituted a condoning of her acts by her husband.

Vivien closed her eyes for a moment, shutting out the sight of the courtroom. When she opened them again a tiny smile caressed her softly curved mouth. She was apparently recalling something she and Larry had shared in the past, but whatever had crossed her mind in that brief time made her appear suddenly stronger. The hand-wringing ceased and her voice became quite clear and confident as she raised her head and looked the lawyer and the world straight in the eye.

A private detective testified that he had found "Miss Plowright and Sir Laurence in nightclothes in a London apartment last June." Both willingly signed a statement to that effect.

"In October 1958," Vivien, in a brave voice, told the court, "my husband came to see me in my theatre dressing room. There were a number of newsmen outside because a magazine story had appeared concerning his love for Miss Plowright. I asked him if it was the case and he admitted he had been in love with Miss Plowright for three months."

Under English law when two parties in a dissolving marriage confess adultery it is up to the judge to determine which shall be accorded the divorce. In this case the judge awarded it to Vivien, and Olivier was made to pay the court costs in both Gage's and Vivien's divorce actions.

When it was all over Vivien got up and walked with a regal composure from the courtroom, but once safely ensconced in the rear seat of the Rolls she leaned back against the fine wool upholstery and sobbed softly as her chauffeur drove her out of sight of gaping onlookers. The proceedings had had a terrible sense of unreality.

Although she was an independent woman without Larry, she knew the only way for her to survive the future was through self-delusion. Gertrude, Bumble, and Jack were waiting for her at Eaton Square as she walked sobbing into the flat that was now hers alone.

She felt warmly comforted by Jack, but it was as though he was help-ing her through the death of someone close to her and unable to lift her heavy heart, for she could not let go of her grief.

What saved her from self-pity again was work. Two days before the divorce the announcement had been made that she was to por-tray Karen Stone, the none-too-successful actress who gives up her career for a life of infatuation with gigolos in *The Roman Spring of Mrs. Stone*.

A physical examination was required for the company's insur-ance and there were some tense moments when the producers thought Vivien might not pass. If this had happened she could not have been cast. But by some miracle she was approved.

Originally the film was to be shot directly on location in Rome, but the Italian censors were distressed over the content of the script and so it was filmed at Elstree studios not far from London. It was theatre director José Quintero's first film and he was understandably unnerved. Vivien, made up and in a blond wig for the part of Karen Stone, was the first performer on the set. As she walked across the enormous set, the eyes of all the crew were upon her. There were whispers, but she passed through them with tremendous pride, wear-ing a leaf-green coat trimmed in silver fox that gave her a regal look. The grips were the first to applaud her, and Vivien raised her arm to them in a queenly fashion. The camera crew and soundmen joined in the welcoming tribute. Vivien bowed. Quintero made his way to her and embraced her, and later remarked that her hands were icy. She had not made a film since *The Deep Blue Sea* in 1955, and she was terrified.

"Please, everybody," Quintero said loudly, holding and warming Vivien's hands in his. "I know that it is customary to make a speech at the beginning of a picture or on the first day of play rehearsals. Usu-ally that speech is supposed to be inspiring and its purpose to give confidence to everyone working with you from the start. But here stands a director who doesn't even know when to call action and when to call cut."

Vivien then stepped forward and free of his grasp, shouted to the crew, "We are with him, aren't we all?" A resounding "Yes!" echoed through the soundstage.

She and Jack maintained separate flats, but they were together almost constantly when Vivien wasn't shooting. In a letter she dated February 23, she wrote him:

In fact my darling love it is the 26th and what does that matter when this should have been written on February 14th—St. Valentine's Day. It really only matters that I love you. Thank you dear dear one—you have made what is nearly a year now—a time of happiness that I never thought possible. My very best and most beloved of Angels I hope you will look back on it with gladness too—you are so closely precious to me and I love you sweet darling Jack—

Your Vivien

I do love my lilac today and thank you for it.

Though she loved Jack, her emotions were still torn between him and Larry, who was appearing in New York in *Becket*, only a few streets from where Joan Plowright was playing in *A Taste of Honey*. Rumors were circulating that the two were planning to wed soon, and Vivien became convinced that she must see Larry before he married. The plan to preview a new wide-screen version of *Gone With the Wind* in Atlanta in mid-March gave her just the excuse she needed. *Roman Spring* was in the last two weeks of filming, which meant it would be delayed by her absence if she went.

Quintero and Vivien had become good friends, Quintero often returning to Eaton Square after the day's shooting with Vivien—or to a local pub called The Purple Apple. "Do a few lines from *Gone With the Wind*," he would often ask her.

"Fiddle-dee-dee, fiddle-dee-dee, Melanie," Vivien would say, falling into a Southern accent as she pretended to mark up purchases on a cash register, "even if they are Yankees!"

"Oh, José," she begged when she heard about the Atlanta "preview," "the only ones who are left are Olivia and myself. I haven't seen Atlanta in over twenty years. I know it may delay you one or two days but you can shoot some of the scenes with Warren [Beatty] or Lotte [Lenya]. Oh, José, darling, *please*."

Quintero suspected the truth and tried to dissuade her, but it was no good, so he reluctantly agreed to let her take the time off. "Please don't harm yourself," he warned her.

"Thank you, dear José." She smiled gratefully, and a few days later she was on her way.

Mr. Jack Merivale
6 Sloane Gardens
London, SW1, England

March 8th, '61

My darling—they have handed me this nice little pad of writing paper and I can think of nothing I want to do more than to write to you on it.

We are stationary in the sun before take-off—I did *love* your telegram and have read it 4 times already—thank you my dear sweet love for your thoughtfulness. We had a swift drive to the airport with poor Mr. M.G.M. [studio representative] very nervous. Arrived in good time— Trudie [her housekeeper] and I had a small brandy or at least ½ of one (I think Bernard [her chauffeur] polished off the remainder) and here we are. A pretty stewardess has just shown us what to do with life jackets— oh, my dear—I shall miss you—keep safe and well—I will look forward to hearing your voice tonight. Thank you too for my lovely-scented present. Darling, we are just taking off now. We are coming down at Shannon where I am going to get some *Ma Griffe* perfume because it is so economical to buy it at an airfield! (Tell Bumble) We are in the air now. I shall post this in Ireland— I kiss you, my darling dear— I hope at whatever time of the day this reaches you it finds you happy and well—feeling fondly towards your loving—demanding (I know) but above all loving— Angelica.

But in New York Olivier agreed only to see her when he was accompanied by Joan and at a public place. This came as a great blow to Vivien. Olivier perhaps assumed that such an ultimatum would cause Vivien to change her mind about the meeting. But he underestimated Vivien's tremendous determination to see him under any circumstances. He booked a table at Sardi's and Vivien agreed to meet them at the restaurant. She dressed as carefully for the appointment as a woman might for a first rendezvous with a prospective lover and allowed enough time for Olivier and Plowright to have been seated. It was early, before curtain time, Sardi's was packed to capacity, and Vivien did not have an easy time as she was led to their table. The lovers faced her, seated close together. Olivier rose but did not come around the table to greet her. Vivien sat down stiffly across from the man who had been her husband and the great love of her life and whom she still worshiped. It was almost impossible for her to shift her glance so that it would take in the woman he had chosen to replace her. When she finally did look at Joan she flinched. Joan Plowright was exceedingly plain, with a nice enough face but certainly not one that would make heads turn as they had just done for Vivien when she entered Sardi's.

Before theatre curtain time the noise decibel level in Sardi's is high and the packed tables are jammed close together, making privacy almost impossible. It was not an easy place to hold a private conversation, and perhaps that was intentional on Olivier's part. In this bustling and impersonal atmosphere Olivier broke the news to

Vivien that he and Joan were to be married in a few days' time. He took Joan's hand in his for strength and she smiled at him with adoration. They did not dawdle over dinner or wait for coffee. Less than an hour later Sir Laurence Olivier and the future and second Lady Olivier escorted the first Lady Olivier out of Sardi's and saw her to a taxi.

Brokenhearted, Vivien boarded the plane the next morning for Atlanta with her old friend Radie Harris. They stopped at the Georgian Terrace Hotel, where she and Olivier and Gable and all the stars of *Gone With the Wind* had stayed for the first premiere. The hotel now sadly fitted her mood. It was aging badly and much of its glamour was fading. Jack was her only hope for the future, and she clung to the thought of him constantly and wrote him as often as she could.

To Mr. Merivale Esq.
6 Sloane Gardens
London, SW1, England

Friday 10 Mar '61

My Angel Darling
Just somehow I did not get around to writing this last night because I was in real late! And just fell into bed—but sent you waves of love just the same. This morning there is brilliant sunshine and we are on our way to Aunt Fanny's Cabin (if you please) for a brunch—then somewhere for lunch perhaps—then bed for a little lay down before Eugene does my hair for tonight and at 5 my sweet we shall talk—this is only a line to tell you I love you—

Angelica.

She quite enjoyed the film but thought the gala "preview" was a rather sad idea. Margaret Mitchell, Gable, Lombard, Fleming, Leslie Howard, and Hattie McDaniel had all died; and Vivien and Olivia were, though certainly still beautiful ladies, middle aged. Nevertheless the new wide-screen version of the film was even more spectacular than the original.

Vivien returned to London on March 17, and two days later the news broke that Joan and Larry had been married in a simple ceremony and feted at a party at Richard Burton's New York apartment (Burton was appearing in *Camelot*) after all three had completed their evening performances in different theatres.

The press were waiting for Vivien when she came home from the studio the day Olivier rewed. "You know it happened this morning in New York? Do you have anything to say?" they asked.

Vivien had not heard the news yet and she looked puzzled. "About what?"

"Sir Laurence and Miss Plowright were married this morning."

For a split second Vivien lost her footing, and Quintero, who was by her side, grabbed her arm and steadied her. Then Vivien straightened, threw back her head, and gave the reporters a perfect Scarlett smile. "Of course I knew it, and when I went to New York I wished them all the happiness in the world," she declared.

The four weeks before her work on *Roman Spring* was complete was a difficult time for her. She did not get along with Beatty, whom she found arrogant and uncooperative, and she had a painful fall from a horse after refusing to allow a double to do the required shot. The horse, a magnificent chestnut animal, had been ridden by Olivier six years before in *Richard III* and had been schooled to break into a canter the moment it heard the sound of the clapper board. Vivien was supposed to trot to the far end of a field where there was a tree with a low-hanging bough and a roundabout beyond. This location had been selected because it was symbolic of Mrs. Stone's own dilemma—an inability to know which path to take in her life. Vivien was a more than competent horsewoman and not at all afraid of her mount. When the clapper board was slapped, the horse took off, heading straight toward the low-lying branch. Vivien leaned forward, pressing her face into the horse's neck. Even so, the branch tore off her blond wig as it struck the top of her head, knocking her off the horse and stunning her. Miraculously she was not injured. She insisted on remounting the same animal so that the scene could be refilmed. And indeed she got back on and put the horse through its paces so that the shot could be completed before lunch.

One day she was moved to a new dressing room because the old one had plumbing problems. She entered it for the first time with her housekeeper, Trudi Flockart, who went with her everywhere that Jack could not. In a short time Trudi had become Vivien's good friend, companion, and secretary as well as her housekeeper. Vivien stood in the doorway of her new quarters with Trudi peering over her shoulder. Vivien's eyes swept the room, taking everything in in a matter of moments. "Those curtains are dirty," she said. "I can't possibly dress in here until they are cleaned." She shuddered with distaste. "They are disgraceful, in fact." She sat down and would not budge until Trudi got on the telephone to the front office.

"Miss Leigh's dressing-room curtains must be changed for clean ones immediately," Trudi insisted, "or she simply will not be able to prepare for her next scene."

Within minutes fresh curtains were brought from somewhere and the dirty ones removed, and Vivien sat down at her table to make up. There seemed to be no injured feelings, nor did the staff believe she was being difficult. She was a meticulous person who lived by and up to certain standards. Once the clean curtains were up, she was ready to do her job.

But when the film was completed there was a tremendous sense of letdown. Vivien began to drink again, and those "little signs" began to show. Those close to her were now able to see them. The wildness would come into her eyes. The frivolous, high-spirited, loving woman would disappear and in her place would be a clawing, desperate person.

Chapter Twenty-eight

During her manic periods Vivien would eat abnormally—sometimes two enormous meals, one immediately after the other—and she would gain a considerable amount of weight in a matter of days. This happened directly after the last day of shooting on *The Roman Spring of Mrs. Stone*. It was a "sign" that Jack now had come to recognize and he got her to Dr. Conachy immediately for a series of ECT's, which helped to control the attack in a rather early stage. But she had to do something about her weight, since they were leaving shortly on an overseas tour for the Old Vic Company.

The tour had been decided upon when they had been in Paris for the costume fittings with Balmain, even before *The Roman Spring of Mrs. Stone* had gone into production. They were to visit five Australian cities—Melbourne, Brisbane, Sydney, Adelaide, and Perth—before continuing on to New Zealand to play in Auckland, Christchurch, and Wellington. And as work on the film ended and she began her plans for the tour, her thoughts could not help but zig-zag back and forth from the tour in 1948 that she had made with Larry to the present. There was a sense of unreality to it, something dreamlike. She was going with Jack, who was to appear in all three plays they were doing (*Twelfth Night*, *Duel of Angels*, and *The Lady of the Camellias*); but it did not seem right to her, and the confusion of thoughts between the two periods almost sent her into a serious manic phase.

After the shock treatment she decided to go to a very discreet reducing spa. She took a little room for a week, starting on a Wednesday. By Friday she rang Jack and told him she was coming home for the weekend and returning on the Monday.

"Well, my darling," Jack replied, "if you do that, there goes the two pounds a day you're losing, because you won't be able to resist the temptations of wine and good food," he warned.

"That's all nonsense," she insisted. "I've been allowed home and I'm going to be a good girl and follow instructions to the last period."

Indeed she was true to her word, eating only lettuce with lemon-juice dressing while everyone else was gorging himself on Trudi's hearty German cooking. She was disciplined to the extreme, a deep facet of her personality that carried over into everything she did when not manic.

Before they were due to leave for Australia, Robert Helpmann came up with the idea of extending the tour to include South Africa. This created a good deal of controversy within the troupe. Jack was the most disturbed, positively refusing any thought of such a thing because he was afraid that Vivien, who had absolutely no feelings for differences in people—ethnic or otherwise—and being a very bold woman to boot, would speak her mind out against the political suppression of South African blacks the moment she set foot in the country and that if she entered a manic phase while there, could easily do something that would result in her being jailed.

Dame Sybil Thorndike, on the other hand, thought they should go—even though she also detested the system—so that the South Africans could be exposed to another point of view. Finally Jack won and the idea of appearing in South Africa was abandoned, though later a decision was made to extend the tour instead to Mexico and South America, a decision that kept the company abroad for over nine months.

They arrived in Melbourne early in July 1961 and opened at Her Majesty's Theatre for a six-week engagement on July 12. They stayed at the Hotel Windsor, and while they were preparing to dress for the theatre on opening night Vivien wrote Jack a note on hotel stationery and placed it on his bureau top with a gift box containing a lovely silk ascot.

> Dear dear heart—you are going to have such a wonderful success. I know it and oh how I hope you will be happy in it. I love you and thank God for you. Sweet one my love is all around you—you don't have to wear this pressie—you know! your proper one will come in a proper place—for pressies I mean! Your Angelica.

And on July 15 she wrote Ted Tenley, a good friend who had been in the cast of *Duel of Angels:*

Dearest Ted,

The first night was a BEAST. The house very late in coming in because the ladies wanted to be snapped in the foyer. I really thought a pack of Huskies had been let loose in the stalls. There were so many white fur stoles! They sat in uncomprehending restlessness. True monsters! The notices good and the houses since then very fair and impressive, but nothing like that darling U.S.A.!

Trudi wrote Tenley on July 31, *"Twelfth Night* goes very well indeed and got good critics. Now we are sweating about *Camellia."* She didn't have to worry, because *The Lady of the Camellias* was the best-loved play of the tour.

Vivien was once again treated like visiting royalty, as she had been during the first tour, and expected to make numerous public appearances in addition to her performances. Not only was Jack constantly by her side, but also Trudi and Bobby Helpmann were there to be counted upon, and the most amiable company contained some old and fast friends. There were also flying visits from "Uncle Cecil" and Michael Benthall, the director of the Old Vic. But although everyone's greatest concern was still for Vivien's health, amazingly she appeared to have greater vitality and stamina than anyone else in the troupe.

They played eight shows a week, and often Vivien would make numerous personal appearances as well. They had no time off between the last show in Melbourne on August 26 and their opening in Brisbane on August 28, but finally there was a twelve-day hiatus before they were to open at the Theatre Royal in Sydney. She and Jack spent the time on Orpheus Island in the Great Barrier Reef where she wrote Tenley on a postcard:

Dearest Ted—I have been *very* bad about writing—forgive me please— The Brisbane Theatre was pleasant with *Lady of the Camellias* the smashingest success. Now we are on a very remote island—7 of us all together! *Very* beautiful and peaceful. My little house is the one on the far right (PIC). Nothing to do but swim, play, shell, sleep, and commit an occasional sin! Jack is writing you a proper letter I see. [Arrive] Sydney 26th. So much love to you dear Ted always— Vivien.

In Sydney they stopped at the new Hilton Hotel, but the windows could not be opened as the hotel was centrally air-conditioned, and Vivien was unable to bear the claustrophobic feeling. She recalled a man whom she and Larry had met on the first tour and who owned a lovely estate called Fernley Castle on Rose Bay which had recently been made over into a hotel, so they moved there. Her condition immediately improved, but Jack was still concerned, for he was learning how to detect the smallest indication that she might not be quite as well as she seemed.

And after the second week in Sydney she seemed less spirited than usual. Up until that time she refused to be dissuaded from accepting any public appearance requested of her. Now she tried to postpone whatever she could. One night she shook badly before a performance and then afterwards sat quite remotely in her dressing room speaking to no one. The spells of crying followed. Jack had the letter from Dr. Conachy and wanted her to see a doctor in Sydney before she went from the depressive to the manic phase. But she was adamant that she would be all right without shock treatments. She did not trust any other doctor, and nothing could convince her that her refusal to consult anyone else was detrimental to her health.

All the members of the troupe were tremendously helpful. Helpmann was constantly infusing as much humor into the tour as possible. "Uncle Cecil" flew over again from London. The shakes stopped. The crying ceased. She smiled and laughed again. She went out on the hottest days looking cool and impeccable, shook hands with dignitaries, accepted bouquets of flowers, and gave short speeches. She seemed herself again, and Jack was confident that she was going to survive the long ordeal of the tour.

Saturdays they played two performances. Early one Sunday in the third week of their run (Vivien was always awake by eight A.M. no matter what time she had gone to bed the previous night) she announced that she had accepted an invitation for them to drive out to visit a couple they had met, John Thompson and his wife. The Thompsons lived two hundred miles from Sydney and Jack reminded her rather curtly that it was entirely too much of a trip for her when she had to be back for a performance the very next night.

"I said we would go and we will," she retorted angrily. "And if you don't want to go I'll drive there alone."

Before Jack could stop her she was outside and had moved toward the car they had rented. There was little else he could do but follow and get in beside her, as she refused to let him drive. Silence shrouded them as they drove through the heat of the day. Suddenly

Jack looked up to see the Sydney Harbor Bridge come into view. "I'm very sorry but we've got to do a U-turn here," he told her.

"Why?"

"Because we are going in the wrong direction," he advised.

She swung the car around and they drove at least a hundred miles again in complete silence. Jack knew there was nothing he could do to get her to return to the hotel and, fearing she could do serious harm to herself if he asked her to stop and let him out of the car, did nothing. Suddenly Vivien seemed to have lost control, and the car swerved madly. Jack grabbed the wheel and pulled the vehicle to the side of the road. They had a puncture and Jack, Vivien fast at his heels, got out to change the tire, sweating in the terrible heat as he worked.

Immediately droves of buzzing flies surrounded them. Still refusing to speak to him, Vivien nonetheless grabbed a road map from the glove compartment of the car and worked furiously swatting and sweeping away the flies that hovered over Jack's sweaty figure.

They arrived at their destination at half past five, exhausted from the drive and the terrible tensions of the day, to be informed that the Thompsons had planned a huge gala at the local country club in Vivien's honor. Over one hundred people, Jack was informed, had been gathered to meet "Scarlett O'Hara." Vivien had collapsed in bed by then and could not be awakened. Jack rather nervously agreed to leave her and to go with his host, while Mrs. Thompson waited behind to accompany Vivien when she awakened.

Not long after Jack and Mr. Thompson arrived at the country club another guest excused himself, returned to the Thompsons' house, and there took a shotgun and killed himself. Vivien had mercifully slept through the terrifying event, but when she awoke the house was filled with people and the terrible sound of uncontrolled sobbing. If she had been headed into a manic phase as Jack feared, the shock of the suicide seemed to have affected her like a series of ECT's. She was once again a sweet and tender woman, contrite as she got into their car early the next morning—this time giving Jack the wheel.

"I'm not afraid to die," she confided after an hour or so of silence. "But you won't let them put me away will you?" she pleaded softly.

"It would have to be over my dead body," he assured her.

From this point in the tour, there were strong parallels to Vivien's behavior on the *Titus Andronicus* tour in 1957. Trudi was less and less able to cope with seeing Vivien in this state. Helpmann was always able to make Vivien laugh, for he was a marvelous quick-witted jester and a wonderful storyteller. But he hated to see her when she was manic and would disappear at those times (though when she was in a state of depression he was the most supportive and helpful of all those close to her). Her friends could not bear the Jekyll and Hyde change that would take place in her personality. She became a different person; rather than being the impeccable and well-mannered Vivien they knew, she would become sluttish and slovenly and say things that she would ordinarily never allow anybody to repeat in her presence. She was capable of stripping naked in front of people and screaming obscenities. She had a deliciously witty yet naughty sense of humor ("Mummy," she once asked the prim and quite proper Gertrude in front of guests, "have you ever slept with another woman?"), but while manic she became coarsely obscene. At such times Jack did his utmost to keep her away from people.

From Sydney they went to Adelaide, then Perth, Wellington, and Christchurch, winding up the Australian tour at Her Majesty's Theatre in Auckland on St. Patrick's Day 1962. There were only twelve days before they were to open in Mexico City on the first wing of their Latin American tour.

While they had been received well everywhere they went in Australia, in Latin America their reception was even more enthusiastic. Language seemed no barrier. They had cut *Duel of Angels* from the repertoire, and *Twelfth Night* and *The Lady of the Camellias* were familiar enough so that an audience who did not understand English could still follow the story.

From Mexico City they went to Caracas, Venezuela. They were there at the Hotel Tamanaco on April 8, which Vivien and Jack considered their anniversary. Vivien could not let the day pass without giving Jack a present, although he had begged her not to do so.

> My Darling [she wrote in the letter that accompanied the gift]—Before you become upset (quite unnecessarily) by this present remember I chose it long, long ago in Vence [France] and give it to you now in remembrance of a day that changed my whole life—a change for the very best my darling love. I am grateful to you for so many things—you have taught me more than you imagine—dear love— Happy anniversary— Your very own—Angelica.

The present was a ring she had worn, and which was now attached to a gold chain for him to wear about his neck.

From Caracas they went to Lima, Peru; Santiago, Chile; Buenos Aires, Argentina; Montevideo, Uruguay; Sao Paulo, Brazil; and finally, on May 11—Rio de Janeiro. Perhaps Rio's hot, humid climate brought back memories of Ceylon, or perhaps the extensive and enervating tour was beginning to become too much for her, but a deep depression again set in. Jack wanted her to fly back to London, but she insisted on visiting Lucinda and Howard Dietz in New York for a few days first, and he agreed.

Vivien had previously deferred to Olivier's wishes. Now Jack deferred to hers.

Chapter Twenty-nine

The loss of Notley had been a difficult adjustment for Vivien. It had been more than a country home, it had been a way of life. She dearly loved the weekend guests, the beautiful gardens, and the roots it had given her.

Before she had left on the Australian tour, she had managed to find her own country house. It was Dirk Bogarde who had put her on to Tickerage Mill, a Queen Anne house situated about forty-five miles from London, a short distance from a lovely old village, and on a mill pond. She wasted no time in buying it. Within a few weeks she hung her pictures on the walls; and though the house was being completely renovated and was in a state of chaos, her friends navigated the extremely narrow unpaved stony long private road to its front door to visit her.

Jack Merivale, of course, was by her side. Poo Jones, after a six-month quarantine made necessary by his American adventure, was regally stretched out before the sitting-room fireplace. But there was something strangely amiss. Vivien was almost the same magnificent hostess as she had been at Notley. Yet it always seemed as though the master of the house was away.

Tarquin had been traveling in Indonesia, writing while he lived with the people. He returned to London a short time before she and Jack had left for the Australian tour. One night Vivien and Tarquin sat up late surrounded by many of her beautiful possessions that had once graced Notley's rooms. Everyone else in the house was asleep, and in those quiet hours Tarquin and Vivien were trading private thoughts.

"Leigh taught me how to live," Vivien said softly, "your father how to love, and Jack how to be alone."

Tarquin understood what she was saying. For the first time in her life Vivien—who had been married to or living with a man continually since she was eighteen—believed in her own identity. Jack's position was not easy, and Tarquin and those close to Vivien admired the manner in which he handled a most compromising situation. And Suzanne, with Jack now at her mother's side, appeared more relaxed in her visits, frequently accompanied by her family. The house at Tickerage had a more comfortable atmosphere than any Larry and Vivien had shared. To Suzanne it was "Mummy's house," to her boys "Grandmama's house." They loved visiting, and Vivien truly liked having them there.

On May 26, 1961, shortly before the tour, Vivien had written Ted Tenley:

Dearest Ted— Your *beautiful* little cup arrived this week and goes down to Tickerage today. Thank you for the dear sweet *pet*. The house is an absolute dream and I am miserable at the thought of having to leave it [for Australia]. The swan had 7 cygnets—the Moor has had 4 Moorlets or whatever they are called—the duck had 3 ducklings—and to cap it all a pigeon with a message around its leg landed on the lawn! We soon discovered what the message read—"Get the hell in and learn your lines!" [Helpmann's practical joke.] Rehearsals going well. Bobby is being marvelous. The company are charming and they are ach-tung! All the costumes are lovely but the ones for *Lady of the Camellias* are just the most ravishing I have seen. Poo comes home today [from quarantine]. It is 7 A.M. and I am so excited I cannot sleep for he will be here at 9:30. We have a tiny poodle at Tickerage called Sebastian and a small fry pussycat called Nichols. I do hope they all get on together!

She was home—for Tickerage, not Eaton Square, would from this time represent home to her. Curiously, she never referred to England as home, never thought of herself as English, for that matter. She was an *International*. "After all, my parents were French and Irish and our family even has Spanish blood—and I do so love the United States and consider myself part American," she would often say.

Jack and Vivien spent a few days at Sands Point, New York, with Cindy and Howard Dietz after the long tour. When they got back to London, Dr. Conachy had seen her a few hours after her arrival at Eaton Square, and within a few days and after a series of shock treatments she was well enough to travel down to Tickerage. On arriving, she wept with joy as she cradled Poo Jones in her arms and was careful not to step on Sebastian and Nichols, who were fighting for equal time. Jack wanted her to rest, but that was an impossibility for Vivien. She was home, with people and friends sharing her days and evenings. A new member of the staff, Mrs. Macaulay, immediately became her right arm. Mrs. Mac, as Vivien called her, was of a much easier, calmer nature than Trudi, possessing the ability to cope under any circumstances, and Vivien felt safe and protected in her care.

While Jack and Vivien had been in Australia she had been sent a playscript of a musical version of *Tovarich*, a play by Jacques Deval and Robert Sherwood.

"Ridiculous. I can't sing," Vivien had said, putting it aside without even opening the cover.

"Now, just a minute," Jack had reminded her. "I remember that story. The part of the Grand Duchess is ideal for you, and certainly you dance. God knows you are always complaining you have no one to dance with and chiding Bobby Helpmann about his neglect in this matter. [Helpmann was a great dancer long before he moved to acting and directing.] And Rex Harrison did not think he could sing when he was first handed the playscript of *My Fair Lady*."

Vivien had picked the playscript up dutifully, if rather reluctantly, found it enchanting, and considered accepting the role. Shortly after, the producer, Abel Farbman, had flown to New Zealand to see her, and she had even stood on the stage of the theatre where she was appearing one hot afternoon and sung a chorus of "Alone" for him. Obviously her rendition had not been too bad, because he had become so persistent that he then flew to Mexico City when she was appearing there and had her listen to a recording of the score, and from there to Buenos Aires to discuss the script alterations. Finally she had agreed to open with the play in New York that following spring. It gave her time to take some singing and dancing lessons and to rest up at Tickerage for five or six months before flying to New York for rehearsals. More important, she could plant the gardens and finish decorating the house and with the arrival of summer fill it with friends and flowers.

The parade of dear friends began from the start of June 1962. Rachel Roberts and Rex Harrison were among the first, with Harrison giving Vivien advice on singing in a musical. Her brown leather guest book with "Tickerage Mill—April 1961" hand-tooled in gold on its cover was filled with a scramble of famous names during that period. Tarquin wrote his name in Chinese, Gielgud's neat small script appears and reappears, as does Leigh's open, friendly hand. The Redgraves came, Terence Rattigan, George Cukor, Noël Coward, and many others.

Vivien, who loved and needed the stimulation that the intelligence and wit of her friends gave her, thrived on good conversation. Although Tickerage was minuscule compared to Notley, there still was enough room for five or six houseguests on a weekend and many more for luncheons and dinners. Mrs. Mac was a marvelous cook; and mealtimes, either in the dining room or on the terrace overlooking the mill pond, were as elegant and as much fun as they had ever been at the Abbey.

It was obvious to everyone that she adored Jack for "saving her." But no one speculated anymore that they would marry. With Tickerage Vivien seemed to have found peace. She seldom spoke of Larry, but his picture remained by her bedside, as well as a small box containing the arrow ring she had received from him when the film plans for *Macbeth* had fallen through. And in the drawer of her bedside commode inside a leather wallet were two letters he had written her, worn thin from constant folding and unfolding. When he was at Chichester in *Uncle Vanya* she had gone to see him twice but had not stepped backstage. Writing Lucinda at the time, she said, "What a rare thing Larry has made of Uncle Vanya. His Astrov was one of my favorite of his performances. I have seen it twice."

She still thoroughly enjoyed the role of Lady Olivier; it seemed most unlikely that she would ever give it up by remarrying.

On November 5, 1962, she celebrated her forty-ninth birthday with a weekend of festivities at Tickerage. Her guests came on the second, a Friday, and remained through the fifth, which was a Monday, and included Alan Dent, Hamish Hamilton, Gertrude, Jack, Bumble, and Leigh.

The day before her departure for New York to do *Tovarich*, Vivien, with Gertrude and Jack, returned to London. Judy Garland, married at the time to Mark Herron, was living near Eaton Square and invited the three of them for dinner. At least Vivien assumed Gertrude had been included in the invitation. Judy seemed happy to see them, but nonetheless was in an agitated state. Dinner was announced, and they all went into a small dining room. The table was one place-setting short, but neither Judy nor Herron did anything about repairing the mistake. Judy filled the seats with her guests, leaving none for herself. Then she dashed in and out of the kitchen during dinner, hovering over the table, seemingly not eating a morsel of food. Gertrude sat through the dinner in appalled silence, Vivien and Jack chatted about superficials. Eventually Judy disappeared into her bedroom. It was a terribly upsetting evening for everyone, especially for Vivien.

Since Jack was scheduled to appear in a John Huston film, *The List of Adrian Messenger,* he remained in London, and Trudi accompanied Vivien to New York on November 12. Jack was already apprehensive about letting her go alone, but he knew he had to pursue his own career. She wrote him during the flight:

> Angel—my Angel— This is altogether very painful and miserable sitting here without my darling. We have been in the air about ten minutes. The plane is quite empty. I have been looking at your pictures—the one of you at 20—just a very little younger than you are now! And then the one with a very large beaker of some dubious liquid in a garden in Buenos Aires—I also have lots of your cards and letters—I cling to them because they make you seem not so far away— Oh, my darling—it is difficult to know what to hope for. When shall we be together again? You have been so adorable during these last months in spite of all the pain you have been in [he suffered a bad back], and I admire and love you and oh how I miss you already—so what the coming weeks and months will be like I fear to think.

She was met at the airport by Abel Farbman, Ted Tenley, Radie Harris, Delbert Mann, and several other friends and driven to the Dorset Hotel, where a suite had been reserved for her. There was a cable waiting from Jack to reassure her, and all the welcoming committee came up to her suite for sandwiches and drinks while Trudi unpacked. Radie stayed on for a time. But finally Vivien was alone.

"I have taken a pill," she wrote Jack, continuing her letter, "because I want to have a proper sleep and know I should be awake fretting and missing you so dreadfully otherwise and I have a script conference at noon."

The letters flew back and forth across the Atlantic in the same passionate profusion as when she had been separated from Larry before doing *Gone With the Wind*—at least a letter every day and sometimes two or three. Her letters reaffirmed that she was uneasy about appearing in a musical. But Vivien's appetite for loving admirers seemed as insatiable as her appetite at times was for food. She had not changed since she was a little girl at Roehampton, a young woman married to Leigh, or Olivier's wife. Even if she had to remind herself (and the letters helped in this way), she wanted to be assured that love was hers just for the reaching out. She wrote Jack the next evening:

> Angel Darling— I have been longing for the day to finish so that I could write to you. Abel arrived at noon and we talked over the script. Delbert Mann [then the director] at 2:30—I had a session with him over it—then to the office with the lot of them to hear the new songs! and new ideas!—oh, dear—one wonders how anything ever gets settled. I came *home* (great Heavens!)—back! at 6:30 bewildered as to how I should ever get through it. I feel so alien to this medium and not at all sure of what is right and what is not. Everyone seems to have a different view of what they believe right for a musical—they all have the experience I lack . . . I feel utterly lost and wish only for news of you— Sweet—sweet one—you were *naughty* to put that lovely pressie in my pocket but I do thank you—what an angelic—generous thought—I hope you are alright in the flat with Mrs. Mac and Poo Jones—are they treating you kindly and fondly? My sainted boy—goodnight—I love you—I love you so deeply—I read your letters all of the time to give me courage— How dearly and *clearly* you write—unlike your most loving—Angelica.

She then added, "Do you think Poo Jones misses me at all? I do him dreadfully—please play an extra game with him for me."

She was never left alone except to sleep. The daytime hours were filled with learning the songs ("They really are pleased with my voice isn't that comforting?") and the dances ("Byron Mitchell is taking me to buy some dancing shoes—I am truly frightened. I do not think they really realize what they are in for!") and deciding on an interpretation of the role.

Evenings were spent with good friends like Tennessee Williams, Arnold Weissberger, Milton Goldman, and Radie Harris. Noël Coward was in town, and that gave her great delight. Dining with him one night, she took a torn letter from her wallet. "You sent this to me when I was in Netherine Hospital during my breakdown," she told him. "I've never gone anywhere without it since."

Weekends she spent with the Dietzes at Sands Point. She wasn't drinking to excess, but she could not stop smoking. Her sleeping pattern was the same. Even with the aid of pills she never slept more than four to five hours. Trudi appeared about eight A.M., but by that time Vivien would have finished the *Times* and done the daily crossword, written Jack, and already had her breakfast sent up from room service.

Vivien begged Milton Goldman, the agent and her good friend, to see if he could find a play for Jack to do in New York, now that his work on the Huston film was complete. Then she rang Kay Brown to see what she could do. With each day she grew more fearful that she would not be able to withstand the pressures of the actual production without him.

She threw herself into the hard work of the rehearsals and visited her old friend Leueen MacGrath as often as she could at her new home on East 62nd, as Leueen had Poo Jones's sister and the two cats greatly resembled each other. Thanksgiving was spent with the Kanins (Garson and Ruth Gordon). Throughout this time she kept calling Goldman to ask, "Have you found something for Jack yet?"

When they moved rehearsals from the rehearsal hall to the Broadway Theatre on December 11, Vivien wrote Jack:

> Great heavens! What a theatre—so ugly—but really it does not seem much bigger to me than the opera house in Manchester! Jean Pierre [her co-star] has a very large, low voice—Noelie says it is much worse than mine. I saw my dressing room at the theatre for the first time—it is indescribable—a most fearful battleship grey—a sort of passage—with odd walls jutting out—it makes the Royal Adelaide Theatre look like Versailles!

Leigh was undergoing an operation back in England and, unable to put him out of her thoughts, Vivien had Jack call him and keep her informed. "Do visit Leigh. He would like that!" she urged. She corresponded with Leigh as she always did when she was away from England and kept him up to date on her life.

They rehearsed straight through Christmas. It was Vivien's first experience with the chaos of mounting a musical and the insecurity instilled by the removing and replacing of performers and crew. Just after 1963 was ushered in, they took the show to Philadelphia and Trudi wrote Ted Tenley:

> Dear Ted— How sweet of you to send me the wire for opening night. Many thanks. Well, I presume you have heard by now that they did not throw eggs or rotten tomatoes. In fact, the place roared with applause. The show still needs tidying up, but I am certain it can be

done. Vivien and Byron's Charleston stops the show every night and even though the reviews have been mixed, word of mouth must have been terribly good. In spite of bitterly cold weather and a transport strike the lines at the box office are tremendous, business is marvelous. Delbert Mann has left the show and we are expecting Peter Glenville any day now. With his reputation it should be no problem at all for him to straighten out those few weak spots. Vivien has lost a lot of weight and I am very concerned about her health. I hope she is strong enough to carry on for a long time. The play is so demanding. A lot of her friends are here for the premiere. Nöel Coward, Garson Kanin and Ruth Gordon, Radie and many more, and they unanimously raved about her performance. Nöel had a lot to criticize but he really went overboard and I only hope Vivien does not take his words too much to heart.

Vivien was, in fact, seriously ill in Philadelphia, but somehow she managed to conceal it. She had asked to have Dr. Conachy send her the pills she used to combat her periods of depression, and the bitter cold of Philadelphia heightened her false sense of exhilaration. She also began to drink heavily again.

The show played Boston before going to New York on March 18, where it opened during a protracted newspaper strike, so the only reviews appeared on television. "First nighters rocked the rafters with spontaneous applause," one reviewer reported. The show was a great hit and Vivien the jewel in its tinseled crown. It probably was just as well that the reviews did not appear in print, because artistically it was not a show that the critics could have lauded; but Vivien—as in Philadelphia—stopped the show doing the Charleston with Byron Mitchell, and she looked incredibly beautiful. Shortly after the opening she won the Tony award for her performance, and when the newspaper strike was over all the critics were unanimous in their admiration of her charm and talent. Appearances were that it would enjoy a long run, but Vivien was not well and her friends were grateful when Jack joined her in New York to appear as a replacement in *The Importance of Being Earnest* at the Madison Avenue Playhouse until it closed on July 13. He arrived to find her in the worst state he had ever known her to be in.

It was a difficult spring, and an even more trying summer. They moved into a lovely house with a beautiful garden that Gielgud had formerly sublet. Her friends still surrounded her. Although Tennessee was upset by the terminal illness of his longtime friend Frank Merlo, he still found time for her. He had loved her performance in *The Roman*

Spring of Mrs. Stone, considering it the best film translation of his work and Vivien his truest film heroine. Vivien seemed able to control herself in the presence of good friends like Nöel Coward and the Dietzes, but lost control when she was alone with Jack, and often backstage at the theatre as well.

One night before going on she became more manic than anyone had ever seen her. Ted Tenley was there and helped Jack try to restrain her, but she fought like a tiger for nearly an hour, trying to hurl herself against the door and totally dismantle the room. That frightening catlike quality surfaced; and when she was at last subdued she sobbed and clung to Jack, and finally, looking like a small pussycat, she curled up terrified and horrified at the damage she had done in the room. On October 6, with Jack fearing she might truly be losing her sanity, and with Vivien in an even more progressed state of manic behavior, she played the Grand Duchess for the last time. Jack and Trudi took her under heavy sedation back to London and put her into Dr. Conachy's care. After a longer than usual series of treatments, Jack and Bumble drove her back to Tickerage Mill, but it was winter and the trees were barren of leaves and the mill pond was frozen over.

Chapter Thirty

Vivien rested at Tickerage waiting for an early, early spring, waiting for the flowers to bloom, sharing the eternal hope with Jack that a miracle would happen and that she would never again suffer the indignities of another manic attack. Leigh's steadying influence was more important to her than ever. They spent her birthday quietly with Leigh at his home, Old Manor Farm, in Zeals, Wiltshire, and returned to Tickerage for Christmas. The next day they drove to south Devon to spend the weekend with Olivier's two nieces—Caroline and Louise, of whom Vivien was most fond, returning to Leigh's to spend a night before traveling on to London and Eaton Square. New Year's Eve they ventured across the Square to have a drink with Bobby Helpmann and Michael Benthall, and then over to another friend's to greet the New Year, but they came home directly thereafter.

"She's really very well again now," Jack wrote Ted Tenley. "Thank God, and we are off to Tobago on Tuesday for a month which should do her a world of good."

Tickerage—so beautiful in all seasons save for the bitter winds of winter—had grown depressing and lonely. The long road to the house was so icy and difficult to navigate that not even Leigh wanted to attempt it. Jack was concerned that loneliness and restlessness could trigger a recurrence of her condition, so he arranged for them to meet the Dietzes on the island of Tobago, knowing how much Vivien adored them and how impossible it would thus be for her to refuse. They had also visited the island once before on a short visit prior to

the Australian tour, and she had been enchanted with it and enthusiastic about going back.

They met Howard and Lucinda and stayed at the Arnos Vale
Beach Hotel, which was set high on a hill that overlooked the un-
spoiled Robinson Crusoe beach and was surrounded by thickly
greened trees and a wild profusion of exotic flowers. It was warm and
the clear and limpid water revealed literally thousands of tropical fish
beneath its rippling surface.

One day they sailed over to a nearby island that was a bird sanctuary and which contained a large aviary boasting birds with all kinds
of tropical plumage. The aviary was about to close when they arrived
late in the afternoon and the ticket taker did not want to accept their
entrance fee. Jack was livid and refused to turn away, so reluctantly
they were allowed in. Called the "Oasis," it had splendid gardens and
rare and lovely birds. Vivien took a fancy to a large white cockatoo,
which, according to the plaque outside its aviary, was supposed to be
able to imitate human speech. Drawing as close to it as she could, she
repeated over and over with full Shakespearean intonations, "Fuck
the Oasis, fuck the Oasis, fuck the Oasis . . ." for a solid and patient
five minutes. Then, after a moment the cockatoo repeated in imita-
tion of Vivien's precise English pronunciation, "Fuck the O-*a*-sis,
fuck the O-*a*-sis, fuck the O-*a*-sis . . ."

They returned to Tickerage Mill in March, in time for Vivien to
begin the spring planting. Dr. Conachy had died, which came as a
great shock to her, but she was placed in the care of Dr. Linnett,
whom she respected. She and Jack spent a fairly idyllic early spring.
They had no sooner arrived back from Tobago than she received an
offer from Stanley Kramer to appear in *Ship of Fools*. She wrote
Cindy Dietz in March, "Tomorrow I see Stanley Kramer about a film
he is making this summer—it would be nice if it is anything
interesting."

It apparently was, because a week later she wrote Cindy that the
meeting with Kramer was interesting and the film sounded as if it
might be possible. "I shall have the first draft in a week. Meanwhile I
shall try to struggle through the 700 pages of the book!"

Noël Coward and Cole Lesley came to spend a week. Vivien
wrote Cindy on March 15:

> Noelie has been here for a week which has been a huge joy. He is
> looking perfectly wonderful and seems really totally recovered from the
> horrors he has had to put up with. [He had been quite ill.] He is now
> painting huge canvases and Cole counted 422 pairs of feet in one! They

are really very attractive (Canvases and feet!) and his pleasure in them is adorable. I am hoping to go and stay with him in Switzerland sometime this spring and am determined to pick up my brushes again. At last the country is starting to hint of spring. The wild daffodils are out at Ticker-age and the anemones about to burst into bloom and if those rotten little bullfinches don't nibble the blossoms it should be wonderful this year.

She never did visit Coward, because she decided to accept the role offered to her by Kramer in *Ship of Fools*. On April 27, 1964, she wrote Cindy:

How dear of you both to say I could come to you on my way through—but I very much doubt if I shall have the time. There seems to be so much to do before leaving. I decided on the film because I really think it might be interesting and the part though not well motivated very arresting in the book and with great possibilities. Kramer is the director and producer and I do think he is one of the very few one can look forward to working with. . . . Jacko has been playing the film star part in *Mary, Mary* in Windsor and very, very good indeed he was. . . . Jose [Quintero] whisked in and out of London. George [Cukor] came and visited. I saw him again just before he left. Larry has made the most glorious success in *Othello*. We go to see it tomorrow night. Today as I was picking daffodils and narcissus and forget-me-nots and tulips I longed for you to be with me. The sun was shining and it all looked lovely enough for *you* to see. God bless you. Vivien.

Cindy had been relieved to see her on the island of Tobago, for she had looked rested and well. The last time Cindy had been with her, during the run of *Tovarich*, she had been "a poor little, exhausted, thin child—so exhausted, yet the same Vivien—for as worn and sick as she was she simply insisted she dress and go into town to buy personal presents for all the members of the cast and crew. And the same impeccable houseguest. Her bedroom never looked used and each night she would remember to carefully fold her soiled clothes and cover them with a beautiful square of lace-trimmed crepe de chine."

The Dietzes were two of the people with whom Vivien behaved well. Noël, Leigh, George Cukor and Howard Dietz were all older men, extremely knowledgeable, possessed of great charm and wit. (Dr. Conachy had fallen into the same category.) All were men who appeared to hold no sexual attraction for her, and with whom she never misbehaved.

Merivale was reassured to know that Cukor would be out on the

Coast, because Vivien had to fly there alone. He was completing work on a television segment and could not follow for a few days. Cukor had moved her into a lovely house on Thrasher Avenue arranged for by Kramer and had taken enormous trouble to redecorate for her before her arrival. The house was set high up in the hills and overlooked all of Hollywood, and it was a breathtaking sight to Jack as he stepped into the living room the first night he arrived. "I think we ought to take out citizenship papers and stay here," Vivien announced, but she dropped the idea by morning.

Kramer had considered only two actresses for the role of Mary Treadwell in *Ship of Fools*—Vivien and Katharine Hepburn. Hepburn did not want to return to films at that precise time because Spencer Tracy (whom she had lived with for years) was seriously ill. Vivien was Kramer's only other choice, and he was delighted that she had agreed to do the film. Her arrival had been set a week before the start of principal photography so that costume fittings would be completed in time.

Jack wrote to Howard and Cindy on June 16, the day following her first day on the film:

> She is very well and seems much happier to be here than either she or I expected. The house is charming and the weather is perfectly dreadful. There's a heated swimming pool which is like a sulphur pool giving off clouds of steam in the damp, chilly California mornings. Vivien off for the studio about an hour ago looking twelve and a half.

Later that day on the back of the letter Vivien added:

> Oh, my darlings, what an adorable welcome! Yours were the first flowers I saw—amaryllis, white and blue, huge shasta daisies, peonies of all colors. Too lovely and your sweet note! I do thank you. I have been kept hard at work since the moment I arrived which is why I have not written earlier. Goodness how I wish you were here. There is a glorious spare room????!!!! The work goes well I feel. I like the script writer [Abby Mann] and he seems to like what I write so we get along well. George [Cukor] and Kate [Hepburn] have been saints. It's so lovely to have each here. I have a charming chauffeur and a car, a sweet, French good cook who brings her cat which is nice.

There was no location shooting, since the entire picture was filmed first at Columbia studios and then the Paramount process stages. Ironically, Kramer never used a ship, nor was a single ship photographed for the film. Unlike her relationship with Kazan, Vivien's comments and discussions on the script were welcomed by Kramer, and he allowed her great leeway in her interpretation. Out of these discussions emerged the way she finally played the makeup scene at the mirror and the Charleston scene. But even surrounded and supported by friends and working under superior conditions, Vivien spun into a manic phase within a short time. She had been drinking and Jack, feeling that alcohol was partially responsible, rang her friends to ask them not to serve cocktails before dinner if at all possible. She turned on Simone Signoret, who played the Condesa in the film, but the French star was marvelous and supportive and quickly became someone Jack could count on for assistance. Katharine Hepburn was by her side whenever she was not at Tracy's, and accompanied her to the periodic shock treatments she was forced to undergo during the making of the film. Kramer was completely aware of her condition, indeed knew of it even before he signed her. He had always admired her and says to this day, "Her courage was magnificent. Only occasionally were there problems. I cannot emphasize Vivien Leigh's courageous attitude enough. Any lesser person could not even have attempted to keep busy during such pressure, yet she was one of the hardest working and most professional performers I have ever worked with."

But the effort cost Vivien a great deal in her health, and Jack was alarmed when it was suspected that her tuberculosis had flared up again. Vivien did everything she could to fight the manic attacks and seemed much more terrified than ever of an attack coming on. She made sure that she was surrounded with all the people with whom she seemed to behave best, such as Kate and Cukor. She even sent for Gertrude, and persuaded John Gielgud to prolong his stay.

One day Vivien was sunning by the pool and Gielgud was in it. Vivien assumed that he could swim, because he would remain in the water for hours at a time. But he actually waded back and forth at the shallow end, making it appear that he was swimming. When Vivien heard a faint cry—"Help! Help!"—she looked up. Gielgud had stepped accidentally into the deep end and was flailing his arms about. Down he went. Vivien thought he was clowning about and paid no attention. Up he came again. "Oh, do please help," he whimpered, swallowing water as he gasped the words and sank below the surface again. Vivien leaped to her feet, dashed to the edge of the pool, dove in, pulled him from under the water, and swam with him to the edge of the pool. Somehow she managed to push him onto the ledge, whereupon she jumped out and began mouth-to-mouth resuscitation.

She seldom had any recall at all of what she did or who she might have offended during a manic attack, and this worried her terribly. "You must tell me who I might have hurt," she would beg Jack as she once had Olivier. "You must. I have to write them an apology." It was this gallant attitude of hers that won everyone's heart.

Lee Marvin, who was known to have an occasional drink, often came on the set breathing heavily and exhaling gusts of stale-scotch breath. More outspoken than she had been able to be with Gable during the shooting of *Gone With the Wind*, she would order him off the set and refuse to do a scene with him until he took care of his bad breath and his disrespectful behavior. In spite of it, they had a mutual admiration for each other. "God, you have talent!" she lauded him after the playing of their last scene together.

In the mirror scene she hummed and sang snatches of a popular song of the 1920s, and to use it in the film would have cost $30,000 to clear the rights. Kramer asked her to hum something else. She fixed her big beautiful eyes on him and smiled her famous Cheshire cat smile. "My husband was one of the greatest directors in the theatre and films. *He* would permit me to do any song I liked!" she replied. Kramer let her have her way but then dubbed in another song that needed no clearance and was hummed by another singer whose voice was of the same timbre as Vivien's.

She would talk about Larry often and to everyone. When she wrote him he replied. Enough time had passed since the divorce that he obviously felt in a more secure position. He was now a family man, a new father. Once again his picture appeared by her bedside, and the mementos from their life together were reinstated as well.

Jack was thankful to get back to London with Vivien on September 23. "We arrived bang on time," he wrote the Dietzes, "to find blue skies and sunny warmth and London looking clean and lovely, and Gertrude [who had returned before them] there to meet us looking clean and lovely too. She is amazing. She had got up at half-past five in order to be at the airport at nine and arrived looking like a two year old!"

That weekend they were back at Tickerage. Vivien was in a state where she wasn't quite herself but was not completely wild. The doctor came down from London to see her and a young Australian nurse,

Adelaide, was engaged. Gertrude, Mrs. Mac, and Cal Darnell (Linda Darnell's brother and a fond friend) were with her as well. Jack was terrified of what was to become of her. She had managed to get through the Kramer film with his kindness and the marvelous cooperation of Lee Marvin and Simone Signoret, but she was hallucinating much more frequently than she had, and he was fearful she might not be able to get the insurance companies to cover her for another film. And he could not see how she could continue to live on the scale she insisted on living if she did not do a film every couple of years. It seemed to him he had to do what he could to further his own career to supplement their income. Feeling assured she was in good hands, he went to London to speak to his agent.

Vivien then became hysterical and she rang him on the phone. "You've got to come home," she cried. "Things are very bad at Tickerage. I'm all alone!" Jack returned immediately, but she was, of course, as he had immediately upon disconnecting verified, not alone. For days he and Gertrude seemed to be holding a hospital vigil. Then one evening the three of them sat in the sitting room, Vivien curled up tensely in her favorite chair looking as though she might spring out of it at any moment; Poo Jones circled her neck like a fur collar; Sebastian was at her feet; the giant labrador, Jason, who had recently joined the family, was asleep by the fire. For a week Vivien had worn a troubled look, one that Jack and Gertrude and all those close to her recognized as a sign that she was in the manic phase of her illness. She was, in fact, not Vivien at all, reacting and acting like a totally different woman. Jack stared across the room at her, but she did not see him. Suddenly the troubled look seemed to simply melt away and she became incredibly serene. Her hands, which had tensely grasped each other moments before, had relaxed and she was stroking Poo Jones, and the attitude of her entire body was different.

Jack turned to Gertrude and whispered, "My God, I think I may go to church on Sunday."

"Church, dear?" Gertrude replied, not having noticed Vivien at that moment. "Why, dear, why?"

"Because she's returned to us." Jack sighed with relief.

And so she had, and once again Tickerage was filled with friends and Vivien was the Lady of Tickerage Mill. On October 18 she had recovered sufficiently to have Princess Margaret and Lord Snowdon for luncheon. Lord Snowdon had once lived in the house as a child, and the luncheon was thus an even more special occasion. Vivien adored royalty as much then as she always had, and she went to great extremes to make the visit perfect. She spent hours picking and arranging flowers, planning the menu (they had a halibut mousse, stuffed Cornish hens, green beans, salad, and an apple flan), selecting the linens and the china. The house had to be cleaned from top to bottom, the hedges trimmed, the gardens pruned. First she had decided to lunch on the terrace and then, fearful it might grow too cool, changed all the preparations to the dining room. The wines were chosen with great care, and she was truly thrilled when Lord Snowdon commented on their delicacy. When an occasion like the Snowdon luncheon was planned, Jack was always apprehensive until it was over. The strain of not knowing what he might expect at any minute was beginning to tell on him. But Vivien was so excited about the luncheon that she called Lucinda Dietz in New York to tell her about it. Any uneasiness Jack suffered seemed worth such genuine and childlike delight.

Her birthday was spent as it had been the previous year, with Leigh. Writing Ted Tenley, she commented, "I had a perfectly lovely birthday staying in Wiltshire with my first husband. It was peaceful and gay and the countryside was a wonder. Merivale was in fine humor. He goes to California tomorrow. I may go to Katmandu on the 30th. No joking!"

She wasn't. Jack had been offered a film role and after great deliberation had decided to take it. Vivien had behaved badly when he came to his decision. He suggested she come with him, but she refused. To Vivien a pattern seemed to be repeating; and she was not entirely wrong, because like his predecessor, Olivier, Jack had begun to fight for his own identity and self-preservation.

Chapter Thirty-one

Through Roger Furse Vivien had been introduced to Mr. and Mrs. Stebbins, who had lived in India and were planning to return. "Why don't you join us?" they asked Vivien after seeing how enthusiastically she asked questions about India and their life there, and hearing that she had been born in Darjeeling. When Vivien found she could not change Jack's plan to take the film assignment, she told the Stebbinses she would indeed go with them to India and then join Roger Furse and his wife on the island of Corfu, where they had a home.

Nothing Jack or Gertrude said made her change her mind, and so, leaving on November 19, earlier than she anticipated, she began what she glibly titled "a return to my roots." What follows are the letters she wrote Jack, which form an encapsulated journal of the trip.

November 22nd (1964)

Dearest Angel

Arrived in Delhi in a glorious sunrise welcomed by absolutely charming Americans and given a delicious breakfast. Now we are in the air in a tiny plane seating about 10 flying towards Katmandu. The Stebbins are completely good and sweet and gay and gentle. The sun is shining and the air very clear. Oh—the first sight of these extraordinary mountains— Oh dear, how I wish you were here seeing them with me.

November 23rd

The flight became too bumpy and uncomfortable to write any more— The Stebbins given a tremendous welcome at the airport—and I drove with his second in command and his wife who was in the middle of playing Elvira in *Blithe Spirit* for a week— I must tell you the first sight of the Himalayas is unforgettable— Peaks of blue white that you think *must* be clouds. The Embassy here is charming—lots of rooms, but simple—some have 2 beds lovely views and no bath. I do not know how to describe the place. It is by far the most enthralling I have ever seen— Temples everywhere—*beautiful* faces—Tibetan and Nepalese— After lunch we drove to the funeral city—all along the river are alcoves where the dead are burned and dowsed into the river. Above—lines of small temples heavily carved gutted windows and in the center the worshipped Penis sometimes surrounded by flowers and little offerings. Dear heart you will have been home two days when you get this. [He only did a cameo bit and then returned to London.] I am in bed. All the others still up. I am so sleepy and have not really recovered from the shots—the 2nd was far worse-than the first but I think with a real night's rest tonight I shall feel quite well again. I wish you were here to see these astonishing things. But I think just the same you would be restless!!— Goodnight my love—I'll add a little in the morning.

November 25th

Already we have seen so much—so many marvels—one's eyes are just kept swiveling. My darling one I do long to know how it all was with you—how it all is with you—whether you are spending most of the time at Tickerage or at the flat. Did little Poo give you a good welcome? We leave here Saturday and from then on I really am not sure of the itinerary as schedules are of the very vaguest in these regions—so plans are continually switching— All I know is that I shall be with Roger [in Corfu] on the 18th [of December] where I trust I shall find you my beloved. [Jack had promised to join her there.] This is a very healthy holiday dearest—early bed—lots of air—I am very well indeed— My breakfast is just coming in brought by a gentleman whose name translated means "moon God"! Not bad is it? My love my darling my most dearly missed darling— Your Angelica—

November 28th

In the air to Delhi

Darling one— I do hope this reaches you on your birthday [December 1st] and I hope you will have a happy day—how earnestly I wish you were here for it. The week in Katmandu was a truly marvelous experience— The Stebbins were the most enchanting hosts—you would love them— It was a warm and comfortable and charming house. Our inspections of the various temples and villages were all fascinating. The Nepalese are a dear people smiling and warm—truly beautiful faces—also the warmth of the Tibetans and some Chinese. One walk I shall never,

never forget up to a tiny village with a miraculously beautiful temple where we watched a Buddhist Ceremony— Then one day we flew to a place called Pokra—a very funny day on arrival at the airport. We asked for horses to take us to the lake—no horses. Mules? No mules—so I said "There are two bullocks—please attach them to a cart and we shall get in *it!*" This we did sitting on straw! The lake water was the color of pale jade and very warm. Yesterday we chartered a little plane (the Raj's in fact!) and flew all day over the range of these fantastic mountains and as close as we could get to Everest— It was so thrilling. Darling the only unhappiness has been your absence— I long for news and ache to hear your voice.

December 9th

Dear One . . . this morning we rode on elephants—a most peaceful and charming notion—their dear faces were all painted with flowers— Yesterday afternoon we went up a beautiful river which is a bird sanctuary— as amazing to see as our tropical fish [a recent hobby, for which a tank had been installed at Tickerage]—much colors and strange shapes— I took a lot of pictures and was given the nest of a Weaver bird—you shall see. The weather is most pleasant warm and sunny in the day and cool in the evenings— The dusk is positively Australian. The other day we passed a bus called "Public Transport"!!!—the markets are just too fascinating but I have been a very good angel only 4 earrings today and some bangles. I pray God it may not be very long before I see you. A thousand kisses.

December 15th

Dearest Love,

A letter—a letter— I keep reading it—it does indeed seem years since I saw you! We are flying over the Bay of Bengal landing any minute in Madras. With your letter came one from Cal (hilarious as ever)—a cable from Winston [Churchill] thanking me for his birthday flowers— one from Fursie saying how much he was longing to see us on the 18th— an Xmas card from Abby Mann saying he liked his jacket and that Stanley was getting pleased with the picture and me in it—oh—thank goodness—and a wonderful one from George—very funny and dear. You shall see them all on Corfu— Oh my Darling love! I miss you so and long for you and kiss you and kiss you and kiss you Dear love my love— Angelica.

To Jack's and Gertrude's great relief she had survived the Indian journey without any attacks and with seemingly little difficulty. Jack flew to meet her in Corfu on December 18, 1964, feeling some ease at having just received her last letter before boarding the flight. It was raining when he finally reached the island, a steady, depressing, humid rain which kept up the entire time they were there. Only a few hours after they were reunited it appeared to have a violent effect on Vivien. She became badly depressed. Jack wanted to return home with her immediately, but she would hear nothing of it. Before he could convince her, she had suffered a manic attack. Alan Webb had been visiting in Corfu with them, and the two men managed to get her onto a boat train (a plane would have been impossible). It was a terrifying trip, with Vivien in a terrible state, hysterical, trying to jump off the train, tearing at her clothes. Most people were frightened of her when she was in this condition (Trudi had been, as well as many other members of their staff), but Jack never feared that she would harm him, and he was able to restrain her.

During these violent attacks she wanted to get rid of Jack because she thought of him as her custodian. But at the same time, because deep down there was still an awareness of the love they had for each other, she wanted him to be there. So she would suffer these wrenching and terrible schisms of behavior. One moment she would be screaming for him to go away, to get out, and the next shrieking that he must never, ever leave her.

They arrived home before the New Year. Vivien felt a desperate need to see her grandchildren; so Suzanne and Robin and her three small boys—Jonathan, Rupert, and Neville—stayed from December 31 until January 3, 1965, with Vivien, Jack, Gertrude, and Leigh at Tickerage. Vivien had seemed miraculously to snap back to normal. Shortly after she had returned she was told that Winston Churchill had accepted an invitation she had previously extended him to lunch with her at Tickerage on the third. Pamela and Leland Hayward were also there, and Vivien appeared happier than she had been in years. She greeted Sir Winston as though he were a god, then led him into a discussion of Lord Nelson, whom she knew he worshiped. He once again told her how many times he had seen her film *Lady Hamilton* and how marvelous he thought it was. Afterward they walked in the gardens of Tickerage and discussed painting.

The parade of weekend guests at Tickerage began anew—Frederick Ashton, Laurence Harvey and Joan Cohn, Alan Webb, Jack and Dereen Hawkins—and on Valentine's Day Tarquin brought down his new bride, Riddelle. He was writing then and had published a book. On February 28, Peter Finch came to visit. Vivien was charming and gay, the perfect hostess, the best companion.

When Leland Hayward had visited, he had discussed with her the possibility of her appearing in a play, *La Contessa*, that Paul Osborn had adapted from a work of Maurice Druon's. Osborn had spoken many times with Vivien about this project during the preceding year. Druon's novel had been called *The Film of Memory*, and it was based on the extraordinary life of the Marquesa Casati, who had died only nine years before. The Contessa—with her white face, orange hair, and eyes rimmed with black tape—had been a famous personality of the 1920s. When she lived at the Palais Rose, near Versailles, where she kept tame leopards and panthers as domestic pets, she used to give enormous parties and not surprisingly ran through several fortunes. The play was financed by Seven Arts Productions, a film company, and it was thought that it might have strong film potential providing it was a successful play.

The play, with Vivien as the Contessa Sanziani (the fictional name for the Contessa), looking exquisite in gowns Bumble had designed for her, previewed on a Tuesday, April 6, 1965, in Newcastle under Helpmann's direction. Helpmann told the press, "This is not a play of ideas. It is nothing to do with kitchen sinks. It is a romance."

"Well nobody is going to quibble about that assessment," the critic of the Newcastle *Daily Express* said the morning after the opening. "It is in fact as stylized and as conscientiously romantic as a novelette—but it is a quite impossible play."

On the tenth of May Vivien wrote Cindy Dietz from Manchester:

My Darling Cindy,

It seems forever since I heard from you. I think about you and miss you. You will have heard from Paul [Osborn, the author] of our troubles. He was so dear and helpful when he was here, and I am so deeply hurt for him over the disappointment. It just doesn't seem to be the sort of play they want to see here at this time. Anyway, when I think of the years and work he put into it, it is heartbreaking. I do hope all his present ventures will make up for it in some measure. I simply do not know what I shall do next. This is the last week and of course it is distressing playing on knowing we are not going in [to London].

The show closed in Manchester and Vivien returned to Tickerage. On August 20 she wrote Cindy:

My darling Cindy— I did not come over for the *Ship of Fools* premiere for a number of reasons. Principally because of having to be available to see whatever characters turned up for Tickerage—moreover film premieres are not my idea of bliss! I read and read plays old and new but so far have found nothing I really find fascinating enough to do. I do not care for this enforced idleness one bit.

Ship of Fools had had one of the most gala invitational premieres in Hollywood history, almost equal to that of *Gone With the Wind*. Vivien received good personal notices, but the film was considered pretentious and a bore. Just the same, Vivien flew to Paris on November 1 to receive an Étoile Crystal, awarded her for her performance as Mary Treadwell. She again wrote Cindy:

> I have forgotten if I told you I had been asked to play Madame Van Meck in the joint American-Russian film on the life of Tchaikovsky. Naturally I am fascinated by the idea of such a venture and await the English script daily.

The project never materialized, but she waited during a beautiful autumn at her beloved Tickerage Mill.

> Today Jack and I are at Tickerage—no guests—a gentle rain—a rather cross swan gliding by on the mill pond—the labrador and the poodle chasing each other across the lawns. Yet Sunday was a divine autumn morning—a summer mist and the wild life on the lake doing their balletic best. We both said—if only Cindy and Howard were here.

Although Vivien no longer seemed disturbed by the gibes of critics, neither was she content—though she adored each blade of its grass and each fallen petal of its flower gardens—to retire to Tickerage. As she had long ago told Maureen O'Sullivan, "I am going to be a *great* actress." And this was still her lifelong dedication.

Chapter Thirty-two

Winston Churchill had died short months after visiting Vivien at Tickerage. Then Olivier became seriously ill and Vivien was beside herself with worry. It was doubtful that she would ever be capable of cutting the cord that bound her to Larry. Simply the very fact of his existence was a source of energy for her to draw upon. He had committed many unkind and hurtful acts toward her since Joan had entered his life. Indeed, there had been strained and difficult times dating back to their Australian tour before his meeting with Joan. Still, Vivien blamed Joan for her loss and felt that this was Larry's greatest betrayal of her. What appeared to be petty incidents—the luring of Vivien's maid one time to the Oliviers' staff; his staying with Joan at Margalo Gilmore's New York flat, where Vivien and Larry had been so happy—took on great significance to her. By this time all their painful years together had faded away and she remembered only the golden ones of their great passion for each other.

Though she wrote letters of apology for her behavior during a manic phase, and though she confessed to Jack her fear of madness, she otherwise never discussed her "illness," nor did she speculate on how her behavior during the illness might have been too much for Olivier to live with. She could, after all, be the most refined and tasteful woman—the woman he fell in love with—but she could also be incredibly vulgar, downright sluttish. She could be the quietest and most companionable of creatures, and she could be a wild, uncontrollable madwoman. She could be the kindest and sweetest and most thoughtful of people, and she could be cruel. Olivier had not been able to cope. Neither had Trudi, who by this time seemed to have faded away. And at times even Jack, who loved her perhaps more than Olivier had, because he had entered their relationship with full awareness of the fierceness of her illness, despaired of their future together. Yet Vivien refused to admit to herself that Olivier had left her because of her condition. She was convinced she would never have deserted him no matter what he had suffered. It was Joan, all Joan's fault, and she would never forgive her—though she still had no bad words for Larry.

She had written Cindy that she was not able to go to the States for the *Ship of Fools* premiere because she had to be available "to see whatever characters turned up for Tickerage." Few did turn up in the autumn of 1965. Vivien had lost weight and was not at all well. There was a cold sore on her lip that refused to heal, and she suffered extreme coughing spasms. Her tuberculosis was reappearing, but she refused to accept the seriousness of her condition.

Inactivity was the most painful state she could endure, and so it was with great exultation that she agreed to tour the east coast of Canada and the States as Anna Petrovna in a production of Anton Chekhov's *Ivanov*. It was adapted and directed by John Gielgud, and the cast included Jack, Roland Culver, Jennifer Hilary, Ronald Radd, Edward Atienza, and Dillon Evans, with Gielgud in the title role.

On December 21 Jack wrote Cindy Dietz from Eaton Square:

Have you heard the charming news that Vivien and I are coming to New York? I suppose you must have. I have been told that Radie devoted a paragraph or was it a whole column [in the *Hollywood Reporter*] to the fact that V was to play in *Ivanov*. What a pity she took it upon herself to cast her in the wrong part! Poor Radie. She's always putting her foot into it. We are rehearsing quite hard and finding it quite impossible either to learn or to act. V is obviously going to be exquisite in the part though her performance is being forged on the anvil of total despair.

A constant battle had raged between Radie and Jack, and both got in their licks against the other whenever they could. Radie had known Vivien from the days of her first arrival in the States and through the casting of *Gone With the Wind* and the halcyon days when the Oliviers had been one of the most romantic couples in the world, and she never was able to accept Jack in Olivier's place.

On December 29, 1965, Vivien wrote Cindy:

The present arrival date is February 3rd, but we have not settled where to stay in New York during the two weeks rehearsals. They will be pretty

278

hectic, I imagine, as quite a hunk of the cash will be needed. We are rehearsing whenever possible here. I spent Christmas with the whole family [Gertrude, Jack, Suzanne, Robin, the three children, and Leigh]. Very noisy it was! But great fun too!

The play had been produced the preceding season in London with Yvonne Mitchell in Vivien's role of Ivanov's Jewish wife who is dying of tuberculosis, and Claire Bloom in Jennifer Hilary's role of the young heiress intent on marrying Ivanov once he is a widower. Vivien need not have worried about the show's capitalization, because the venture had cost Alexander Cohen, its producer, only about $65,000 to import from London, and he had recovered that in its pre-Broadway tour (New Haven, Boston, Philadelphia, Washington, and Toronto). They were on a limited engagement that was to extend until June 11 if business warranted.

Paula Laurence and Ethel Griffies joined the show during its New York rehearsals. Gielgud greeted his company on the vast old stage of the Broadway Theatre (the company was only to rehearse there and open at the Shubert) beaming and trim in a bright sports jacket. Vivien entered punctually and stood in the center of the stage looking breathtaking in a raspberry wool suit. No time was wasted. The stage floor was taped, the rehearsal furniture in place, the cast was shown a picture of their set, and the rehearsals began.

They opened at the Shubert in New Haven on February 21 to good notices. New Haven was bitter cold and there was a terrible wind the entire time they were there, which kept them confined either to the Hotel Taft or to the theatre, which adjoined it. New Haven, of course, had wonderful memories for Vivien and Jack. It is where their love first bloomed, and Vivien felt quite elated to be there. But the cold was penetrating and she suffered chills and fever from the very onset of the tour.

The weather in Boston was sunnier, and Vivien and Jack even hosted an outing to Marblehead. Ethel Griffies, who was eighty-eight years old at the time, tripped over a chair in her hotel room the day of the Boston opening and broke a rib, yet went on that night strapped up and obviously in pain. Katharine Cornell came back after the performance. "Does it hurt?" Miss Cornell queried.

"Only when I speak," Miss Griffies replied.

Paula Laurence was relieved to hear the game Miss Griffies singing "Avalon" in her dressing room in Philadelphia, the next stop on the tour. "How nice to hear you singing again," she shouted over Miss Griffies' strident voice.

"The last time I played this theatre," the grand old performer recalled, "I not only sang but I did high kicks, and I was seventy!"

They stayed at the Hotel Sylvania in Philadelphia, which at the time also sheltered José Greco and his dancing gypsies, the casts of *The Trojan Women* and *Any Wednesday*, a visiting symphony orchestra, and the Harlem Globetrotters. But the *Ivanov* cast was closely meshed, and they remained together during their off-hours. Vivien, as she had always done in the past, entertained individual members of the cast nightly. It had been a precedent that she and Larry had begun with *Romeo and Juliet*.

Snow and rain plagued them in Toronto, and by the time they reached Washington, Jack was concerned that Vivien might not be able to continue on. But Vivien persisted.

They opened at the Shubert in New York on Tuesday evening, May 3, 1966, to a glittering, star-studded first-night audience after a three-hour rehearsal demanded by Gielgud (who was forever changing exits and entrances and bits of business as well as readings). A good deal of coughing and restlessness was heard from the audience. Clearly the show was slow, at times downright boring. The critics had seen a preview performance the previous night, as Alexander Cohen had insisted on an opening night curtain of eight-thirty, which meant they would have missed the last act if they were to meet their newspaper deadlines. But the play was as much lacking in dash opening night as it had been in preview.

Vivien's role hit terrifyingly close to home, and she would often at the end of the play and her final confrontation scene be shaken and have difficulty casting off the mood it engendered. Hers was a relatively small part, and as one reviewer said, "When she is off-stage the play too often falters."

During the five and a half weeks the play ran in New York, Vivien and Jack stayed in a house at 160 East Seventy-second Street that belonged to Joan Fontaine—Vivien having exchanged living quarters so that Fontaine remained at Eaton Square in London during the New York run of *Ivanov*.

Jack wrote to Cindy on July 27 from London:

Our homecoming was made hectic and hideous by the discovery that some precious things were missing from the flat. [There had been a burglary.] Poor V was distracted as some of them belonged to Larry. So the insurance people and the CID have been in and out and made our life rather miserable. But there is one bright bit of news to relate. The new gardener and his wife have turned up trumps. The garden at Tickerage has never looked better and the inside of the house was as clean and orderly as I have ever seen it.

Vivien was ill, and though she would not admit it she did pay more attention to the doctor's orders and rest more often than she had previously done. Yet she still had to fill Tickerage with her dear friends. On July 30 she returned there to celebrate World Cup Final Day with a host of them, Gielgud and Alan Webb among them, and to cheer England to a 4-to-2 win over West Germany. She then remained in the country for almost the entire winter, only traveling up to London on rare occasions. One time she decided the day had arrived when her little grandson Neville should be inaugurated into the grand family custom of tea at Brown's. The six-year-old was picked up by his grandmother in the chauffeured car for the gala occasion. Jack met them directly after and Vivien was beaming and extremely proud, claiming Neville's manners had been most exemplary and that he had to her delight invented a new dessert—ice cream with hard sauce—and his precocious taste convinced her that he would become a gourmet. Indeed she was so delighted that she insisted they repeat the rendezvous the following week at the same time.

Once again she picked the little boy up and drove him to Brown's and once again Jack met them directly after. This time both Grandma and the child glowered at each other. It had been a terrible afternoon, and Neville had obviously behaved in a rather commonplace six-year-old manner. "He was beastly, simply dreadful. He sloshed his sauce all over the table, and spilled milk all over the tea sandwiches. I shall never take him to tea again!" she announced and, leaving the child on the curb, got into the back seat of the car. Jack helped Neville into the front and they rode without speaking to each other—the child as furious at Vivien as she was at him.

Vivien spent a quiet birthday, her fifty-third, with Jack, Bumble, and Leigh at Tickerage. She was again becoming restless, and everyone, fearing idleness might adversely affect her, was happy when she was asked to star in the London stage production of Edward Albee's *A Delicate Balance*, which was set to open on the road in late summer before coming into the West End early in the fall. She was terribly enthusiastic about the idea of doing a play in London, although she was not at all sure about the merits of *A Delicate Balance*. Michael Redgrave came by often and they would rehearse together.

She wrote Cindy on May 19, 1967:

I cannot understand the grand success of Gadge's book [Elia Kazan's *The Arrangement*]. Noël has been here, which is always a joy. Actually well again thank heaven. I think—I *think* it all goes according to plan. I think I start rehearsals in July. But as all is not completely settled yet, I had better leave it at that. But it will be a great relief to be working again. Jack starts rehearsals for *The Last of Mrs. Cheyney* [playing the Gerald du Maurier part] on the 29th. They play Guildford for three weeks, and hope to bring it in. He is well and of course sends his dearest love. Beloved George Cukor is here preparing for *Nine Tiger Men*. He thinks there may be something in it for Jack. That is good news.

On May 28 Hamish and Yvonne Hamilton and Bumble were with her at Tickerage. The next day she wrote Jack at Guildford:

My Darling one—this is to tell you that you are going to be wonderful—Please try to enjoy it dear heart— All my thoughts and love are with you every minute. You are only wicked not to allow me to share tonight with you. I love you. Your Angelica.

She returned to London that Monday, and Gertrude and Bumble were terribly alarmed at her weakened condition. She seemed suddenly to have lost a great deal of weight, her coughing spasms were worse, and Mrs. Mac said she was spitting up blood.

She was put to bed immediately and the doctor called. To everyone's surprise, including Vivien's, he told them the tuberculosis had spread to both lungs and that the state of her health was very critical. He begged Vivien to let him transfer her to the hospital, but she adamantly refused. The next day he tried to convince her again that she should go where she could get constant care and treatment. The answer was the same. It would take at least three months, he told her, of not moving from her bed for her to get well. She promised she would behave and take all the dreadful medications he prescribed, not to smoke or drink, to rest all the time, and to see people for only a few minutes each day. The last promise was the only one that she found almost impossible to keep.

On June 17 she scribbled a note to Cindy on the backs of two picture postcards ("Greetings from Long Island" in fire red over a map of the island, and a card from the Phillips Collection, Washington, with a photograph of Degas' "Women Combing Their Hair"):

My Darling—isn't this *too* silly—I am so cross— However everyone has been so kind and thoughtful and the play is only postponed mercifully. I am like a lying chemist shop. All sorts of perfectly repellent things to take. They say it will be three months—*much* shorter than the last time at least. I read and write and look at my play [*A Delicate Balance*] endlessly. Think of you and dearest Howard and how I would dearly love to see you, Your devoted Vivien.

On July 2 she wrote a more proper letter:

My darling— I am so silly and outraged to the eyeballs these days—I cannot remember whether I answered your angelic cable. Isn't this a fair beast? So unexpected, too. Everyone has been angelic. The play is only postponed, not cancelled. I study it all the time in the hope I might understand it all one day. Forgive this more than usual dreadful handwriting, but the drugs they give me make me sillier than ever. Needless to say, I am far more worried about Larry. He writes me a lot but I think he is going through hell. Noël is here, which is a joy. Jack has made a whacking success in *The Last of Mrs. Cheyney* at Guildford. They soon come into the Phoenix. (He seems rather pleased with himself—for him!) My love to you both my darling Cindy— Vivien.

That week she seemed to improve and everyone was heartened. Olivier was recuperating quite satisfactorily from surgery. Jack was still in Guildford, and he rang every night from his dressing room before going on stage. On Friday, July 7, when he rang as usual, Vivien sounded very sleepy and her speech somewhat slurred. Deeply concerned, Jack drove back from Guildford directly after the show, arriving at the flat at ten past eleven. When he peeped into Vivien's room he saw that she was sound asleep—Poo Jones on the bed beside her. There were flowers on her desk—late peonies flown in from Holland—and a neat stack of letters and cables from friends from all over the world wishing her well. Her bed linens looked fresh, and there was no sign of soiled clothes or handkerchiefs. The scent of her favorite perfume, Joy, filled the air. There was, in fact, nothing medicinal in the room except the bedside tray with its many pill bottles placed carefully so that they were almost completely hidden by the same picture of Larry that had always been by her bedside—Larry when he was young and beautiful, the Olivier Jack remembered as Romeo and the Larry Vivien knew in her heart no other woman would ever possess.

Jack quietly closed the door and went into the kitchen to make himself something to eat. Fifteen minutes later he returned to check if Vivien was still sleeping. When he opened the door, to his horror he found her lying on the floor, face down. His immediate reaction was that she had stumbled while trying to reach the door. The doctor had warned her not to get up if she was alone, and Jack had in the past few weeks found her uneasy and uncertain on her feet as she watered plants in the sitting room. He ran to her and started to lift her up. Her body was warm, but she was not breathing. Kneeling over her, he desperately tried mouth-to-mouth resuscitation. But his frantic efforts were to no avail. She had obviously awakened and been overcome with a choking spasm, reached for the thermos on the nightstand to pour herself a glass of water, and knocked it over. She had struggled to her feet and staggered toward the door of her bedroom. A viselike feeling of claustrophobia must have overwhelmed her. She could not know at that moment that her lungs had filled with fluid and that she was drowning in her own liquid. No one had told her that was how the end might be, that tuberculosis often claimed its victims in that way.

Jack lifted her frail form from the floor and gently placed her on the bed. Poo Jones cried from beneath the bed, and Jack, fighting for his own control, rang the doctor and told him to come right over. Then he rang Bumble, Alan Webb, and Peter Hiley, an old friend who had been with them on the Australian tour. Bumble and Webb arrived only a short time after the doctor had declared her legally dead. Bumble spent the night on the living-room sofa so that Jack would not be left alone with Vivien's body. The next morning Gertrude, Suzanne, Leigh, and Larry were notified. Larry, still in the hospital, got straight out of his bed and came directly to the flat, where he remained with Jack for the entire day, not leaving until Vivien's body had been removed.

To Gertrude's horror, Vivien's will specified cremation, meaning a Catholic burial was out of the question; but she did accompany Jack down to the country to stand by as he carried out Vivien's last wish—that her ashes be scattered over the grounds of her beloved Tickerage.

All Vivien's friends were stunned by her death. It was inconceivable to believe that her warm, humorous letters would no longer cross the Atlantic, that her merry laugh had been stilled. The gift-giving had not stopped with her death, for her will carried bequests to each and every friend. It seemed no one was forgotten. To Cindy she had written the year before, "I have just made out my will and given all the things I have and many that I haven't." But she was richer than anyone had thought.

On Tuesday, August 15, 1967, her English friends gathered at the Royal Parish Church of St. Martin-in-the-Fields to pay her tribute. It was as star-studded an audience as Vivien had ever played to. The three men who had loved her—Leigh, Olivier, and Merivale—each sat by himself, each with his own private memories. Readings were given by John Clements, Emlyn Williams, and Rachel Kempson, Lady Redgrave. It was Gielgud who gave the final tribute.

"She will not be forgotten," Gielgud said, "for her magic quality was unique. A great beauty, a natural star, a consummate screen actress and a versatile and powerful personality in the theatre—she had a range that could stretch from the comedy of Sabina in *Skin of Our Teeth* to the naturalistic agonies of Blanche DuBois in *Streetcar*, and the major demands of Lady Macbeth and Cleopatra. Even in *Titus Andronicus*, when she had only a few short scenes, she contrived the most beautiful pictorial effects. Who can forget the macabre grace with which she guided the staff with her elbows to write in the sand with it, a ravished victim gliding across the stage in her long gray robe. . . ."

But in Hollywood memory of Vivien was more vivid and dazzling. To the friends she had there she would always be Scarlett O'Hara. On March 17, 1968, The Friends of the Libraries at U.S.C., who had in previous years honored Aldous Huxley, Somerset Maugham, and Cole Porter, chose to honor the first actress, Vivien Leigh. No Academy Award ceremony ever had a more stellar audience. The Town and Gown dining hall of the university was decorated with three huge blow-ups of Vivien—two as the fiery Scarlett O'Hara and one from her final film, *Ship of Fools*. No matter where you looked, there was Vivien flashing her green eyes as she smiled that unique and bewitching Cheshire smile that was singularly hers. This night there were no hymns or prayers. A sense of good theatre pervaded the evening, and Vivien would have approved. Those who spoke—Gladys Cooper, Greer Garson, George Cukor, Chester Erskine, Joseph Cotten, Wilfrid Hyde White, Judith Anderson, Walter Matthau, Rod Steiger, Claire Bloom, and Stanley Kramer among them—mainly told anecdotes. Then the lights dimmed and there was Vivien, nineteen and exquisite; Vivien and Olivier, youthful and handsome, in a scene from *Fire Over England*; Vivien singing and dancing with Charles Laughton in *St. Martin's Lane*, and sparring with Lee Marvin in *Ship of Fools*. The lights came on for a moment.

"And now," Chester Erskine announced, "the original tests Vivien made for *Gone With the Wind*."

The theatre darkened. There was a scratchy sound, a clapboard chalked with "Miss Vivien Leigh—Test—Scarlett O'Hara." The lighting was poor, the color muddy. Then there she was, holding all her tomorrows in as she caught her breath as Mammy laced up her corset. The head tilted back, there was fire in her eyes, electricity in each movement. There was no doubt why she had been chosen to play Scarlett O'Hara. Vivien was unique. Somehow she had managed to capture life and contain it within herself in such a manner that made her seem invincible.

The lights came up, the audience applauded, they stood and cheered, and then they filed out glancing up at Vivien as she dazzled them from the immense posters.

Acknowledgments

Tennessee Williams says of Vivien, "Having known madness, she knew how it was to be drawing close to death." Having often been close to death, I might add, gave her a fearlessness, a daring, a sort of insolence toward life, and a kind and tender and incredibly affectionate regard for the living. She was a good deal more than a film star who received two Oscars for two of the most celebrated roles in film history (Scarlett O'Hara and Blanche DuBois), or a stage actress who won acclaim for her Juliet, Antigone, and Cleopatra. Vivien Leigh was a woman of great extremes and greater excesses. A woman whose candle surely did burn at both ends, and yet refuses, through the incandescence of her friendships and her film portrayals, even now to be extinguished. I found myself wanting to know why Vivien Leigh would not recognize defeat, why in the face of it she would raise her exquisitely molded chin and stare uncomprehendingly at it with fiery eyes.

I traveled to London, Paris, the South of France, Hollywood, and New York to find that answer. I sat in darkened projection rooms watching almost every foot of film she had shot, spent weeks poring over her private letters and papers, talked to those closest to her and those who only had brushed her life. I walked her school halls, sat in her garden, studied her medical reports. These pages were written fortunately with the cooperation of many wonderful people: first and foremost, Mr. John (Jack) Merivale, who shared the last seven years of her life; Mr. Tarquin Olivier, whose sensitivity and insight were invaluable; Mr. Leigh Holman, her first husband; and Mrs. Suzanne Farrington, her daughter.

I am beholden as well to Doris Nolan and Alexander Knox, Sir John Gielgud, Sir Cecil Beaton, Mr. Elia Kazan, Ms. Maxine Audley, Ms. Maureen O'Sullivan, Mrs. Lucinda Ballard Dietz, Mr. Howard Dietz, Mr. Peter Hiley, Dame Flora Robson, Viscountess Lambert (Patsy Quinn), Mr. Theodore Thaddeus Tenley, Mr. Stanley Kramer, Mr. Arnold Weissberger, Ms. Paula Laurence, Mr. Charles Bowden, Mr. Angus McBean, Ms. Radie Harris, and Mr. Tennessee Williams.

Also, I must again thank Jack Merivale, Leigh Holman, Suzanne Farrington, Sir Cecil Beaton, Lucinda Ballard and Howard Dietz, Tarquin Olivier, Vicountess Lambert, and Dame Flora Robson for contributing photographs from their personal collections for use in this book.

I owe a debt of gratitude as well to the Mother General and the Sisters of the Sacred Heart Convent, Roehampton, the staffs of the British Film Institute, Mr. Steve Rubin and the Academy of Motion Picture Arts and Sciences, Ms. Martha A. Mahard and the staff of the Harvard Theatre Collection, and the staff of the Lincoln Center Library of the Performing Arts. This book could not have been written without the great enthusiasm of Mr. Michael Korda; the fine editorial help of Ms. Joan Sanger; the encouragement of Ms. Monica McCall; the tremendous help of Mr. Mitchell Douglas and Ms. Marlene Marks, who had the difficult task of transcribing many, many hours of taped interviews; and the invaluable research assistance given by Ms. Marcelle Garfield. I am also most grateful to the many, many others who answered my queries, letters and newspaper advertisements so graciously.

Vivien Leigh molded her life from dream and fantasy, which never contain defeat, lived in the future, where almost anything could happen, and truly believed, like Blanche, that everyone had a right to magic. And magically she lived her life.

Anne Edwards
New York City
July 1976

Chronology

THEATRE CHRONOLOGY

THE GREEN SASH by Debonnaire Sylvester and T. P. Wood
Opened at the Q Theatre, London, February 25, 1935
Produced and directed by Matthew Forsyth
CAST: Vivian Leigh (Giusta), Kathleen Boutall (Piccarda), David Horne (Marco), Margo Hawkins (Simonetta), Marion Fawcett (Amalia), Eric Berry (Giovanni di Campiglione), Tristram Butt (Ugoline), Douglas Vigor (Niccolo Niccoli), Eward Dudgeon (Gregorio), Ashton Pearse (Franco)

THE MASK OF VIRTUE by Carl Sternheim (English version by Ashley Dukes)
Opened at the Ambassadors' Theatre, London, May 15, 1935
Presented by Sydney W. Carroll
Directed by Maxwell Wray
CAST: Vivien Leigh (Henriette Duquesnoy), Jeanne de Casalis (Mme de Pommeraye), Frank Cellier (Marquis d'Arcy), Viola Tree (Mme Duquesnoy), Douglas Matthews (Footman), Jenny Barclay, Adeline Hook, Olive Hinton, Antonia Brough (Maids)
Moved to the St. James's Theatre May 29, 1935

RICHARD II by Shakespeare
Opened at Oxford (OUDS), February 17, 1936
Directed by John Gielgud and Glen Byam Shaw
CAST: Vivien Leigh (Queen), David King-Wood (King Richard), Florence Kahn (Duchess of Gloucester), Helen MacInnes (Duchess of York), Michael Denison (Lord Fitzwater), remainder of cast were students

THE HAPPY HYPOCRITE by Clemence Dane, from a story by Max Beer-
bohm, music by Richard Addinsell
Opened at His Majesty's Theatre, London, April 8, 1936
Directed by Maurice Colbourne
CAST: Vivien Leigh (Jenny Mere), Ivor Novello (Lord George Hell), Viola
Tree (Lady Otterton), Carl Harbord (Mercury), Philip Disborough (Sir
Follard), Charles Lefeaux (Beau Brummell), Isabel Jeans (La Gambori),
Marius Goring (Amor), Ffwlass Llewellyn (Bishop of St. Aldred's), Wil-
liam Dewhurst (Garble), Stafford Hilliard (Mr. Aeneas)

HENRY VIII by Shakespeare
Opened at the Open Air Theatre, Regent's Park, London, June 22, 1936
Presented by Sydney Carroll
Directed by Robert Atkins
CAST: Vivien Leigh (Anne Boleyn), Gyles Isham (Duke of Buckingham), C.
N. Anson (Campelus), Lyn Harding (King), Baliol Holloway (Wolsey),
Lawrence Baskcomb (Lord Chamberlain), Ion Swinley (Earl of Surrey),
Franklyn Kelsey (Griffiths), Phyllis Neilson-Terry (Queen), Hilda Tre-
vllyan (Old Lady)

BECAUSE WE MUST by Ingaret Giffard
Opened at Wyndham's Theatre, London, February 5, 1937
Directed by Norman Marshall
CAST: Vivien Leigh (Pamela Golding-Ffrench), Margaret Emden (Mrs. Gold-
ing-Ffrench), Enid Lindsey (Mrs. Mainwaring), Mary Hinton (Margaret
Chansy), Catherine Lacey (Diana Fellows), Peggy Talbot-Daniel (Mary),
Alan Napier (Sir Basil Graham), Jill Furse (Judith Chansy), Anne Firth
(Olga Jevins), Ann Casson (Hilda Mainwaring), Wallace Douglas
(Richard Dobbs), Denys Blakelock (Harold Dering), Anthony Ireland
(Hugh Greatorex), Margery Weston (Preston), Elizabeth Gilbert (a girl)

BATS IN THE BELFRY by Diana Morgan and Robert MacDermot
Opened at the Ambassadors' Theatre, London, March 11, 1937
Directed by A. R. Whatmore
CAST: Vivien Leigh (Jessica Morton), Evelyn Ankers (Susan Enderley), Ivor
Barnard (Rev. Morton), Charles Hawtry (Jerry Morton), Henry Kendall
(Edward Morton), Leslie Wareing (Nora Morton), Michael Shepley
(Harold Shaw), Lilian Braithwaite (Miranda Bailey), Lydia Sherwood
(Lila Carnworthy)

HAMLET by Shakespeare
At Kronborg Castle, Elsinore, June 1937
Directed by Tyrone Guthrie
CAST: Vivien Leigh (Ophelia), Laurence Olivier (Hamlet), John Abbott, Dor-
othy Dix, Anthony Quayle, Leo Genn, Torin Thatcher, and George
Howe

A MIDSUMMER NIGHT'S DREAM by Shakespeare
Opened at the Old Vic Theatre, London, December 27, 1937
Directed by Tyrone Guthrie
CAST: Vivien Leigh (Titania), Robert Helpmann (Oberon), Ralph Richardson (Bottom), Gordon Miller (Puck), Stephen Murray (Lysander), Frank Tickle (Quince), Anthony Quayle (Demetrius), Gyles Isham (Theseus), James Hoyle (Egeus), Sidney Bromley (Philostrate), Frederick Bennett (Snug), Alexander Knox (Snout), Jonathan Field (Starveling), Althea Parker (Hippolyta), Alexis France (Hermia), Agnes Lauchlan (Helena)

SERENA BLANDISH by S. N. Behrman, from the novel A *Lady of Quality* by Enid Bagnold
Opened at the Gate Theatre, London, September 13, 1938
Directed by Esme Percy
CAST: Vivien Leigh (Serena Blandish), David Tree (Edgar), John Teed (Nikkle), Trevor Reid (Walter), Aubrey Dexter (Sigmund Traub), Greta Wood (Mrs. Blandish), Michael Morice (Frederic), Jeanne de Casalis (Countess Flor di Folio), Lawrence Hanray (Martin), Rosamund Greenwood (Lady), Stewart Granger (Lord Ivor Cream), Bidley Briggs (Sir Everard Pyncheon), Harold Scott (a stranger)

ROMEO AND JULIET by Shakespeare
Opened at the 51st Street Theatre, New York, May 9, 1940, after a tour including San Francisco, Chicago, and Washington
Directed by Laurence Olivier
CAST: Vivien Leigh (Juliet), Laurence Olivier (Romeo), Dame May Whitty (Nurse), Edmond O'Brien (Mercutio), Cornel Wilde (Tybalt), Alexander Knox (Friar Laurence), Wesley Addy (Benvolio), Halliwell Hobbes (Capulet), Katharine Warren (Lady Capulet), Ben Webster (Montague), Barbara Horder (Lady Montague), Frank Downing (Paris), Hazel Brown (Rosaline), Morton L. Stevens (Old Capulet and Friar John), Walter Brooke (Chief Officer), Jack Merivale (Balthasar), Robert Busch (Abraham), Joseph Tomes (Gregory), William Barrows (Sampson), Wilton Graff (Escalus), Ralph Brooke, Earle Grey, Oliver Cliff, Raymond Johnson, Clara Speer, Nan Merriman, Patricia Knight, Mary Kane, Nancie B. Marsland, Virginia Burchfield, Charles Prescott, Howard T. Stark, John Straub, Charles Martin, Tileston Perry, H. Robert Edwards, Ted Huish, Brant Gorman, and Ralph Grayson
Scenery and costumes by Motley

THE DOCTOR'S DILEMMA by George Bernard Shaw
Opened at the Haymarket Theatre, London, March 4, 1942
Directed by Irene Hentschel
CAST: Vivien Leigh (Jennifer Dubedat), Cyril Cusack (Louis Dubedat), Austin Trevor (B.B.), Frank Allenby, Charles Goldner, George Relph, and Morland Graham

THE SCHOOL FOR SCANDAL (two scenes) by Richard Brinsley Sheridan
Presented at the Haymarket Theatre, London, April 24, 1942
(This was a special matinee performance in aid of Stage Charities and on the
occasion of Cyril Maude's eightieth birthday)
CAST: Vivien Leigh (Lady Teazle), Cyril Maude (Sir Peter)

SPRING PARTY, a revue
Toured North Africa entertaining troops, spring 1943
Produced by John Gielgud
CAST: Vivien Leigh, Beatrice Lillie, Dorothy Dickson, and Leslie Henson
(Vivien Leigh recited "You Are Old, Father William" by Lewis Carroll,
"Plymouth Hoe" by Clemence Dane, and a satirical poem about Scarlett
O'Hara)

THE SKIN OF OUR TEETH by Thornton Wilder
Opened at the Phoenix Theatre, London, May 16, 1945
Directed by Laurence Olivier
CAST: Vivien Leigh (Sabina), Cecil Parker (Mr. Antrobus), Joan Young (Mrs.
Antrobus), Terence Morgan (the Antrobus son), and Ena Burrill (the
Antrobus daughter)

THE SKIN OF OUR TEETH by Thornton Wilder
Revival opened at the Piccadilly Theatre, London, September 11, 1946
Directed by Laurence Olivier
CAST: Vivien Leigh (Sabina), George Devine (Mr. Antrobus), Esther Somers
(Mrs. Antrobus)

Australian and New Zealand tour of the Old Vic Company
Departure February 14, 1948; return November 1, 1948

RICHARD III: Vivien Leigh (Lady Anne), Laurence Olivier (King Richard)

THE SCHOOL FOR SCANDAL: Vivien Leigh (Lady Teazle), Laurence
Olivier (Sir Peter)

THE SKIN OF OUR TEETH: Vivien Leigh (Sabina), Laurence Olivier (Mr.
Antrobus)

Old Vic Repertory Season 1949
At the New Theatre, London
Directed by Laurence Olivier

RICHARD III (opened January 26)
CAST: Vivien Leigh (Lady Anne), Laurence Olivier (King Richard), Mercia
Swinburne, George Relph, Terence Morgan, Peter Cushing, Peggy
Simpson, Derrick Penley, and Dan Cunningham

ANTIGONE (opened February 10)
CAST: Vivien Leigh (Antigone), Laurence Olivier (Chorus), George Relph (Creon), Terence Morgan, Dan Cunningham, Mercia Swinburne

A STREETCAR NAMED DESIRE by Tennessee Williams
Opened at the Aldwych Theatre, London, October 11, 1949
Directed by Laurence Olivier
CAST: Vivien Leigh (Blanche DuBois), Bonar Colleano (Stanley Kowalski), Renée Asherson (Stella Kowalski), Bernard Braden (Mitch), Theodore Bikel (Pablo Gonzalez)

CAESAR AND CLEOPATRA by George Bernard Shaw
Opened at the St. James's Theatre, London, May 10, 1951
Directed by Michael Benthall
Sets by Roger Furse, costumes by Audrey Cruddas
CAST: Vivien Leigh (Cleopatra), Laurence Olivier (Caesar)

ANTONY AND CLEOPATRA by Shakespeare
Opened at the St. James's Theatre, London, May 11, 1951
Directed by Michael Benthall
Sets by Roger Furse, costumes by Audrey Cruddas
CAST: Vivien Leigh (Cleopatra), Laurence Olivier (Antony)
(The two plays alternated nightly)

CAESAR AND CLEOPATRA by George Bernard Shaw
Opened at the Ziegfeld Theatre, New York, December 19, 1951
Presented by Gilbert Miller
Directed by Michael Benthall
Sets by Roger Furse, costumes by Audrey Cruddas
CAST: Vivien Leigh (Cleopatra), Laurence Olivier (Caesar), Robert Help-mann (Apollodorus), Wilfrid Hyde White (Britannus), Harry Andrews (Lucius Septimius), Pat Nye (Ftatateeta), Niall MacGinnis (Rufio)

ANTONY AND CLEOPATRA by Shakespeare
Opened at the Ziegfeld Theatre, New York, December 20, 1951
Presented by Gilbert Miller
Directed by Michael Benthall
Sets by Roger Furse, costumes by Audrey Cruddas
CAST: Vivien Leigh (Cleopatra), Laurence Olivier (Antony), Donald Pleas-ence (Lemprius Euphronius), Harry Andrews (Enobarbus), Mairhi Rus-sell (Iras), Robert Helpmann (Octavius Caesar), Wilfrid Hyde White (Lepidus), Niall MacGinnis (Pompey), Edmund Purdom (Thydeus), Katharine Blake (Charmian)

THE SLEEPING PRINCE by Terence Rattigan
Opened at the Phoenix Theatre, London, November 5, 1953
Directed by Laurence Olivier

CAST: Vivien Leigh (Mary Morgan), Laurence Olivier (the Prince), Martita Hunt (the Grand Duchess), Jeremy Spenser (the King), Richard Wattis (Peter Northbrook)

TWELFTH NIGHT by Shakespeare
Opened at Stratford-upon-Avon, April 12, 1955
Directed by John Gielgud
CAST: Vivien Leigh (Viola), Laurence Olivier (Malvolio), Keith Michell (Orsino), Mervyn Blake (Sea Captain), Alan Webb (Sir Toby Belch), Angela Baddeley (Maria), Michael Denison (Sir Andrew Aguecheek), Edward Atienza (Feste), Maxine Audley (Olivia), Lee Montague (Fabian), William Devlin (Antonio), Trader Faulkner (Sebastian)
Scenery and costumes by Malcolm Pride

MACBETH by William Shakespeare
Opened at Stratford-upon-Avon, June 7, 1955
Directed by Glen Byam Shaw
CAST: Vivien Leigh (Lady Macbeth), Laurence Olivier (Macbeth), Maxine Audley (Lady Macduff), Keith Michell (Macduff), Geoffrey Bayldon (Duncan), Trader Faulkner (Malcolm), Ian Holm (Donalbain), William Devlin (Ross), James Grout (Lennox), Robert Hunter (Menteith), Gabriel Woolf (Caithness), Ralph Michael (Banquo), Paul Vieyra (Fleance), Lee Montague (Seyton), Dilya Hanilett, Nancye Stewart, Mary Law (Weird Sisters), David King (Servant), Patrick Wymark (Porter), George Bayldon (Doctor), Rosalind Atkinson (Gentlewoman)

TITUS ANDRONICUS, attributed to Shakespeare
Opened at Stratford on Avon, August 16, 1955
Directed by Peter Brook (who also designed the sets and composed the incidental music)
CAST: Vivien Leigh (Lavinia), Laurence Olivier (Titus Andronicus), Maxine Audley (Tamora), Frank Thring (Saturninus), Anthony Quayle (Aaron), Alan Webb (Marcus Andronicus), Michael Denison (Lucius), Kevin Miles (Chiron), Ralph Michael (Bassianus), Lee Montague (Demetrius)
(The above three plays were performed in repertory by the Old Vic Company for the Stratford Festival)

SOUTH SEA BUBBLE by Noël Coward
Opened at the Lyric Theatre, London, April 25, 1956
Directed by William Chappell
CAST: Vivien Leigh (Lady Alexandra Shotter), Ian Hunter (Sir George Shotter), Arthur Macrae (John Blair Kennedy), John Moore (Edward Honey), Joyce Carey (Cuckoo Honey), Alan Webb (Punalo), Peter Barkworth (Captain Christopher Mortlock A.D.C.), Nicholas Grimshaw (Admiral Turling), Eric Phillips (Robert Frome), Ronald Lewis (Hali Alani)

TITUS ANDRONICUS, attributed to Shakespeare
Opened at Stoll Theatre, London, July 1, 1957, after a tour of Paris, Venice, Vienna, Belgrade, Zagreb, and Warsaw beginning May 6, 1957
Presented by the Shakespeare Memorial Theatre Company
Directed by Peter Brook
CAST: Vivien Leigh (Lavinia), Laurence Olivier (Titus Andronicus), Anthony Quayle (Aaron), Maxine Audley, (Tamora), Alan Webb (Marcus Andronicus), William Devlin, Basil Hoskins, Paul Hardwick, and Rosalind Atkinson

DUEL OF ANGELS by Jean Giraudoux (*Pour Lucrece*), translated by Christopher Fry
Opened at the Apollo Theatre, London, on April 24, 1958
Directed by Jean-Louis Barrault
CAST: Vivien Leigh (Paola), Claire Bloom (Lucile), Derek Nimmo (Joseph), Peter Wyngarde (Marcellus), Fiona Duncan (Gilly), Basil Hoskins (Armand), Pauline Jameson (Eugénie), Freda Jackson (Barbette), Robin Bailey (Mr. Justice Blanchard), Lawrence Davidson (Clerk of the Court) (Miss Bloom was replaced later by Ann Todd and then Mary Ure)

LOOK AFTER LULU by Noël Coward, adapted from *Occupe-toi d'Amélie* by Georges Feydeau
Opened at the Royal Court Theatre, July 29, 1959; transferred to the New Theatre, September 8, 1959
Directed by Noël Coward
CAST: Vivien Leigh (Lulu d'Arville), Anthony Quayle, Richard Goolden, Michael Bates, Meriel Forbes, George Devine, Max Adrian, and Robert Stephens

DUEL OF ANGELS by Jean Giraudoux (*Pour Lucrece*), translated by Christopher Fry
Opened at the Helen Hayes Theatre, New York, April 19, 1960
Presented by Roger L. Stevens and Sol Hurok
Directed by Robert Helpmann
CAST: Vivien Leigh (Paola), James Valentine (Joseph), Peter Wyngarde (Marcellus), Aina Niemela (Gilly), John Merivale (Armand), Mary Ure (Lucile), Ludi Claire (Eugénie), Felix Deebank (Mace Bearer), Margaret Braidwood (Barbette), Ken Edward Ruta (Servant), Alan MacNaughtan (Mr. Justice Blanchard), Donald Moffat (Clerk of the Court), Theodore Tenley (Servant)

Old Vic Overseas Tour, July 12, 1961, to May 16, 1962

TWELFTH NIGHT, directed by Robert Helpmann, designed by Loudon Sainthill

DUEL OF ANGELS, directed by Robert Helpmann, designed by Felix Kelly

THE LADY OF THE CAMELLIAS, directed by Robert Helpmann, designed by Carl Toms

(The three plays were performed in repertory. Vivien Leigh portrayed Viola in *Twelfth Night*, Paola in *Duel of Angels*, and Marguerite Gauthier in *The Lady of the Camellias*)

Schedule of Australian tour:
July 12 to August 26, Her Majesty's Theatre, Melbourne
August 28 to September 16, Her Majesty's Theatre, Brisbane
September 28 to December 9, Theatre Royal, Sydney
December 11 to December 30, Theatre Royal, Adelaide
January 1 to January 13, 1962, Her Majesty's Theatre, Perth
January 24 to February 10, Opera House, Wellington
February 12 to February 24, Theatre Royal, Christchurch
February 26 to March 17, Her Majesty's Theatre, Auckland

Schedule of Latin American tour, which included only *Twelfth Night* and *The Lady of the Camellias:*
March 29 to April 3, Mexico City, Mexico
April 6 to April 9, Caracas, Venezuela
April 12 to April 13, Lima, Peru
April 17 to April 18, Santiago, Chile
April 23 to April 29, Buenos Aires, Argentina
May 2 to May 4, Montevideo, Uruguay
May 7 to May 9, Sao Paulo, Brazil
May 11 to May 16, Rio de Janeiro, Brazil

TOVARICH, a musical based on the play by Jacques Deval and Robert E. Sherwood, book by David Shaw, lyrics by Anne Crosswell, music by Lee Pockriss
Opened at the Broadway Theatre, New York, March 18, 1963
Presented by Abel Farbman and Sylvia Harris
Directed by Peter Glenville
CAST: Vivien Leigh (Tatiana), Jean Pierre Aumont (Mikail), George S. Irving (Charles Davis), Louise Kirtland (Grace Davis), Byron Mitchell (George Davis), Margery Gray (Helen Davis), Alexander Scourby (Gorotchenko), Paul Michael (Vassily), Michael Kermoyan (Admiral Boris Soukhomine), Gene Varrone (Count Ivan Shamforoff), Katia Geleznova (Baroness Roumel), Rita Metzger (Marina), Don McHenry (M. Chauffourier-Dubieff), Louise Troy (Natalia), Maggie Task (Louise), Tom Abbott (Ballet Master), Barbara Monte (Nadia), Pat Kelly (Mme Van Hemert), Eleonore Treiber (Mme Van Steuben), Bettye Jenkins (Kukla Katusha), William Reilly (Ivan), Larry Roquemore (Sergei), Harald Horn (Baron General Rasumov), Michele Franchi (Baroness Rasumov), Antony De Vecchi (Prince Dobrynin), Marion Fels (Princess Dobrynin), Dale Malone (General Boruvsky), Joan Trona (Lady Soukhomine), Will Parkins (Count Rostoff), Lorenzo Bianco (Essaul), Charlene Mehl (Elena), William Glassman (Igor)

Musical numbers staged by Herbert Ross
Production designed by Rolf Gerard
Costumes by Motley

LA CONTESSA by Paul Osborn, adapted from the novel *The Film of Memory* by Maurice Druon
Closed out of town; previews at Newcastle, April 6, 1965; Liverpool, April 19, 1965; Manchester, May 4, 1965
Presented by H. M. Tennent Ltd. and Leland Hayward and Flerts Productions Ltd.
Directed by Robert Helpmann
Settings by Desmond Heeley, costumes by Beatrice Dawson
CAST: Vivien Leigh (Contessa Sanziani), David Knight (Peter Somers), Joseph Furst (Vittorio Vicaria), Stanley Lloyd (Walter), Gerald Cross (Pavelli), Bruce Montague (Clerk), Nicola Paget (Carmela), Anna Middleton (Valentina), John Gay (Revato), John Gill (Do Wolf), Percy Marmont (Count Sanziani)

IVANOV by Anton Chekhov, adapted by John Gielgud
Opened (after tour of United States and Canada) at the Shubert Theatre, New York, May 3, 1966
Directed by John Gielgud
CAST: Vivien Leigh (Anna Petrovna), John Gielgud (Ivanov), Ronald Radd (Mikhail), Edward Atienza (Count Shabelsky), John Merivale (Dr. Ivov), Paula Laurence (Zinaida Savishna), Helen Christie (Marfa Babakina), Dillon Evans (Kossykh), Ethel Griffies (Avdotya Nazarovna), Roland Culver (Pavel Lebedev), Jennifer Hilary (Sasha), Guy Spaull (Butler), Anna Minot (Maid), Michael Miller (Pyotr)

RADIO APPEARANCES

(U.S.A.)
A *British Tribute to King George and Queen Mary*, NBC, February 1939 (Vivien Leigh read "A Woman's Last Word" by Elizabeth Barrett Browning)

(U.K.)

April 8, 1941	*For Us the Living*
May 11, 1941	*My Life in the Theatre*
May 8, 1942	*School for Scandal*
December 27, 1942	*School for Scandal*
February 10, 1944	*Sunday Night Poetry Reading*
September 2, 1952	*Desert Island Discs*
May 5, 1956	*Theatre* (Italian exchange program)
August 8, 1956	*A Message to India*
April 28, 1957	Interview
July 31, 1957	Interview
August 20, 1957	*Antony and Cleopatra*

September 24, 1957   *Woman's Hour: Conversation in Ebony Street*
May 8, 1958   *Toast of the Town*
June 6, 1966   *What Makes an Actor?*
(All of the above were done for the B.B.C.)

TELEVISION APPEARANCES

Several excerpts from plays that Vivien Leigh appeared in were shown on television.

FILM CHRONOLOGY

THINGS ARE LOOKING UP, Gaumont British
Opened in London, February 25, 1935
Produced by Michael Balcon
Directed by Albert de Courville
Screenplay by Stafford Dickens and Con West
CAST: Vivian Leigh (small role as schoolgirl), Cicely Courtneidge, Henrietta
   Watson, Dick Henderson, Jr., Suzanne Lenglen

THE VILLAGE SQUIRE, Paramount British
Opened in London, April 1935
Produced by Anthony Havelock-Allen
Directed by Reginald Denham
Screenplay by Arthur Jarvis Black
CAST: Vivian Leigh (Rose Venables), Leslie Perrins, David Horne

GENTLEMAN'S AGREEMENT, Paramount British
Opened in London, June 1935
Produced by Anthony Havelock-Allen
Directed by George Pearson
Screenplay by Jennifer Howard
CAST: Vivian Leigh (Phil Stanley), Frederick Peisley, Antony Holles, David
   Horne, Ronald Shiner

LOOK UP AND LAUGH, Associated British Film Distributors
Opened in London, August 4, 1935
Produced and directed by Basil Dean
Screenplay by J. B. Priestley
CAST: Vivian Leigh (Marjorie Belfer), Gracie Fields, Robb Wilton, Kenneth
   More, Douglas Wakefield, Billy Nelson, Harry Tate

FIRE OVER ENGLAND, London Films
Opened in London, February 25, 1937; New York, March 4, 1937
Executive producer, Alexander Korda

Produced by Erich Pommer
Directed by William K. Howard
Screenplay by Clemence Dane and Sergei Nolbandov, from the novel by A. E. W. Mason
Photography by James Wong Howe
Special effects by Ned Mann, Lawrence Butler, and Edward Cohen
Designed by Lazare Meerson
Music by Richard Addinsell
Musical director, Muir Mathieson
Film editor, Jack Dennis
Costumes by René Hubert
Sound by A. W. Watkins and Jack Rogerson
CAST: Vivien Leigh (Cynthia), Flora Robson (Queen Elizabeth), Laurence Olivier (Michael Ingolby), Leslie Banks (Earl of Leicester), Raymond Massey (Philip of Spain), James Mason (Hillary Vane), Robert Newton (Don Pedro), Herbert Lomas (Richard Ingolby), Morton Selten (Burleigh), Tamara Desni (Elena), Robert Rendell (Don Miguel), Charles Carson (Admiral Valdez), Henry Oscar (Spanish Ambassador), Lawrence Hanray (French Ambassador), Roy Russell (Cooper), Howard Douglas (Lord Amberley), Cecil Mainwaring (Illingworth), Francis de Wolfe (Tarleton), Graham Cheswright (Maddison), George Thirlwell (Gregory), A. Corney Grain (Hatton), Donald Calthrop (Don Escobal), Lyn Harding (Sir Richard)
American distributor, United Artists
Won the 1937 Gold Medal of the Comité International pour la Diffusion Artistique et Littéraire pour le Cinéma

DARK JOURNEY, London Films
Opened in London, March 28, 1937; U.S.A., April 2, 1937
Produced by Alexander Korda
Directed by Victor Saville
Screenplay by Arthur Wimperis from a story by Lajos Biro
Photography by Georges Perinal
Special effects by Ned Mann, Lawrence Butler, and Edward Cohen
Designed by André Andrejew and Ferdinand Bellan
Music by Richard Addinsell
Musical director, Muir Mathieson
Film editors, William Hornbeck, Hugh Steward, and Lionel Hoare
Costumes by René Hubert
Sound by A. W. Watkins and Charles Tasto
CAST: Vivien Leigh (Madeleine Godard), Conrad Veidt (Baron Karl von Marwitz), Joan Gardner (Lupita), Anthony Bushell (Bob Carter), Ursula Jeans (Gertrude), Eliot Makeham (Anatole), Margaret Pickard (Colette), Austin Trevor (Dr. Muller), Sam Livesey (Major Schaeffer), Cecil Parker (Captain), Edmund Willard (German Intelligence Officer), Charles Carson (Fifth Bureau Man), William Dewhurst (Killer), Henry Oscar (Magistrate), Reginald Tate (Mate), Robert Newton (Officer), Philip Ray (Fa-

ber), Lawrence Hanray (Cottin), Percy Walsh (Captain of the Swedish Packet), Laidman Browne (Rugge), Martin Harvey (Bohlan), Anthony Holles (Dutchman)
American distributor, United Artists
Reissued in 1953 as *The Anxious Years*

STORM IN A TEACUP, London Films
Opened in London, June 6, 1937; U.S.A., November 22, 1937
Produced by Victor Saville
Directed by Victor Saville and Ian Dalrymple
Screenplay by Ian Dalrymple and Donald Bull from James Bridie's adaptation of the play *Sturm im Wasserglas* by Bruno Frank
Photography by Mutz Greenbaum (Max Greene)
Special effects by Ned Mann and Edward Cohen
Designed by André Andrejew
Music by Frederic Lewis
Musical director, Muir Mathieson
Film editors, William Hornbeck, Hugh Steward, and Cyril Randell
Sound by A. W. Watkins and Charles Tasto
CAST: Vivien Leigh (Victoria Grow), Rex Harrison (Frank Burdon), Sara Algood (Mrs. Hegarty), Cecil Parker (Provost Grow), Ursula Jeans (Lisbet Skirving), Gus McNaughton (Horace Skirving), Arthur Wontner (Fiscal), Edgar K. Bruce (McKellar), Robert Hale (Lord Skerryvore), Quinton MacPherson (Baillie Callender), George Pughe (Menzies), Arthur Seaton (Police Sergeant), Cecil Mannering (Police Constable), Cyril Smith (Councilor), Scruffy the dog
American distributor, United Artists

A YANK AT OXFORD, Metro-Goldwyn-Mayer
Opened in New York, February 25, 1938; London, April 1, 1938
Produced by Michael Balcon
Directed by Jack Conway
Sceenplay by Malcolm Stuart Boylan, Walter Ferris, and George Oppenheimer
CAST: Vivien Leigh (Elsa Craddock), Robert Taylor (Lee Sheridan), Lionel Barrymore (Dan Sheridan), Maureen O'Sullivan (Molly Beaumont), Griffith Jones (Paul Beaumont), Edmund Gwenn (Dean of Cardinal), C. V. France (Dean Snodgrass), Morton Selten (Cecil Davidson), Edmund Breon (Captain Wavertree), Norah Howard (Barmaid), Edward Rigby (Scatters)

ST. MARTIN'S LANE, Associated British Picture Corporation (U.S. title *Sidewalks of London*)
Opened in London, October 18, 1938; New York, February 15, 1940
Produced by Erich Pommer
Directed by Tim Whelan
Screenplay by Clemence Dane

CAST: Vivien Leigh (Libby), Charles Laughton (Charles), Rex Harrison (Harley), Larry Adler (Constantine), Tyrone Guthrie (Gentry), Maire O'Neill (Mrs. Such), Basil Gill (Magistrate), Claire Greet (Old Maud), Helen Haye (Selina)

TWENTY-ONE DAYS, London Films, Denham Productions (U.S. title 21 Days Together)
Opened in London, January 7, 1940; U.S.A., May 16,1940
Produced by Alexander Korda
Directed by Basil Dean
Screenplay by Basil Dean and Graham Greene from the play *The First and the Last* by John Galsworthy
Photography by Jan Stallich
Designed by Vincent Korda
Film editors, William Hornbeck, Charles Crichton, and John Guthrie
Music by John Greenwood
Musical director, Muir Mathieson
Sound by A. W. Watkins
CAST: Vivien Leigh (Wanda), Laurence Olivier (Larry Durrant), Leslie Banks (Keith Durrant), Francis L. Sullivan (Mander), Robert Newton (Tolley), Hay Petrie (John Aloysius Evans), Esme Percy (Henry Walenn), Victor Rietti (Antonio), Morris Harvey (Alexander Macpherson), Meinhart Maur (Carl Grunlich), Lawrence Hanray (Solicitor), David Horne (Beavis), Wallace Lupino (Father), Muriel George (Mother), William Dewhurst (Lord Chief Justice), Frederick Lloyd (Swinton), Elliot Mason (Frau Grunlich), Arthur Young (Asher), Fred Groves (Barnes), Aubrey Mallalieu (Magistrate)
American distributor, Columbia Pictures

GONE WITH THE WIND,* David O. Selznick Production for Metro-Goldwyn-Mayer
Opened in Atlanta, Georgia, December 15, 1939; London, April 17, 1940
Produced by David O. Selznick**
Directed by Victor Fleming* (additional scenes by George Cukor, Sam Wood, William Cameron Menzies, and David O. Selznick)
Screenplay by Sidney Howard* (F. Scott Fitzgerald, Oliver Garrett, Ben Hecht, John Van Druten, Jo Swerling, and David O. Selznick also worked on the screenplay and contributed to the final version), based on the book *Gone With the Wind* by Margaret Mitchell
Designed by William Cameron Menzies**
Art director, Lyle Wheeler*
Photography by Ernest Haller, A.S.C.* (associate, Ray Rennahan)
Technicolor associates, Ray Rennahan, A.S.C., Wilfrid M. Cline, A.S.C.
Music by Max Steiner (associate, Lou Forbes)
Special effects by Jack Cosgrove (associate for fire effects, Lee Zavitz)
Costumes by Walter Plunkett
Scarlett's hats by John Frederics

Interiors by Joseph B. Platt
Interior decoration by Edward G. Boyle
Film editor, Hal C. Kern* (associate, James E. Newcom)
Scenario assistant, Barbara Keon
Recorder, Frank Maher
Makeup and hair styling by Monty Westmore (associates, Hazel Rogers, Ben Nye)
Dance directors, Frank Floyd, Eddie Prinz
Historian, Wilbur G. Kurtz
Technical advisers, Susan Myrick, Will Price
Research by Lillian K. Deighton
Production manager, Raymond A. Klune
Technicolor supervision by Natalie Kalmus (associate, Henri Jaffa)
CAST: Vivien Leigh* (Scarlett O'Hara), Clark Gable (Rhett Butler), Leslie Howard (Ashley Wilkes), Olivia de Havilland (Melanie Hamilton Wilkes), Hattie McDaniel* (Mammy), Thomas Mitchell* (Gerald O'Hara), Barbara O'Neil (Ellen O'Hara), Evelyn Keyes (Suellen O'Hara), Ann Rutherford (Carreen O'Hara), Butterfly McQueen (Prissy), Victor Jory (Jonas Wilkerson), Oscar Polk (Pork), Isabel Jewell (Emmy Slattery), Ona Munson (Belle Watling), Zack Williams (Elijah), Fred Crane (Brent Tarleton), George Reeves (Stuart Tarleton), Alicia Rhett (India Wilkes), Rand Brooks (Charles Hamilton), Carroll Nye (Frank Kennedy), Marcella Martin (Cathleen Calvert), Howard Hickman (John Wilkes), Laura Hope Crews (Aunt Pittypat Hamilton), Harry Davenport (Doctor Meade), Leona Roberts (Mrs. Meade), Jane Darwell (Mrs. Merriwether), Albert Morin (René Picard), Mary Anderson (Maybelle Merriwether), Terry Shero (Fanny Elsing), Eddie Anderson (Uncle Peter), William McClain (Old Levi), Jackie Moran (Phil Meade), Cammie King (Bonnie Blue Butler), Mickey Kuhn (Beau Wilkes), Ward Bond (Tom, a Yankee Captain), and with Cliff Edwards, Ed Chandler, George Hackathorne, Roscoe Ates, Eric Linden, John Arledge, Tom Tyler, William Bakewell, Lee Phelps, Paul Hurst, Ernest Whitman, William Stelling, Louis Jean Heydt, Robert Elliott, George Meeker, Wallis Clark, Irving Bacon, Adrian Morris, J. M. Kerrigan, Olin Howland, Yakima Canutt, Blue Washington, and Lillian Kemble Cooper

WATERLOO BRIDGE, Metro-Goldwyn-Mayer
Opened in New York, May 17, 1940; London, November 17, 1940
Produced by Sidney Franklin
Directed by Mervyn LeRoy
Screenplay by S. N. Behrman, Hans Rameau, and George Froeschel, based on the play by Robert E. Sherwood
CAST: Vivien Leigh (Myra), Robert Taylor (Roy Cronin), Lucile Watson (Lady Margaret Cronin), Virginia Field (Kitty), Maria Ouspenskaya (Madame Olga Kirowa), C. Aubrey Smith (the Duke)

*indicates Oscar winners; **special award

LADY HAMILTON, Alexander Korda Films, Inc. (U.S. title *That Hamilton Woman*)
Opened in New York, April 4, 1941; London, July 30, 1941
Produced and directed by Alexander Korda
Screenplay by Walter Reisch and R. C. Sherriff
Photography by Rudolph Mate
Designed by Vincent Korda
Set decoration by Julia Heron
Costumes by René Hubert
Film editor, William Hornbeck
Music and musical director, Miklos Rozsa
Sound by William H. Wilmartin
Production assistant, Andre De Toth
CAST: Vivien Leigh (Emma Hamilton), Laurence Olivier (Lord Nelson), Alan Mowbray (Sir William Hamilton), Sara Allgood (Mrs. Cadogan-Lyon), Gladys Cooper (Lady Nelson), Henry Wilcoxon (Captain Hardy), Heather Angel (Street Girl), Halliwell Hobbes (Reverend Nelson), Gilbert Emery (Lord Spencer), Miles Mander (Lord Keith), Ronald Sinclair (Josiah), Louis Alberni (King of Naples), Norma Drury (Queen of Naples), George Renavent (Hotel Manager), Leonard Carey (Orderly), Alex Craig (Gendarme), and George Davis
American distributor, United Artists
Won Academy Award for sound recording

CAESAR AND CLEOPATRA, United Artists
Opened in London, December 11, 1945; New York, September 6, 1946
Produced and directed by Gabriel Pascal
Screenplay based on the play by George Bernard Shaw
Decoration and costumes by Oliver Messel
Art director, John Bryan
Music by Georges Auric
CAST: Vivien Leigh (Cleopatra), Claude Rains (Caesar), Flora Robson (Ftatateeta), Francis L. Sullivan (Pothinus), Basil Sydney (Rufio), Cecil Parker (Britannus), Stewart Granger (Apollodorus), Raymond Lovell (Lucius Septimius), Antony Eustrel (Achillas), Ernest Thesiger (Theodotus), Michael Rennie (First Centurion), Esme Percy (Major Domo), Stanley Holloway (Belzanor), Leo Genn (Ben Affris), James McKechnie (Wounded Centurion), Felix Aylmer (First Nobleman), Valentine Dyall (First Guardsman)

ANNA KARENINA, London Films
Opened in London, January 22, 1948; New York, April 28, 1948
Produced by Alexander Korda
Directed by Julien Duvivier
Screenplay by Julien Duvivier, Guy Moran, and Jean Anouilh from Leo Tolstoy's novel
Photography by Henri Alekan

Special effects by W. Percy Day and Cliff Richardson
Designed by André Andrejew
Film editor, Russell Lloyd
Costumes by Cecil Beaton
Music by Constant Lambert
Musical director, Dr. Hubert Clifford
Sound recording by John Cox
CAST: Vivien Leigh (Anna Karenina), Ralph Richardson (Alexei Karenin), Kieron Moore (Count Vronsky), Sally Anne Howes (Kitty Shcherbatsky), Niall MacGinnis (Levin), Martita Hunt (Princess Betty Tverskoy), Marie Lohr (Princess Shcherbatsky), Michael Gough (Nikolai), Hugh Dempster (Stepan Oblonsky), Mary Kerridge (Dolly Oblonsky), Heather Thatcher (Countess Lydia Ivanovna), Helen Haye (Countess Vronsky), Austin Trevor (Colonel Vronsky), Ruby Miller (Countess Mezhkov), John Longden (General Serpukhovskoy), Leslie Bradley (Korsunsky), Michael Medwin (Doctor), Jeremy Spenser (Giuseppe), Gino Cervi (Enrico), Frank Tickle (Prince Shcherbatsky), Mary Martlew (Princess Nathalia), Ann South (Princess Sorokina), Guy Verney (Prince Makhotin), Beckett Bould (Matvey), Judith Nelmes (Miss Hull), Valentina Murch (Annushka), Theresa Giehse (Marietta), John Salew (Lawyer), Patrick Skipwith (Sergei)
American distributor, Twentieth Century–Fox

A STREETCAR NAMED DESIRE, Warner Brothers
Opened in New York, September 20, 1951; London, March 2, 1952
Executive producer, Elia Kazan
Produced by Charles K. Feldman
Directed by Elia Kazan
Screenplay by Tennessee Williams from his own play; adaptation by Oscar Saul
Costumes by Lucinda Ballard
CAST: Vivien Leigh (Blanche DuBois), Marlon Brando (Stanley Kowalski), Kim Hunter (Stella Kowalski), Karl Malden (Mitch), Rudy Bond (Steve), Nick Dennis (Pablo), Peg Hillias (Eunice), Richard Garrick (Doctor), Anne Dere (Matron), Edna Thomas (Mexican Woman)
Vivien Leigh won an Academy Award for her performance

THE DEEP BLUE SEA, London Films
Opened in London, August 24, 1955; New York, October 13, 1955
Executive producer, Alexander Korda
Produced and directed by Anatole Litvak
Designed by Vincent Korda
Screenplay by Terence Rattigan from his play
CAST: Vivien Leigh (Hester Collyer), Kenneth More (Freddie Page), Emlyn Williams (Sir William Collyer), Eric Portman (Mr. Miller), Moira Lister (Dawn Maxwell), Arthur Hill (Jackie Jackson), Miriam Karlin (Barmaid), Heather Thatcher (Lady Dawson), Dandy Nichols (Mrs. Elton)
American distributor, Twentieth Century–Fox

THE ROMAN SPRING OF MRS. STONE, Warner Brothers
Opened in New York, December 29, 1961; London, February 15, 1962
Produced by Louis de Rochemont
Directed by José Quintero
Production designed by Roger Furse
Music by Richard Addinsell
Screenplay by Gavin Lambert from the novel by Tennessee Williams
CAST: Vivien Leigh (Karen Stone), Warren Beatty (Paolo), Coral Browne
(Meg), Lotte Lenya (Contessa Gonzales), Jeremy Spenser (Young Man),
Jill St. John (Barbara Bingham), Ernest Thesiger (Stefano), Paul Stassino
(Barber), Bessie Love (Bunny), Carl Jaffe (Baron), Cleo Laine (Singer),
Elspeth March (Mrs. Barrow)

SHIP OF FOOLS, Columbia Pictures
Opened in New York, July 29, 1965; London, October 20, 1965
Produced and directed by Stanley Kramer
Photography by Ernest Laszlo
Screenplay by Abby Mann, based on the novel by Katherine Anne Porter
Music by Ernest Gold
CAST: Vivien Leigh (Mary Treadwell), Simone Signoret (La Condesa), Oskar
Werner (Dr. Schumann), José Ferrer (Rieber), Lee Marvin (Tenny), Mi-
chael Dunn (Glocken), Heinz Ruhmann (Lowenthal), George Segal
(David), Elizabeth Ashley (Jenny), José Greco (Pepe), Charles Korvin
(Captain Thiele), Christine Schmidtmer, Lilia Skala, Barbara Luna, Alf
Kjellin, John Wengraf, Werner Klemperer, and Gila Golan
Vivien Leigh won the French Étoile Crystal award for her performance

AWARDS

Academy Award, 1939, Gone With the Wind, Best Actress
Academy Award, 1951, A Streetcar Named Desire, Best Actress
Knight's Cross of the Légion d'Honneur, 1957
Étoile Crystal, French, for her performance in Ship of Fools

COURT ACTIVITIES

Presented, as Mrs. Leigh Holman, Tuesday, June 13, 1933, by Mrs. Alwyn
Boot
Accompanied Laurence Olivier to Court for his investiture, Tuesday, July 8,
1947

Index